ADVANCES IN
COMPUTER
VISION
VOLUME 1

T0251224

ADVANCES IN
COMPUTER
VISION

VOLUME 1

EDITED BY

CHRISTOPHER BROWN
University of Rochester

Psychology Press
Taylor & Francis Group

New York London

First Published by
Lawrence Erlbaum Associates, Inc., Publishers
365 Broadway
Hillsdale, New Jersey 07642

Transferred to Digital Printing 2009 by Psychology Press
270 Madison Avenue, New York NY 10016
27 Church Road, Hove, East Sussex BN3 2FA

Library of Congress Cataloging-in-Publication Data

Advances in computer vision/edited by Christopher Brown.
     p.   cm.
  Bibliography: p.
  Includes indexes.
    ISBN 0-89859-648-3 (v. 1). ISBN 0-8058-0092-1 (v. 2)
    1. Computer vision. 2. Brown, Christopher M.
TA1632.A265 1988   87-27282
006.3'7——dc19   CIP

Publisher's Note
The publisher has gone to great lengths to ensure the quality
of this reprint but points out that some imperfections in the
original may be apparent.

CONTENTS

VOLUME 2

CONTRIBUTORS

John Aloimonos Department of Computer Science, University of Maryland, College Park, MD 20742

Dana Ballard Department of Computer Science, University of Rochester, Rochester, NY 14627

Christopher Brown Department of Computer Science, University of Rochester, Rochester, NY 14627

Allen Hanson Computer and Information Sciences Department, University of Massachusetts, Amherst, MA 01002

Robert Haralick Department of Electrical Engineering, University of Washington, Seattle, WA 98195

Alex Pentland Vision Sciences Group, Media Laboratory, Massachusetts Institute of Technology, Cambridge, MA 02139

Tomaso Poggio Artificial Intelligence Laboratory, Massachusetts Institute of Technology, Cambridge, MA 02139

Ting-Chuen Pong Department of Computer Science, University of Minnesota, Minneapolis, MN

Edward Riseman Computer and Information Sciences Department, University of Massachusetts, Amherst, MA 01002

Linda Shapiro Department of Electrical Engineering, University of Washington, Seattle, WA 98195

Allen Waxman   Electrical, Computer and Systems Engineering, College of Engineering, Boston University, Boston, MA 02215

Kwangyoen Wohn   GRASPLAB, Department of Computer and Information Science, University of Pennsylvania, Philadelphia, PA 19104

Allan Yuille   Division of Applied Sciences, Harvard University, Pierce Hall, Cambridge, MA, 02139

 # INTRODUCTION

VISION AND COMPUTER VISION

The series *Advances in Computer Vision* has the goal of presenting current approaches to basic problems that arise in the construction of a computer vision system, written by leading researchers and practitioners in the field. The first two volumes in the series comprise seven chapters, which together cover much of the scope of computer vision. Chapter 1 of Volume 1 is referred to as 1.1, and so forth.

In these volumes, computer vision means computer programs analyzing visual input (like a television image of a three-dimensional scene) and deriving from the image some description of the scene that is helpful to further reasoning or action concerning the scene (Pentland, 1986). The technical aspects of creating images and transferring them to the computer's memory are not addressed here: We are concerned with the techniques of computerized image analysis. Computer graphics, or the computerized production of images, is the inverse of computer vision: Graphics starts with world descriptions and produces images. Since graphics is so closely related to vision, some graphics techniques are indeed interesting to vision researchers (see chapter 2.4).

Vision is our most powerful sense. If we could endow machines with something like the power of sight, their actions and decision-making could be much more effective and efficient. Automatic navigation systems, industrial inspection, biomedical applications, consumer products, interactive systems, and a host of other areas are potential beneficiaries of breakthroughs in computer vision. Of course in a real system vision is purposive, working toward some particular goal. That means that vision is only a component of a larger system for reasoning and action. There are many hard problems yet to be solved in creating intelligent systems, even if the vision problem were overcome. Still, vision has always been a key problem in artificial intelligence (AI), and it is quite possible to make progress in vision without solving all other problems as well.

Despite our intimate association with them, our brains and minds still provide many of science's deepest and most elusive questions. Each generation applies the most powerful mechanisms it can conceive to try to describe and explain the mental functions of memory, cognition, and perception. Thus one of the currently most productive approaches to understanding mental activity and its underlying hardware is to make a computational model of the processing and then explore both its logical behavior and its implications for physical implementations. A computer program is an experimental artifact that can be used to explore theories of brain function, and the methods and representations it employs may have implications for our understanding of biological vision. The neurosciences are making great strides in describing brain structure, and there is increasing interest in relating structure to function. Thus the natural sciences and the sciences of the artificial are working together to understand general vision systems. Much has been learned, but we are a long way from knowing how to do general vision. The chapters in this volume detail aspects of the vision problem and indicate the range of issues that must be addressed.

A HISTORICAL PERSPECTIVE

The First Vision System. Computer vision began in the mid 1960s with what today would be called a vision system that operated in the polyhedral or "blocksworld" domain (Roberts, 1965). The system started with a photographic image of a blocks scene of planar polyhedral shapes built of a small set of primitives that could be scaled, rotated, and combined by gluing. A scanning densitometer converted the photograph to an array of numbers corresponding to brightnesses. The numerical array was analyzed in several stages: Small "edge elements" were detected where the image changed brightness. These small edges were linked together into longer line segments that ideally corresponded with the images of straight edges in the polyhedral scene. The line segments were linked together at vertices that should correspond to the image of polyhedral corners. Rings of connected line segments formed polygons that delineated the blocks' faces in the image.

Topological analysis of the resulting line segments, vertices, and polygons allowed matching between the two-dimensional image and a computer-held data structure representing the three-dimensional polyhedral primitive building blocks. After matching, the program could infer how the scene was constructed from transformed and combined primitives. The final output was a line drawing of the scene from any desired viewpoint.

Besides its many technical contributions, Roberts's work provided a paradigm that in many ways still holds in computer vision: that of using a careful combination of local image evidence (e.g., edge location) and relational image evidence (e.g., how line segments touch) to make a progressive abstraction from the image signal into symbolic representations that can be used in practical jobs such as recognition or navigation.

Vision as Cognition. After Roberts, vision systems continued to be built, but their performance seemed weak on an absolute scale, or even weak compared to the amount of work that went into them. Something was missing. One influential idea, favored also by cognitive psychologists, was that "high-level" (cognitive) processes were at the heart of vision, and that vision should be approached as some form of problem-solving (Ballard & Brown, 1982). This view has its points and also happened to fit in neatly with the economics of computing at the time—low-level vision processing was computationally very expensive. However, the cognitive vision approach faltered because automated symbolic reasoning proved to be very difficult, and because in vision, the input often does not correspond to expectation. Thus, new research directions arose.

Perception of Three-Dimensions from a Two-Dimensional Image. The next major idea was to use physics and applied mathematics to determine the sorts of information available in an image and how it can be extracted (Horn, 1986). An important first question is how to retain and represent image information. In Volume 1, image information is usually represented as the gray-level in the image. Volume 2 presents more ideas for intermediate data representations. Chapter 2.1 discusses the representation of an image as a faceted surface, and chapter 2.2 considers the representation of an image as zero-crossings of an operator (which is something like a representation of the edges in an image).

The next step is computing "intrinsic images," or invariant physical scene parameters, from a potentially varying image signal. With general viewing conditions, the image of a scene can vary widely, while the physical scene itself, including the distance of its objects or their surface reflectance, remains the same. Understanding the physical parameters of the scene is a big step toward being able to make symbolic descriptions that can be used for tasks. By what knowledge and algorithms can the imaging process be inverted to yield a representation of the physical properties of the scene that produced the image? Particular forms of this question have been the most popular topics for computer vision research for the last decade, and have led to work on "vision modules" that might be incorporated into a complete image-understanding system. Usually these modules operate with minimal assumptions about the domain of the scene, and thus fit into a "low level" or "preattentive" role in a system. Usually research on low-level modules avoids the engineering and systems issues of an integrated system. Chapters 1.2 and 1.3 describe state-of-the-art work in extracting three-dimensional parameters from shading, stereo, and motion.

Biological and Computer Vision. Another important trend that started in the mid 1970s was to try to learn technical things about low-level computer vision from biological systems and, conversely, to try to make computational models to explain biological systems (Marr, 1982; Levine, 1985). Biological vision systems work very well compared to computer vision systems. This cross-fertilization between the neurosciences and computer sciences has been increasingly productive and promises to be a major force in the future of the field. Technology is advancing toward the goal of powerful parallel computers that can comfortably accommodate more brain-like models of computation. Chapters 2.2 and 2.3 are indicative of work at the interface between biological and computer systems.

Modern Vision Systems. Recently, in the past few years, another reaction has begun. The work on vision modules has been so productive of results that the community has turned a substantial part of its attention back to the problem of building integrated systems. This activity is resulting in autonomous land vehicles, robotic systems, and laboratory image-understanding systems. The work described in chapter 1.1 is an example of a large-scale integrated system. A system for recognizing objects must have a way to represent the objects, and one of the greatest challenges in "high-level" vision is to represent symbolically the everyday real-world objects of our visual world—objects with biological or manufactured shapes and with complex surface properties. Chapter 2.4 examines techniques for representing texture and shape that could be useful in an integrated system. Chapter 2.3 shows how a hierarchy of abstraction for polyhedral vision can be implemented with nets of neural-like simple computing units.

1 THE VISIONS IMAGE-UNDERSTANDING SYSTEM

A. HANSON
E. RISEMAN
University of Massachusetts

In this chapter we consider some of the problems confronting the development of general integrated computer-vision systems and the status of the VISIONS project, which has become an experimental testbed for the construction of knowledge-based image interpretation systems. The goal is the construction of a symbolic representation of the three-dimensional world depicted in a two-dimensional image, including the labeling of objects, the determination of their location in space, and to the degree possible, the construction of a surface representation of the environment.

Our system involves three levels of processing for static image interpretation. Low-level processes manipulate pixel data and produce intermediate symbolic events such as regions and lines with their attributes. High-level processes focus attention on aggregates of these events via rule-based object hypotheses in order to selectively invoke schemas, which contain more complex knowledge-based interpretation strategies. Intermediate-level processes carry out grouping and reorganization of the error-prone symbolic representation extracted from the sensory data, utilizing both "top-down" control of the processing by the schema interpretation strategies as well as "bottom-up" data-directed organization of interesting perceptual events. Our design is being extended to integrate the results of motion and stereo processing throughout the three levels of processing, with depth arrays at the lowest level, partially correct surfaces at the intermediate level, as well as two-dimensional and three-dimensional motion attributes where appropriate.

In addition, a highly parallel three-level associative architecture is being developed to achieve real-time dynamic vision capabilities by allowing a bi-directional flow of information and processing across the levels. The machine will employ MIMD processing at the high level and Multi-SIMD (i.e., parallel local SIMD) under MIMD control at both the intermediate and low levels.

INTRODUCTION

This chapter discusses a range of problems in computer vision and describes the VISIONS system,[1] an approach to the construction of a general vision system that relies on knowledge-based techniques for image interpretation. The goal of this effort is the construction of a system capable of interpreting natural images of significant complexity. Over the past 12 years, the VISIONS group at the University of Massachusetts has been evolving the system while applying it to natural scenes, such as house and road scenes, aerial images, and biomedical images. Our philosophy is that it is reasonable to expect that each new domain will require a different knowledge base, but most of the system should remain the same across task domains. This paper documents the status of the system in mid-1986 as its development continues. Note that we do not attempt to carefully survey the literature on knowledge-based vision; partial reviews may be found in [16, 17, 29, 31, 54] and some representative individual research efforts are described in [13, 15, 18, 19, 32, 42, 48, 52, 63, 70, 82, 88, 89, 92, 93, 99, 100, 104, 107, 110, 119, 122, 123, 128, 133, 134].

The Problem of Image Interpretation

Our research has concentrated to a large extent on the identification of objects in static color images of natural scenes by associating two-dimensional image events with object descriptions [19, 20, 21, 53, 54, 55, 56, 57, 58, 59, 60, 61, 72, 106, 109, 111, 113, 114, 115, 116, 117, 118, 148, 149, 150]. However, at a more general level, the VISIONS design utilizes many stages of processing in the transformation from "signals" to "symbols," or to use more specific terminology, from two-dimensional image events to object labels and three-dimensional hypotheses. Unless the domain is extremely simple and heavily constrained so that object matching processes can be applied directly to the image (e.g., via template matching), there must be some form of sensory processing that extracts information from an image to produce an intermediate representation.

---

[1]VISIONS: Visual Integration by Semantic Interpretation of Natural Scenes

A FUNCTIONAL PERSPECTIVE

Another way to think about the chapters in this series is in terms of the functional components of a vision system. The organization of chapters is top-down, then bottom-up. Chapter 1.1 starts with a description of a modern vision system that is not only of considerable technical interest, but also provides an example vision system that may help the reader structure the content of the remaining chapters in the two volumes. Volume 1 then goes on in chapters 2 and 3 to concentrate on the extraction of three-dimensional physical parameters from two-dimensional images as part of early vision. Volume 2 moves from representations of the input image that are useful for further processing (chapters 1 and 2) to higher-level vision processes and three-dimensional representations (chapters 3 and 4).

Low-level Input Analysis and Image Representation. The idea that the image can be used to suggest a few clues and then be discarded, leaving perception to cognitive levels, seems indefensible (Fodor, 1983). Chapters 2.1 and 2.2 deal explicitly with image representations. Chapter 2.2 deals with the vital question of the "natural scale" of a vision calculation: How can a system discover the proper spatial resolution in which to perform image analysis? Where is the meaningful signal in the image? Chapter 2.1 provides a scheme in which the original image information is preserved but also put into a form more accessible for later processing. Chapter 1.1 addresses these issues in the context of an integrated system.

Segmentation. The problem of segmentation is related to the psychological phenomenon of figure-ground perception, or the perception of objecthood. Our natural and unconscious ability to see objects as unities and to delineate their boundaries has no easy implementation in a computer vision system. It is likely that biological systems use multiple sources of image information for figure-ground discrimination (motion, color, texture, and so on—see chapter 1.2). Segmentation is a hard problem that practical systems must solve. Most intrinsic image computations assume that segmentation of the scene into objects and background has been done. Certainly high-level vision (say recognition) usually assumes segmentation. Chapters 1.1, 1.3, 2.3, and 2.4 directly address the topic of segmentation.

Intrinsic Image Computations. The purpose of these computations is to extract physical information about the scene from the image. The motivation is that the physical information will be less sensitive to irrelevant variations to which the image is prey (such as lighting effects), and thus will be a more reliable basis for practical decisions such as manipulation, navigation, or recognition. Chapters 1.2 and 1.3 are mainly concerned with intrinsic images calculation, using clues of shading, multiple cameras, and motion.

System Architecture. System architectures for vision are now being designed as part of several major projects in research centers around the country. Often the system is built around a "blackboard" that serves as communications medium, central representation, and sometimes as a form of autonomous inference or geometrical computing engine. In this volume, chapter 1 gives an explicit description of the detailed makeup of such a vision system. The neural architecture that could underlie vision and thinking in general is of course an important topic in the cognitive sciences. Chapter 2.3 outlines a hierarchy of abstractions implemented in a neural-like net of small processing units.

Hardware Architecture. There is much activity today in designing and building special-purpose hardware architectures. Low-level vision (like graphics and image processing) has long been a candidate for such work because of the simplicity and physical locality of many of the operations. Recently high-level vision, or cognitive processes in general, has influenced the development of computational models (chapter 2.3; Feldman, 1985) and actual computers (Hillis, 1986). Advances in the power and packaging of microcomputers have led to new general-purpose architectures involving many computers working in parallel. These and more special-purpose hardware architectures are very promising tools for advancing all levels of the computer vision problem. In this volume the hardware architecture issue is addressed in chapter 1.

REFERENCES

Ballard, D., & Brown, C. (1982). *Computer vision.* Englewood Cliffs, NJ: Prentice-Hall.
Feldman, J. A. Editor. (January–March 1985). *Cognitive Science 9,* 1, Special Issue on Connectionist Models.
Fodor, J. (1983). *The modularity of mind.* Cambridge, MA: MIT Press.
Hillis, D. (1985). *The connection machine.* Cambridge, MA: MIT Press.
Horn, B. K. P. (1986). *Robot vision.* Cambridge, MA: MIT Press.
Levine, M. (1985). *Vision in man and machine.* New York: McGraw-Hill.
Marr, D. (1982). *Vision.* San Francisco, CA: Freeman.
Pentland, A. P. (1986). *From pixels to predicates.* Norwood, NJ: Ablex.
Roberts, L. G. (1965). Machine perception of three-dimensional solids. In J. P. Tippet et al. (Eds.), *Optical and electro-optical information processing* (pp. 159–197). Cambridge, MA: MIT Press.

This representation must then be refined and associated with semantic events by making use of general knowledge and constraints provided by the physical world represented in the scene domains of interest. This implies that the intermediate events must be mapped to hypotheses about the content and structure of the scene. Once a partial mapping is achieved a variety of interpretation strategies can be employed for matching, verifying, and refining contextual structures, and for grouping incomplete and ambiguous image data into organized perceptual structures.

The construction of a three-dimensional representation of the environment from a static image is an additional aspect of our work. We have made some progress toward this goal (55, 98, 149, 159, 160), but it remains a difficult problem. While the results presented in this chapter focus more on the problem of object labeling in a static monocular two-dimensional image, the system presented here can be naturally extended to include stereo and/or motion analysis of multiple images. The presence of three-dimensional data significantly improves the ability to develop a three-dimensional representation of surfaces and would make the interpretation process easier and more robust, although the problem is still extremely challenging. Thus, our current system is being extended to use depth maps of the visual field produced by motion and stereo algorithms as part of the three-dimensional interpretation process.

Ambiguity and Context

The complexity of the visual task can be made explicit by examining almost any image of a natural scene. Even though it is very difficult to be introspective of one's own visual processing, we believe the conjectures and qualitative discussion in this subsection are intuitive and reasonable.

Humans are rarely aware of any significant degree of ambiguity in local portions of the sensory data, nor are they aware of the degree to which they are employing more global context and stored expectations derived from experience (26, 27, 131, 132). However, if the visual field is restricted so that only local information about an object or object-part is available, interpretation is often difficult or impossible. Increasing the contextual information, so that spatial relations to other objects and object-parts are present, makes the perceptual task seem natural and simple. Consider the scenes in Figure 1.1 and the close-up images in Figure 1.2. In each case subimages of objects have been selected which show:

- "primitive" image events—image events which convey limited information about the decomposition of an object into its parts (which

a

b

c

d

e

f

g   h

FIGURE 1.1.   Original images. These images are representative samples
from a larger data base that is used in our experiments. All are 256×256
pixels in spatial resolution; the color resolution is 8 bits in each of the red,
green, and blue components, except *h*, which is monochromatic.

of course is a function at least partly of resolution); note that this
implies that the path to recognition of the object via subparts is not
available to our perceptual system;

- absence of context—information about other objects which might
  relate to the given object in expected ways is limited; note that this
  implies that the path to recognition of the object, via the scenes or
  objects of which it is a part, is not available to our perceptual system.

In Figure 1.2, as some of the surrounding context of the shoes and the
head are supplied, the perceptual ambiguity disappears and the related
set of visual elements is easily recognized. In each of the cases illustrated
in Figures 1.1 and 1.2 the purely local hypothesis is inherently unreliable
and uncertain, and there may be little surface information to be derived
in a bottom-up manner. It appears that human vision is fundamentally
organized to exploit the use of contextual knowledge and expectations in
the organization of the visual primitives. However, it may be impossible
to associate object labels with these ambiguous primitives until they are
grouped into larger entities and collectively interpreted as a related set of
object or scene parts (28). Thus, the inclusion of knowledge-driven processes at some level in the image interpretation task, where there is still a
great degree of ambiguity in the organization of the visual primitives,
appears inevitable.

We conjecture that image interpretation initially proceeds by forming
an abstract representation of important visual events in the image with-

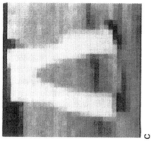

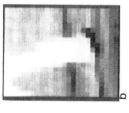

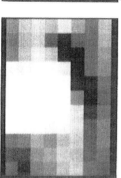

FIGURE 1.2. Closeup subimages from original images. In many cases, the identity or function of an object or object part cannot be determined from a small local view. Only when the surrounding context becomes available can the objects be recognized.

out knowledge of its contents. These primitive elements will be associated with tokens (forming a symbolic representation of the image data), which are then collected, grouped, and refined to bring their collective description into consistency with high-level semantic structures that represent the observer's knowledge about the world.

Issues in Image Interpretation

There are a variety of issues that must be addressed if robust vision systems are to be developed. We have identified some of the key problems that we believe are critical to the interpretation process and which are addressed in the following sections. The reader should note, however, that we are not attempting to discuss all of the issues that are open in vision, since it would lead to a chapter far longer than this one. Thus, in summary, we have abstracted the following set of overlapping problems that must be faced:

- *Reliability of Segmentation Processes.* Segmentation, or low-level, processes vary in quite unreliable and unpredictable ways due to a variety of confounding factors, which include complex uncontrolled lighting, highlights and shadows, texture, occlusion, complex three-dimensional shapes, and digitization effects.
- *Uncertainty.* There is inherent uncertainty in every stage of processing; as the data is transformed it must be kept constrained in a way that preserves some degree of integrity and avoids large search spaces.
- *Information Fusion.* Mechanisms are needed for integrating multiple sources of information, including multiple sensory sources, multiple representations output from low-level processes, and evidence from multiple knowledge sources.
- *Representation.* It is difficult to represent natural objects and scenes that exhibit a tremendous variability in their three-dimensional shape, color, texture, and size and, hence, in many of their measurable characteristics in the two-dimensional image. Yet such a representation is clearly needed in order to capture the structural, geometric, and spatial information required for visual perception.
- *Local vs. Global Processing in Matching.* There is a general need to provide information about the global context to the more localized processes attempting to reach some decision about a portion of the image; the process of hypothesis generation must work in the face of incomplete and inconsistent information.
- *Inference.* Computational machinery is needed for assessing the indirect implication of direct, but uncertain, evidence; this inferencing capability must be able to deal with all of the aforementioned issues.

Difficulties with Segmentation

Probably the most fundamental problem blocking knowledge-based vision development has been the lack of stable low-level vision algorithms that can produce a reasonably useful intermediate representation. Vision systems must deal with the problem of dynamically transforming the massive amounts of sensory data (in an image of reasonable resolution there are $512 \times 512 \cong \frac{1}{4}$ million pixels) into a much smaller set of image events, such as regions of homogeneous color and texture, straight lines, and local surface patches, to which hypotheses will be attached.

There is little doubt that the segmentation problem[2] is a very difficult and ill-formed problem (56). There is no ideal or "correct" segmentation because that is a function of the goals of the interpretation system. The two-dimensional appearance of objects and their parts is affected by variations in lighting, perspective distortion, varying point of view, occlusion, highlights, and shadows. In addition, objects and their parts may or may not be visually distinguishable from the background. Thus, one cannot predict what initial image information relevant to the recognition of objects can be extracted. The only thing that should be counted on is that the process will remain inherently unreliable; certainly some useful information can be extracted, but many errors will also occur, and no optimal solution exists in any nontrivial image domain. In general there is no set of parameter settings for any algorithm that will extract the desired image events without also generating additional nonoptimal or undesirable events. For a given parameter setting, a region segmentation might be too fragmented in one area of an image (i.e., too many regions) while being overmerged in another area of the image (i.e., too few regions). As parameters are varied the partitioning will change, but never will an optimal or near-optimal result be produced throughout the scene. The same is true of line and surface extraction algorithms; they will produce fragmented and overmerged events in a varied and unpredictable manner.

Segmentation vs. the Recovery of Three-Dimensional Surfaces

For the past decade there has been major controversy in the field of computer vision concerning the meaningfulness and validity of segmentation. Some researchers seem to restrict their criticisms to the actual partitioning of images via region segmentation, but feel more open to the process of line extraction. It is our strong opinion that while both

---

[2]Note that we sometimes will use the term *segmentation* loosely to cover not only the usual definition of partitioning an image into connected, nonoverlapping sets of pixels, but also other low-level processes, such as line extraction.

suffer from similar types of unreliability, they both result in descriptions that contain useful information, and therefore, should not be distinguished with respect to the issues being discussed. Researchers who are more theoretically inclined and whose work is sometimes referred to as computational vision (17, 22, 31, 64, 65, 87, 88, 129), have concluded that the recovery of information about the three-dimensional surfaces in the visible environment is the most (and some have implied *only*) appropriate goal. In the extreme, this leads to systems that are restricted to using only those processes that directly recover three-dimensional information (stereo (14, 156), motion (2, 66, 135), shape from shading (65, 68, 157), shape from texture (71), and in general, shape from x, where x is a monocular source of information).

It is our position that even when very good depth information is available, the complexity of the natural world will leave us facing many of the difficult issues that we have been discussing. Consider the problem of interpreting a natural environment, such as a typical crowded city street scene, even if a perfect depth map for all the visible surfaces were available; that is, in addition to the original color information at each pixel, the exact distance to the corresponding visible surface element at each pixel is also recorded. How should the information be partitioned into meaningful intermediate entities such as surfaces, parts of objects, and objects? And then how could this be interfaced to the knowledge base so that control of the interpretation process is feasible? Given that many initial local hypotheses will be inherently uncertain and unreliable, how is globally consistent and reliable integration of the information achieved?

This, in fact, is exactly the set of problems confronting the reliable segmentation of two-dimensional data into regions and lines. It does not appear that the problem of segmentation can be avoided; in some manner the partitioning of the depth map into surface patches of various types and the extraction of three-dimensional lines via depth and orientation discontinuities must be accomplished. We believe that the principles and approaches presented here for analysis of two-dimensional color data of static monocular images will also be applicable to the processing of three-dimensional depth data derived from stereo and laser ranging devices, as well as two-dimensional and three-dimensional motion data derived from a sequence of images.

Overview of the VISIONS System Approach

In response to the issues just outlined, a general, partially working, image-understanding system has evolved over the last 12 years. The system design embodies certain assumptions about the process of transforming visual information. The first assumption is that the initial computation proceeds in a bottom-up fashion by extracting information from the image without knowledge of its contents. A second basic assumption is that every stage of processing is inherently unreliable. A third assumption is that local ambiguity and uncertainty in object hypotheses to a great extent can be removed only by satisfying expected relations between scene and object parts that are stored in a knowledge base about the domain.

Figure 1.3 is an abstraction of the multiple levels of representation and processing in the VISIONS system. The successful functioning of the system involves extracting image events, which are then used to hypothesize scene and object parts for quick access to knowledge structures (called "schemas"), which capture the object descriptions and contextual constraints from prototypical scene situations. The hierarchically organized schemas contain interpretation strategies for top-down control of intermediate grouping strategies and allow feedback from high-level hypotheses to low-level processing.

The general strategy by which the VISIONS system operates is to build an intermediate symbolic representation (ISR) of the image data using segmentation processes that initially do not make use of any knowledge of specific objects in the domain. From the intermediate level data, a partial interpretation is constructed by associating an object label with selected groups of the intermediate tokens. The object labels are used to activate portions of the knowledge network related to the hypothesized object. Once activated, the procedural components of the knowledge network direct further grouping, splitting and labeling processes at the intermediate level to construct aggregated and refined intermediate events that are in closer agreement with the stored symbolic object descriptions. Although the following discussion is motivated primarily via experience with two-dimensional abstractions of the image data (such as regions and lines), the system is being extended to three-dimensional abstractions, such as depth arrays and surfaces, as well as to motion attributes of two-dimensional and three-dimensional tokens.

Briefly, the three levels of representation are:

1. *Low-Level.* Here, numerical arrays of direct sensory data are stored, including the results of algorithms which produce point/pixel data in register with the sensory data (e.g., a depth map produced from stereo point matching).

2. *Intermediate-Level.* This is referred to as the Intermediate Symbolic Representation (ISR) because symbolic tokens for regions, lines, and surfaces with attribute lists are constructed for the image events that have been extracted from the low-level data. Aggregate structures produced by grouping, splitting, and/or modifying the

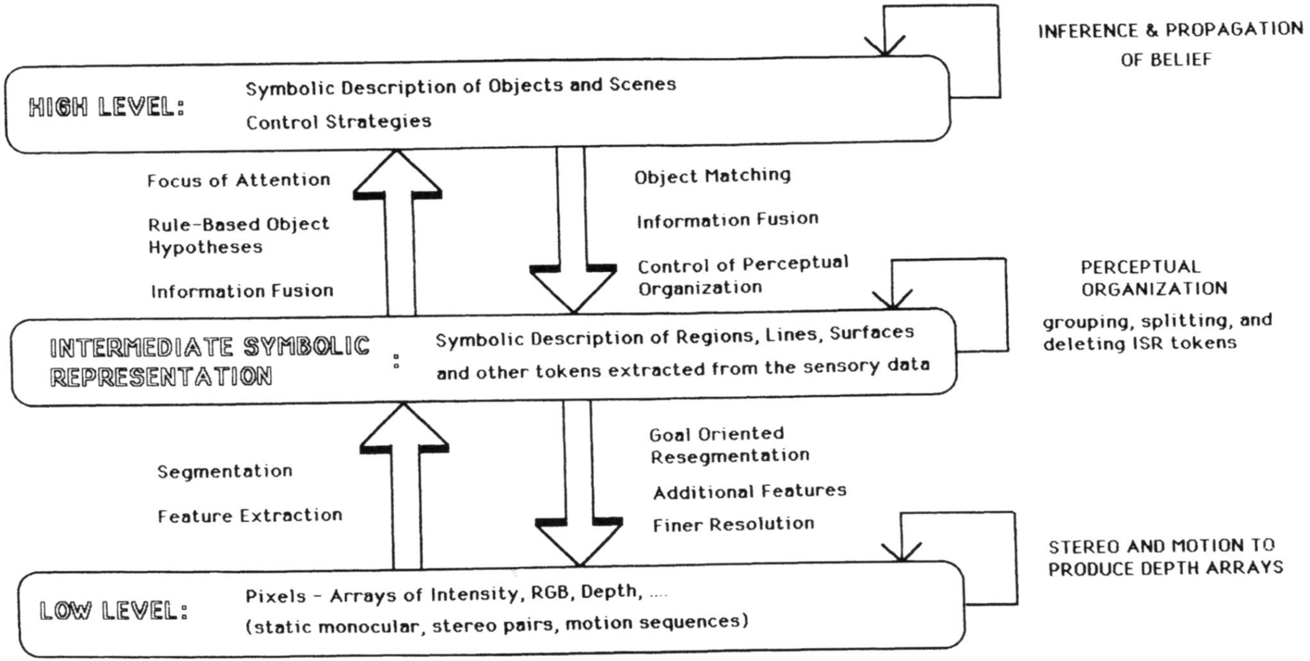

FIGURE 1.3. The VISIONS System: Processing and control across multiple levels of representation are depicted in this system overview.

11

primitive image events or other aggregates are also represented symbolically as tokens in the ISR.

3. *High-Level.* The knowledge base (called "Long Term Memory" or "LTM") consists of a semantic network of schema nodes, each of which has a declarative and procedural component. The network is organized in terms of a compositional hierarchy of PART-OF relations and a subclass hierarchy of IS-A relations. The interpretation process constructs a network in Short-Term Memory or STM, which is composed of image-specific instances of portions of the LTM network.

Now let us consider some of the stages of processing in a bit more detail.

1. *Motion and Stereo.* Multiple frames can be analyzed via motion and stereo algorithms to produce displacement fields, and from these displacement fields, depth arrays can be extracted. It may be possible to process these depth arrays to provide initial surface descriptions of portions of the image.

2. *Segmentation.* Segmentation processes are applied to the numerical arrays of low-level data to form a symbolic representation of regions and lines and their attributes such as color, texture, location, size, shape, orientation, length, and so forth. The region and line representations are integrated so that spatially related entities in either can be easily accessed (124). If depth arrays are available, then three-dimensional surfaces and their attributes can be extracted. Two-dimensional motion attributes can also be associated with regions and lines, while three-dimensional motion attributes can be associated with surfaces and their boundaries.

3. *Focus-of-Attention.* Object hypothesis rules are applied to the region, line, and surface tokens in the ISR to rank-order candidate object hypotheses (20, 21, 118, 148, 149, 155). This initial mapping of spatially organized tokens to object labels provides an effective *focus-of-attention* mechanism to initiate semantic processing. The rules can also be viewed as sets of constraints on the range of attribute values on the ISR tokens (e.g., constraints on the color of region tokens, or length of line tokens, or orientation of surface tokens). Relational rules applied to tokens of a different type (e.g., line-to-region relations) allow fusion of information across multiple representations.

4. *Object Hypothesis and Verification.* More complex object-dependent interpretation strategies are represented in a procedural form within the schema knowledge structures (55, 106, 149, 150). These

local control strategies provide top-down control over the interpretation process. Partial interpretations are extended from "islands of reliability" as in the HEARSAY paradigm (41, 80). General knowledge of objects and scenes is organized around a network of standard two-dimensional views of three-dimensional objects. In cases of simple three-dimensional shapes, such as the planar surfaces forming a polyhedral "house" volume, three-dimensional models and associated processing strategies are employed. Verification strategies exploit particular spatial relationships between the hypothesized object and other specific expected object labels or image features.

5. *Perceptual Organization.* Intermediate grouping algorithms, currently being developed (20, 21, 49, 139, 140), reorganize the region and line elements into larger aggregate structures that are expected to more closely match expected object structures. These include line grouping and region merging capabilities and are intended to be applied in either a bottom-up or top-down manner. There are significant advantages in selective application of knowledge-directed perceptual organization mechanisms, and the schemas provide an effective means for specification of the relevant control knowledge. We hope to evolve similar intermediate grouping strategies for complex three-dimensional shape representations in the future.

6. *Goal-Oriented Resegmentation.* Feedback to the lower-level processes for more detailed segmentation can be requested in cases when interpretation of an area fails, when an expected image feature is not found, or when conflicting interpretations occur. It may also be of utility in motion sequences for extraction of particular objects that have been found in previous frames. Both the region and line algorithms have parameters for varying the sensitivity and amount of detail in their segmentation output. The development and control of such strategies, as well as the integration of their results, is currently being examined in an effort to build a low-level executive (72).

7. *Inference.* Due to the inherent ambiguities in both the raw image data and the extracted intermediate representations, object hypotheses will have a high degree of uncertainty. In order to combine this information into a coherent view of the world, two capabilities are being developed: the capability to combine uncertain evidence from multiple sources of knowledge (116), and the ability to propagate confidences (beliefs or probabilities) through the network of schema nodes (85, 142). The latter capability will allow

inferential capabilities about the presence of object/scene parts for control of the partially completed interpretation. Both heuristic approaches and theoretical formulations related to the Dempster-Shafer theory of evidential reasoning (38, 121) are currently being explored.

THE LLVS: AN INTERACTIVE ALGORITHM SOFTWARE DEVELOPMENT ENVIRONMENT

Interpretive Control for Applying Image Operators

The Low-Level Visions System (LLVS) is a software environment specifically designed to facilitate all low-level image analysis research for the VISIONS image interpretation project. It is a direct descendent of the Image Operating System which has been in use since 1979 (74), and which was originally written in Fortran 77 and CLisp (a UMass dialect of LISP, which computationally is very efficient). The LLVS consists of a high-level interpretive control language (CommonLISP) with efficient "image operators" written in C. The image operators are viewed as local operators to be applied in parallel, at some level of resolution, to all pixels in an input image. The system is useful as both a research tool for algorithm development and as a production system for initial processing of images; it is currently being further developed and extended.

The user interface is one of the most important aspects of any system. LLVS provides a "friendly" environment for both experienced and naive users through the use of LISP as the high-level control language. LISP is particularly well suited for an experimental environment since it is an interpreted language and can therefore be modified interactively. Use of LISP allows interaction with the system to be conducted using LISP expressions. Images appear as LISP objects. On-line help, interactive verification of parameters, and simple installation of new operators are all provided. The environment supports the dynamic definition of experiments with various images and image operators. LLVS provides control mechanisms (*via* LISP) by which the user can compose image operators and control the application of the image operators.

A Parallel Hierarchical Representation for Image Operators

The computational structure of images in LLVS is based on the concept of a *processing* cone proposed by Hanson and Riseman (51, 57); the processing cone is a model for hierarchical parallel array processing and is related to other hierarchical structures (127). At each level of resolution n, the cone contains 2^n by 2^n pixels, with a vector of values, $\mathbf{V}$, stored at each pixel. The corresponding vector element $\mathbf{V}_i$ for all pixels at a given level of resolution can be considered as a single two-dimensional entity; this slice across the cone is referred to as a *plane*. Each pixel at level n has four unique descendents at level $n + 1$ and exactly one ancestor pixel at each level $m < n, m \geq 0$.

A *plane* has attributes of *level, size, location, type, background-value,* and additional user-definable values. Having a size independent of the level and including a location allows part of a plane to be extracted for independent processing in a very efficient way and then related back to the original plane or other parts of the original plane. The type specifies the format in which the pixels of the plane are stored. The background-value provides a value to be used for neighborhood operations which access nonexistent pixels.

Image operators are functions that are evaluated on a set of argument planes and which produce one or more output planes. Execution of an image operator is defined as the local parallel application of a prototype function to all pixels in a plane; the function is applied to a neighborhood around each pixel. This approach will allow the translation to hardware array technology to occur in a natural manner.

A pixel-centered coordinate system and correct system handling of boundary conditions greatly simplify the specification of the prototype image operator, since the operator generally does not need to compute subscripts for neighboring pixels or consider special cases for neighboring pixels that fall outside of the plane. The specification of the image operators is independent of the level of resolution of the data to which it will be applied and it is not necessary to specify the data type of the input plane. Images of different data types and ranges can be handled without any extra code in the image operator, since all access to the image data is through special access functions. Thus, image operators can be interactively applied during the debugging stage to a small window of the image (by specifying *limits* for the processing), or a coarse representation of the data (by doing the operation at a different *level*), and then later applied to the full image at fine resolution. Image operators can be easily added to the system for any function desired by the user.

Image operators conceptually contain four sections. The two most important are the *process* section, which defines the computation to be performed at each pixel, and the *control* section written in LISP. The control section provides the logical association between the plane names utilized in the process section and the actual planes to which the image operator is being applied, and obtains any other parameters required.[3]

---

[3]Because image operators are functions, the input planes and parameters are generally supplied as arguments to the function.

The other two sections are the *initialization* and *termination* sections which may not be needed for particular image operators.

Summary of Distinguishing Features

The three most important characteristics that distinguish LLVS from other image analysis systems are:

1. The partitioning of the image analysis problem into interpretive control and noninterpretive image operators allows good dynamic control of the interactive experimental environment without sacrificing image operator efficiency.
2. The structure imposed on the image operators simplifies the construction of these operators, which minimizes the time and cost of implementing them.
3. The human engineering of the user-interface and automatic documentation make the system easy to use for a novice, yet flexible and convenient for an expert.

SEGMENTATION ALGORITHMS

In an image of a scene there are a variety of sources of low-level information available which can be used to form an initial description of the structure of the image. The extraction of this description, in terms of significant image tokens, is an important precursor to the construction of a more abstract description at the semantic level. It is unlikely that any single descriptive process will produce a description that is adequate for an unambiguous interpretation of the image. Rather, multiple processes are required, each of which views the image data in a different way and each of which produces a partial description that may be incomplete or errorful. As will be seen in later sections, we view one of the functions of the perceptual grouping processes to be the resolution of the multiple descriptions into consistent higher-level symbolic descriptions of the image. Consequently, for the entire history of the VISIONS project, the development of multiple low-level algorithms[4] that are reasonably robust across a variety of task domains has been an important concern, even while recognizing that no single algorithm is sufficient.

---

[4]We will sometimes refer to the spectrum of low-level processes for extracting image events as *segmentation algorithms*, including region and line extraction algorithms, even though some of them do not actually partition in the image into disjoint subsets; thus, sometimes we loosely use *low-level processes* and *segmentation processes* interchangeably.

It should also be noted that all of these algorithms operate initially in a bottom-up mode without any use of knowledge of the task domain. However, rough "sensitivity" settings on parameters of the algorithm, such as "low," "medium," and "high," can be set a priori in order to extract a larger or smaller number of intermediate tokens; these parameters may also be set or modified by other components of the system and the application of the process may be localized to a specified subimage.

While a variety of low-level algorithms have been developed, there are two primary low-level algorithms that are currently in use in our environment: (a) a region segmentation algorithm that is based upon analysis of histogram peaks and valleys in local subimages; and (b) a straight line extraction algorithm that segments the intensity surface into connected subsets of pixels with similar gradient orientation.

In addition to these algorithms there are several others that are used as components of the two main algorithms, or of the perceptual grouping and interpretation mechanisms described later. These will be discussed very briefly in this section; they include an edge-preserving smoothing algorithm (92, 105), a histogram-based multi-valued thresholding algorithm (73), a region-merging segmentation algorithm (49), and a low-level executive for directing goal-oriented low-level processing via feedback from interpretation processes (72).

Histogram-Based Region Segmentation

The region segmentation technique that we employ was first developed by Nagin (94, 95) and later extended by Kohler (75) and Beveridge (24). The approach is in the spirit of the Ohlander–Price algorithms (103, 110), since both their algorithms should be viewed as instances of histogram-based region segmentation. We conjecture that generally our approach will be more robust and computationally efficient because of the problems of recursive decomposition of global histograms in the Ohlander–Price approach (59, 112). The Nagin–Kohler algorithm allows a fixed number of windows to be processed on one pass and significantly reduces the problem of hidden clusters in global histograms that are often encountered in a recursive decomposition approach. However, there has not been a thorough objective comparison of the two approaches.

The histogram-based region segmentation algorithm involves detecting clusters in a feature histogram, associating labels with the clusters, mapping the labels onto the image pixels, and then forming regions of connected pixels with the same label. The process of global histogram labeling causes many errors to occur because global information will not accurately reflect local image events that do not involve large numbers of

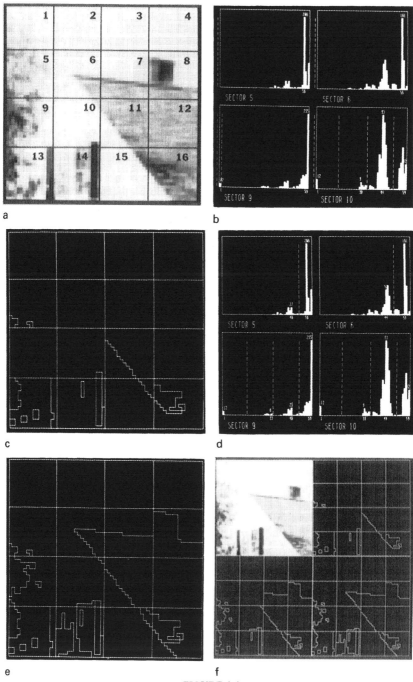

a

b

c

d

e

f

FIGURE 1.4.

18

pixels, but which, nevertheless, are quite clear. Much of the focus of the algorithms will be to organize the segmentation process around local histograms from local windows and then have a postprocessing stage merge regions that have been arbitrarily split along the artificial window boundaries.

The Nagin algorithm overcomes the problem of finding small hidden clusters by partitioning the image into $N \times N$ subimages (usually $N = 16$ or 32) called "sectors"; the histogram segmentation algorithm is applied independently to each sector. Thus, each sector receives the full focus of the cluster detection process and many of the problems of cluster overlap and hidden clusters are significantly reduced. The cluster extraction algorithm determines local maxima and local minima in the histogram, and then sequentially chooses the next "best" maxima, which is that maxima for which the ratio of the local maximum to its adjacent valley is largest and the distance to any previously selected local maximum is greater than some minimum distance. Figure 1.4(b) shows the histograms from four adjacent sectors in the roof/chimney area of Figure 1.1(c); note the significant ambiguity in cluster definition that is (usually) present in the histogram. This suggests a natural "sensitivity" parameter in the segmentation process, achieved by controlling the number of clusters detected. The net result is a set of local maxima and their relationships to the valley separating them, each of which can be considered as a distinct cluster and given a unique label. Theoretically, any N-dimensional clustering algorithm could be used (the rest of the algorithm remains the same), but one must keep in mind that computational simplicity is a primary goal since this clustering algorithm will be executed many times across the image and is only one small step in the entire interpretation process. Each of these labels are then mapped back to the subimage and a connected components algorithm is used to generate a set of labeled regions.

The partitioning of the image into sectors has an obvious weakness. If

---

FIGURE 1.4.   Histogram-based region segmentation. (a) Original image from roof/chimney area of Figure 1.1(c) showing the sector boundaries. (b) Histograms of the four adjacent sectors 5, 6, 9, and 10. Peaks and valleys are extracted, and labels are associated with peaks; the dotted lines mark the valleys and the numbers denote the size of the peaks. (c) Region boundaries formed by mapping the histogram labels to pixels and finding connected components. (d) Augmented cluster set after propagating peaks from adjacent sectors. (e) Region boundaries produced by the augmented cluster set. (f) The original subimage and region boundaries during the three peak-propagation steps; after two iterations of peak propagations, no further peaks are added to any sector and the process terminates. Note that the sensitivity in the peak-extraction process was not sufficient to detect the sky-wall boundary.

an adjacent sector has a visually distinct region that does not overlap the central sector sufficiently, it is quite possible that the cluster will be undetected in the central sector. The small region representing the intrusion into the central sector will then be lost. Nagin (95) attempted to limit this problem, while still preserving the locality of the histogram, by expanding the histogram domain of each sector to overlap adjacent sectors by 25%, while still maintaining the mapping of labels to the central nonoverlapping core.

Nevertheless, if the sensitivity of the peak-extracting process is not sufficiently high, clusters will not be selected and boundaries will disappear. Many of these boundaries will be at corners of a sector window and show results that are inconsistent with an adjacent sector. Figure 1.4(b,c) shows the histograms and resulting individual sector segmentations; the diagonal house wall/boundary disappears.

The Kohler algorithm improves the clustering step by determining correspondences between peaks in adjacent sectors and by adding candidate peaks from surrounding sectors to the set of peaks selected for the central sector. Thus, small variations between peak labels will be accounted for, and if the 25% overlap is not sufficient, small intrusions of regions from one sector to the next will more likely result in a peak to be added. This can be iterated until there are no peak additions between adjacent windows. The augmented set of peaks forms the input to the labeling process. Figures 1.4(b) and 1.4(d) show the set of peaks for four sectors before and after peak addition; Figures 1.4(c) and 1.4(e) show the related individual sector segmentations after mapping cluster labels to pixels and performing a connected components region labeling. Figure 1.4(f) shows the subimage and three steps of the peak addition process in extracting the house boundary. Note that in this example the cluster extraction process was still not set at a sensitivity sufficient to extract the left diagonal boundary between house wall and sky.

The artificial sector boundaries are removed by a region merging algorithm, which considers adjacent regions across sector boundaries. The merge/no merge decision mechanism compares the global mean and variance of the two regions, as well as the local mean and variance of the regions near the sector boundary. More recently, this remerging algorithm has been generalized (49) to use a set of modular feature statistics so that many different remerging strategies can be used; it can also be applied separately from the region segmentation algorithm under discussion here.

The algorithm can be summarized in five steps:

1. Subdivide the image into sectors, compute the histogram of the expanded sectors, and select the cluster labels in each expanded sector.

2. Analyze the cluster labels from adjacent sectors and augment the label set where appropriate.

3. Segment each sector using the expanded set of labels by mapping each pixel value to a label and applying a connected components algorithm.

4. Remove sector boundaries by merging similar regions.

5. Perform small region suppression, which often reduces the number of regions by a factor of 4.

Figure 1.5 shows additional segmentations using this algorithm on several of the images in Figure 1.1. It should be noted that when multi-spectral data is available (e.g., RGB) the algorithm can be applied to each band. Figure 1.5(a,b) shows the result of applying our algorithm to the

a

FIGURE 1.5. Results of histogram-region segmentation. The algorithm has a sensitivity parameter controlling the peak-extraction process and the resulting number of regions produced. In each case the parameter was set to "high" or "very high" sensitivity for each of the 16 × 16 sector sub-images; (a) High sensitivity intensity segmentation; (b) High sensitivity segmentation of the red component (R from RGB); (c) Intensity segmentation at very high sensitivity; (d) Red color plane segmentation at "very high" sensitivity; (e) Intersection of R, G, and B region segmentations at very high sensitivity (or equivalently the union of R, G, and B boundaries). Note the recovery of additional interesting boundaries beyond the intensity segmentation at the expense of additional fragmentation across the image.

b

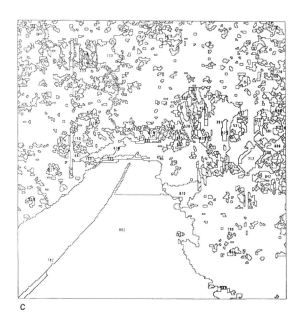

c

FIGURE 1.5. (*continued*)

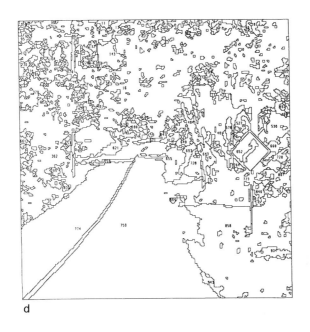

d

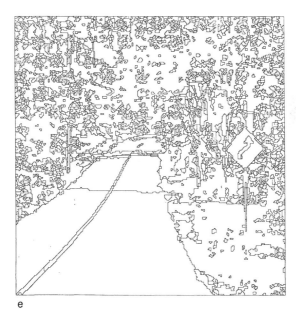

e

FIGURE 1.5. (*continued*)

intensity and red band, respectively. Each of the spectral bands might extract additional boundaries, and the intersection of the region segmentations (or equivalently the union of the boundaries) will usually retain more information than the intensity segmentation at the risk of greatly overfragmenting an image, as shown in Figure 1.5(c–e). The reader should refer to the discussion, "Rule-Based Region Merging" and Figure 1.6 for a technique that will deal with the overfragmentation problem.

Extracting Straight Lines
and Line-Based Texture Features

Despite the large amount of research appearing in the literature, effective extraction of linear boundaries has remained a difficult problem in many image domains. The technique presented here (33, 34) was motivated by a need for a straight-line extraction method which can find straight lines, possibly long and possibly of very low contrast, in reasonably complex images.

A key characteristic of the approach that distinguishes it from most previous work is the global organization of the intensity surface into a "supporting edge context" prior to making any decisions about the relevance of local intensity changes. Pixels are grouped into edge support regions of similar gradient orientation, and then the associated intensity surface is used to determine a gradient–magnitude-weighted planar fit from which a representative line is extracted. A set of line attributes is extracted from the line-support region, the weighted planar fit, and the representative line. These attributes can then be filtered for a variety of purposes.

Figure 1.6(a) is a surface plot of a 32×32 intensity image extracted from Figure 1.1(c); it is the upper roof corner on the right hand side of the image. The vector field of Figure 1.6(b) shows the corresponding gradient image (where the length of the vector encodes gradient magnitude) with a superimposed region segmentation from the gradient orientation algorithm described next. Small 2×2 edge masks are used to compute the gradient so that closely spaced parallel lines will not be missed.

An extremely simple and computationally efficient process is employed to group the local gradients into regions on the basis of the orientation estimates. The 360° range of gradient orientation is arbitrarily partitioned into a small set of regular intervals, say eight 45° partitions, or sixteen 22.5° partitions. Pixels participating in the edge-support context of a straight line will tend to be in the same edge-orientation partitions and adjacent pixels that are not part of a straight line will tend to have different orientations. A simple connected components algorithm can be used to form distinct region labels for groups of adjacent pixels with the same orientation label (Figure 1.6b). The great degree of fragmentation of very low gradient magnitude areas into many small regions can be considered evidence for homogeneity and adjacent elements could be grouped into homogeneous regions.

A line whose local edges have an edge orientation in the vicinity of a partition boundary can be expected to be fragmented. To make the fixed partition technique more sensitive to edges of any orientation, the algorithm actually uses two overlapping sets of partitions, with one set rotated a half-partition interval. Thus, if a 45° partition starting at 0° is used, then a second set of 45° partitions starting at 22.5° is also used. The critical problem of this approach is merging the two representations in such a way that a single representation of each line is extracted from the two alternate line representations. The following scheme is used to select such regions for each line: First, the lengths of the lines are determined for each line support region; then, since each pixel is a member of exactly two regions (one in each gradient orientation segmentation), each pixel votes for the longest interpretation; finally, the percentage of voting pixels within each line-support region is the "support" of that region. Typically the regions selected are those that have support greater than 50%.

The underlying intensity surface of each line-support region is assumed to have a meaningful straight line associated with it. In order to extract a representative straight line, a plane is fit to the intensity surface of the pixels in each edge-support region, using a least-squares method similar to that used by Haralick (62) in his slope-facet model. The pixels associated with the longest line support region are shown as dots on the surface plot of Figure 1.6(c). The pixels are weighted by local gradient magnitude so that pixels in rapidly changing portions of the intensity surface dominate the fit.

An obvious constraint on the orientation of the line is that it be perpendicular to the gradient of the fitted plane. A simple approach for locating the line along the projection of the gradient is to intersect the fitted plane with a horizontal plane representing the average intensity of the region weighted by local gradient magnitude. The straight line resulting from the intersection of the two planes is shown in Figure 1.6(d).

The line-support region and the planar fit of the associated intensity surface provides the basic information necessary to quantify a variety of attributes beyond the basic orientation and position parameters. Length, width, contrast, and straightness can be easily extracted. Based upon these line attributes, the large set of lines can be filtered to extract a set

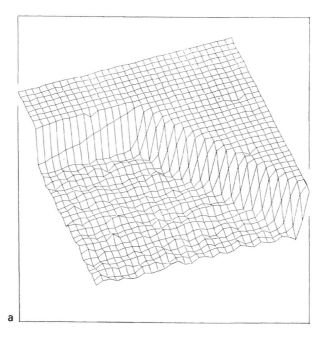

a

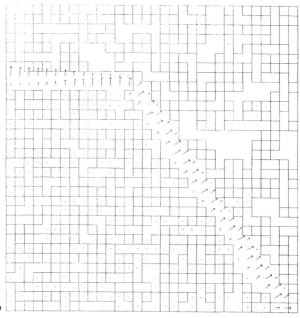

b

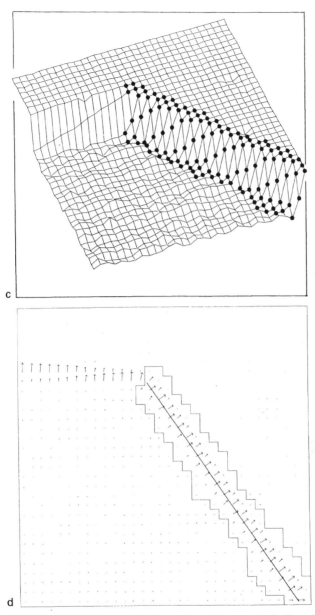

c

d

FIGURE 1.6. Line extraction from gardient orientation. (a) Surface plot of a relatively sharp and high contrast edge; (b) Regions produced by a connected components algorithm applied to the labels of the orientation partitions; (c) Pixels included in the line support region are highlighted by dots; (d) The resulting straight line overlaid on the set of pixels marking up the line support region.

27

with specific characteristics such as short texture-edges, or to select a "working set" of long lines at different levels of sensitivity.

The algorithm described in the preceding sections was applied to two of the house images and two of the road scenes in Figure 1.1. The algorithm is reasonably robust and accurately extracts many low-contrast long lines when overlapping partitions of 45°, staggered by 22.5°, are employed. The results are shown in Figure 1.7, where Figure 1.7(a)

FIGURE 1.7. Results of line-extraction algorithm. (a) Initial line set; (b–e) show the results of filtering the initial line set on various attributes of the lines; (b) High-gradient magnitude lines with gradient ≥ 10 gray levels per pixel; (c) Short high-gradient magnitude lines with length ≤ 5 and gradient ≥ 10 gray levels per pixel; (d) Long high-gradient lines with length ≥ 15 and gradient ≥ 10 gray levels per pixel; (e) Lines with length ≥ 10; (f, g) Two road scenes.

c

d

e

FIGURE 1.7. *(continued)*

shows the unfiltered output of the algorithm applied to the first house
image. Note that all of the short and low contrast edges are still present;
thus, it is necessary to filter the very low magnitude lines and group their
support regions into "homogeneous" regions that are interpreted as
absence of lines, as shown in Figure 1.7(b). We also show the result of
filtering on the basis of weighted gradient magnitude (change in gray-
levels per pixel) followed by a filtering on length that separates the edges
into two disjoint sets, one corresponding to short texture edges as shown
in Figure 1.6(c), and the other to longer lines related to the surface
structure of objects in the image as shown in Figure 1.6(d). Figure 1.6(e)

shows the result of filtering on length alone (length ≥ 5) for one of the other house scenes. The two road scenes are shown in Figure 1.6(f,g).

Additional Low-Level Algorithms

Smoothing

Many segmentation algorithms or low-level processes use some form of smoothing operation as a preprocessing stage. Image data are complicated by errors of approximation due to the discrete nature of the representation, noise intrinsic to the sensors, and variations in the scene itself. Most simple smoothing operators do not remove noise without destroying some of the fine structure in the underlying image.

A technique by Nagao that has been used to counteract this problem is commonly referred to as "edge-preserving" smoothing (92). The goal is to average the value associated with a pixel with only those pixels in a local neighborhood that do not cross a high-contrast boundary, thereby avoiding blurring of information at the boundary. At each pixel a set of masks, each of which contains the pixel but is oriented from the pixel in a different direction, is used to compute the variance in that window. The pixels in the lowest variance mask are used to compute the new pixel average. The major disadvantage is the expensive computation at each pixel.

We have employed both the Nagao algorithm as well as an alternative developed by Overton and Weymouth (105). The latter is a direct weighted average of pixels within a fixed shape mask. An iterative updating process incorporates pixel values in the neighborhood into the calculation of the new average value by means of weights that are decreasing functions of both spatial separation and intensity difference. Values that are more similar (i.e., less likely to cross an edge) are weighted more, and the degree of weighting of the neighborhood versus the current value is increased as a function of the variance in the neighborhood.

This algorithm performs approximately as well as the averaging by the minimum variance mask. Its advantage is that it can be directly computed. Its disadvantage is that the averaging of each pixel in the window is an exponential function of distance, intensity difference, and variance. Thus, the computational cost is also approximately the same. However, it appears that linear approximations to this function might work as well at only a fraction of the cost. The effectiveness of the linear averaging process is currently being examined (35).

Thresholding

Simple thresholding algorithms typically partition an image by assigning one label to pixels with feature values that are equal or greater than some threshold T, and another label to pixels with feature values less than T (141). For some images, such as chromosome images or hand-printed characters, where a clear figure-ground relationship exists, a single threshold often will be able to detect all or most of the object boundaries at the object-background discontinuity. However, those boundaries that correspond to object-object discontinuities or internal structure of the object may not be detected by that threshold. Further-more, in more complex images which do not exhibit a clear foreground-background distinction (such as images of natural outdoor scenes), a single threshold cannot be expected to detect all or even most of the object boundaries in the scene.

Kohler (73) has developed a segmentation algorithm based upon a complex form of thresholding, which uses n thresholds rather than a single threshold. These n thresholds are used to partition the pixel values into $n + 1$ possible classes, and a connected components algorithm is used to produce unique region identifiers. The thresholds are selected sequentially, and each threshold is selected to maximize the global aver-age contrast of edges detected by the threshold across the image. To obtain the final segmentation, an intersection process combines the set of binary segmentations by simply overlaying them and defining a new region label for each distinct combination of the n labels in the set of binary images.

Rule-Based Region Merging

It became apparent during experimentation with the Nagin/Kohler histogram-based region segmentation algorithm that the best results were obtained by making the cluster selection very liberal (i.e., selecting many clusters in order to overfragment the image), and then merging most of the regions in the postprocessing stage. Consequently, the merg-ing process was extracted to form an independent system. The result of that development effort led to a rule-based merging algorithm, which is used to merge regions along the artificial sector boundaries in the Nagin/Kohler algorithm, but which can also be used with any algorithm that produces an overly fragmented region segmentation (49).

The rule-based region merging algorithm starts with an initial seg-mentation as input and selects pairs of adjacent regions, which are candi-dates for merging into a single region. For example, the initial segmenta-tion can be produced by a region growing algorithm with an extremely conservative threshold that produces a highly fragmented segmentation. Because the system only merges (as opposed to splitting) regions, the initial segmentation must contain all the region boundaries desired in the final result.

The merging phase of the algorithm is a locally iterative, but globally parallel, selection and testing of region pairs for merging. For each pair of regions the boundary between them is given a similarity score based on a similarity evaluation function. Then a search for all the local minimal boundaries is made. A boundary is considered locally minimal if, and only if, it is the lowest scoring boundary for both of its associated regions. Those minimal boundaries below the global threshold for region similarity are removed and the statistics for the newly created regions updated; removal of each boundary creates one new region from two old regions. The merging processes is applied iteratively and terminates when none of the remaining boundaries score below the global region similarity threshold. Note that many local pairs can be simultaneously processed.

The similarity function, which of course is the key to the effectiveness of the algorithm, takes into account both global and local information. The global features are extracted from the total populations of the pixels in the two regions, while the local features are extracted from the pixels in the neighborhood of the boundary between the two regions. The similarity function is defined as a set of rules, each of which measures the similarity of two regions on the basis of a single feature, such as means of color or intensity, variance of color or intensity, common boundary length, boundary contrast, or a combination of features. The results of many such rules are combined through a function that computes the overall similarity measure.

The combination function is the product of the score of each of the similarity rules, each of which returns a value centered on one (implying no information about merging); values less than one indicate a vote for a merge (bounded by zero which guarantees a merge), and values greater than one indicate a vote against a merge. In practice the rules are never absolutely certain and often return values close to one.

Expectations of the characteristics of the images and goals regarding the desired segmentation can be encoded in the rules, and the nature of the segmentation produced can be controlled by the choice of rules and relative weights on the chosen rules. The philosophy and methodology of rule-based expert systems can be adapted here to allow modular contributions of features in a situation that is theoretically intractable (see discussion in introductory sections). By defining contributions from a feature set where the features can easily be varied for empirical evaluation or can be varied in situations where the goals of segmentation change, many of the advantages of expert system construction are realized. Currently, the system includes seven rules that can be applied to a pair of regions to determine the desirability of a proposed merge:

1. Difference of the global means normalized by the sum of standard deviations of the candidate regions.
2. Region size—small regions are encouraged to merge with larger regions.
3. Degree of adjacency—regions connected by a relatively long boundary are encouraged to merge.
4. Similarity of the standard deviations.
5. Difference of local means.
6. Maximum allowable standard deviation of the merged region.
7. The degree to which the region could have been caused by mixed pixels during the digitization process (i.e., a narrow region between regions of locally lower and higher means).

Figure 1.8 shows the results of applying the merging algorithm to the output of the histogram-based region segmentation algorithm (de-

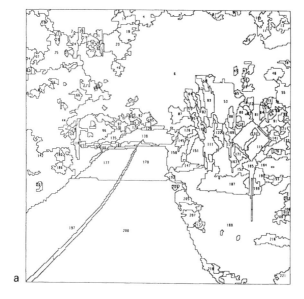

FIGURE 1.8. Region merging. The result of applying rule-based region merging to the output of the histogram-based region segmentation algorithm. (a) After region merging applied to Figure 1.5(e), which is the RGB region segmentation; this result should also be compared to both Figure 1.5(c) and Figure 1.5(e); (b) Intensity segmentation at high sensitivity of the other road scene in Figure 1.1; (c) Three-color intersection of RGB region segmentations at high sensitivity; (d) After region merging; note that portions of the road boundary and telephone pole detail are preserved with relatively few regions in the segmentation.

b

c

FIGURE 1.8. *(continued)*

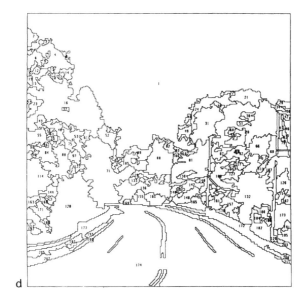

d

FIGURE 1.8. *(continued)*

scribed later) set at very high sensitivity in order to intentionally overfragment the image. In Figure 1.8(a) the algorithm is applied to the
overfragmented three-color segmentation of Figure 1.5(e). This result
should be compared to both Figure 1.5(c) and 1.5(e) since it produces a
qualitatively better segmentation with a smaller number of regions than
either. A second road scene example is shown in Figure 1.8(b–d), with
the intensity segmentation (derived using a high sensitivity setting)
shown in Figure 1.8(b), the additionally fragmented segmentation produced by intersecting regions from the individual R, G, and B segmentations shown in Figure 1.8(c), and the result after rule-based remerging of
the RGB segmentation shown in Figure 1.8(d). In the final result, one
can see the extraction of important detail that was not in the intensity
segmentation; the remerging algorithm was successful in reducing the
number of regions significantly while preserving important detail.

It should be noted that this approach differs significantly from the
approach taken by Nazif (99, 100), although both systems are rule-based.
Nazif's system is more general in that it allows both splitting and merging, and utilizes both lines and regions. However, Nazif's rules are of the
form "If condition, Then action"; it is our position that it is not computationally reasonable to use a production rule paradigm as a full segmentation process. Our rules are all applied simultaneously to any decision to

merge a pair of regions, but require an external control structure to decide globally which merge they execute.

Segmentation of Surfaces

Recently there has been some work on the process of segmenting depth data into surfaces (2, 14, 23, 45, 50, 78, 91, 130, 154, 156, 157). The problems in segmenting depth arrays are very similar to those encountered when segmenting intensity arrays if the scenes are unconstrained natural environments; almost all the issues in processing of intensity and color data will be present. We believe that some of the algorithms that have proven to be robust on intensity and/or color data may be adapted to the problem of segmenting depth data. This is a topic that we intend to explore in the future.

Low-Level Executive

The varying goals, features, and algorithms and their parameters make the problem of delivering the "best" intermediate representation to the interpretation processes an intractable problem. The "best" choices will almost certainly vary across images and vary across different locations in a single image. Consequently, it is unreasonable to expect that an optimal, good, or complete set of image events will be extracted. Rather, the goal is to deliver a usable representation.

We are in the process of developing the feedback loops from interpretation processes to a low-level executive that has knowledge about the set of low-level algorithms previously described. The low-level executive will also be able to accept goal-oriented requests for reanalyzing the sensory data in particular locations in order to extract tokens with particular characteristics. If successful, this capability will change the analysis of the sensory data in a fundamental way.

INTERMEDIATE SYMBOLIC REPRESENTATION

Size of Intermediate Symbolic Representation

It is generally accepted that a computer vision system must perform a variety of transformations of the data during the interpretation process. One of the key abstractions is the transformation of pixels, or more generally arrays of sensory data, into named image events that are more abstract than pixels, but less abstract than concepts of objects such as "house" or "road." The representational level at which the named image events are accessible as tokens is referred to as "the intermediate symbolic representation" (ISR). Examples of symbolic events represented in the ISR are regions, lines, and surfaces and their properties (54, 118); corners and textured areas are others that might prove useful, and in general, any event extractable from the sensory data may be represented.

In many cases, region and line extraction processes produce large numbers of image tokens. Many of these elements have to be repeatedly accessed, as demonstrated in the line grouping algorithm discussed in the next section and further examples in subsequent sections. The size of the intermediate data base can become enormous if the problem domain encompasses multiple sensor modalities, multiple feature representations, and multiple segmentation algorithms with varying parameter settings, motion sequences, temporally or spatially varying image sets, and so forth. This, coupled with the multiple grouping hypotheses that each primitive element could take part in, implies that the amount of data that must be maintained at the intermediate level will often be rather significant.

As we shall see later in the chapter, the high level interpretation processes in the VISIONS system are implemented as schemas using a blackboard system as the communication protocol. Rather than entering all of the intermediate symbolic elements on the blackboard, VISIONS stores this information in an image feature database (124), with a uniform set of access functions forming the interface between the intermediate and high-level processes.

Organizing the ISR into a Database

Image events stored in the ISR generally have the common property of being related to some subset of pixels in two-dimensional arrays of sensory data, either directly sensed data, such as light intensity or depth from a range sensor, or derived data, like normalized color or depth from motion and/or stereo. Thus, the ISR is first organized around "tokens," defined first as sets of pixel from two-dimensional arrays and then as relational groupings of other tokens (described in the following section). A set of tokens of a single type that is selected from an image by some process is called a "tokenset."

Each token has a type and a descriptor for the associated image event. For example, a line token will have a descriptor that includes the end points, angle, length, contrast, and straightness of the line. The specification of the descriptor for a type of token in the ISR is called a "lexicon." There is exactly one lexicon associated with each token type in the ISR, and of course, there will be many tokensets associated with each lexicon of a given type.

The representation of a token consists of a name, a referent to the data it describes, and a list of attributes. Each image is given a unique name, as is each tokenset, and each token in a tokenset is associated with a pointer to the actual token. A token name is made up of its image name, its tokenset name, and its token index. Associated with each token is a specification of the pixels that the token is associated with, represented as a bitplane in the coordinate system of the image. There is also a slot for each of the attributes defined in its lexicon. Tokens are similar to frames in the sense that their slots have procedural attachments for computing the value of the slot. Thus, the definition of an attribute in a lexicon specifies not only the name and data type of the attribute, but a method of computing the value of the attribute. Consequently, token attributes need not be computed until they are required, and this permits flexibility in developing computational strategies.

Some of the grouping processes to be described shortly do not examine the image data directly, but form tokens from groups of other tokens. For example, two perpendicular pairs of parallel lines might be grouped to form a quadrilateral. This more abstract token is still given a name and a list of attributes, and its bitplane can be formed by either the union of the bitplanes of the component lines or the area bounded by the component lines. Tokens can also be formed to represent events that have no referent in the image, such as occluded boundaries or incomplete geometric shapes. Thus, as with the other levels of representation, there are multiple levels of abstraction included within the general intermediate-level representation.

Accessing Tokens

Tokens in the ISR can be accessed either by name or by attribute. That is, one can access the value of an attribute of a particular token (e.g., what is the average intensity of REGION-27?) or access all the tokens with a particular set of attributes (e.g., which lines are longer than 20 pixels?). Some of the accessing modes embody the capabilities of the associative processing that is a key feature of our image understanding architecture (see the conclusion of this chapter). There is special support for the efficient access of spatially related tokens, implemented by coarsely quantitizing $x - y$ space into sectors to allow selective search for tokens "near" some location. This is isomorphic to the spatial organization of the middle level of our image-understanding architecture.

Our approach differs from a straight dataflow approach in which data is restricted to moving up the hierarchy of abstraction. Grouping processes are allowed to incrementally organize tokens under the direction of schema control programs according to the current state and overall goals of the system. This capability is vital if the combinatoric explosion caused by imprudent application of expensive relational measures and grouping operators is to be avoided. For example, a rectilinear line-grouping activity, which would be appropriate for forming a detailed description of a window frame, would be likely to involve an enormous amount of wasted work if applied to an area of coarse tree texture. In our approach, initial results from the application of inexpensive, global processes are examined by specific object interpretation schemas that will selectively apply processes to particular areas of an image. Thus, a schema with knowledge of houses directs productive line grouping in the area of the window, whereas a schema with knowledge of foliage would invoke different processes for grouping inside the random tree texture, which would more likely be productive than rectilinear structures. A more detailed discussion follows.

The ISR provides uniform access functions to different kinds of tokens and, to the degree it makes sense, uniform measurement of the relations between different types of tokens. There are system functions in the ISR for efficiently performing set operations on the bitmaps of tokens. These can be used to compute relations like percent of a line contained in a region and the overlap between a region and the projection of a surface. These relations can be stored directly via pointers or could be maintained as attributes of tokens (e.g., a region has a list of related lines as an attribute). However, caution must be exercised, because the number of computable relations grows exponentially with the number of tokens. Again, advantage is taken of the fact that relatively few of these relations are "interesting"; thus, often, relations will be only selectively computed under top-down control.

FOCUS-OF-ATTENTION, PERCEPTUAL GROUPING, AND INFORMATION FUSION

The mechanisms by which the VISIONS system deals with focus-of-attention, perceptual grouping, and information fusion are related. The attributes of individual tokens and the relations between pairs or sets of tokens in the ISR are the basis for focusing the system's attention. However, this same information is at the heart of both the grouping mechanisms and the methods for fusing information across multiple representations. The relation between a pair of lines can be used to determine whether they can be viewed as an example of a geometric entity, while the presence of a pair of vertical lines properly bounding a dark brown narrow region would increase confidence in a particular object hypothesis beyond the information in a single token.

Some of the experimental results presented in the following two sections are based upon the three region segmentations shown in Figure 1.9. They were derived from the histogram-based region segmentation algorithm, followed by the rule-based region merging algorithm.

The Need for Focus-of-Attention Mechanisms

An important problem in computer vision is the appropriate application of world constraints and expectations; knowledge must be represented in the right form and applied at the right time. We have repeatedly stressed that although the processing of a new image must start bottom-up, more restrictive contexts may be used to selectively focus relevant knowledge as information is accumulated and assessed. In this section we describe a simple rule-based focus-of-attention mechanism for generating an initial set of object hypotheses about the conceptual content of the image (60, 61, 117, 118, 148, 149, 155). The most reliable of these hypotheses are used to form a kernel interpretation, which can be used to activate the relevant schemas in the long-term knowledge base. Once this has been accomplished, object-dependent strategies associated with the schemas are responsible for verifying and extending the kernel.

The object-hypothesis system provides the first link between the image data and the knowledge structures. In many cases, it is possible to construct rules, defined over the tokens in the ISR, which provide evidence for and against the semantic concepts representing the domain knowledge. While no single rule is totally reliable, the combined evidence from many such rules should be more effective in implying the correct local interpretation. The "islands of reliability" thus generated can then be used to extend the hypotheses to surrounding image structures that are spatially and semantically related.

The goal is to focus attention upon particular image events that are likely candidates for particular object labels, rather than the selection of the best object label for each region, line, and/or surface. For example, given a set of regions in an outdoor scene, we might wish to select a few strong possibilities for the object "sky." This approach avoids some of the problems inherent in the traditional approaches to pattern classification where one attempts to classify every region (61). The application of the hypothesis-generation rules can also be utilized top-down as part of a hypothesis verification or extension strategy associated with some active schema.

Rules Applied to a Single Token:
Token Attribute Rules

A constraint on a token feature (or attribute) provides a very simple representation of a unit of knowledge that can be used to generate object hypotheses. For many objects (e.g., sky or tree), there is a natural seman-

a

b

FIGURE 1.9. Region segmentations for interpretation experiments. Each of these images was produced by the histogram-based region segmentation algorithm at high sensitivity, followed by the region merging algorithm to reduce the number of regions.

tics and a descriptive simplicity that can be associated with a set of token attributes; for example, values may be defined as "large" (size), "lightly textured" (texture), "blue" (color), "bright" (intensity), and so forth. A range on each token attribute, even if it is loosely constrained, captures some aspect of the object semantics. Thus, we define a simple rule as a constraint on the range of a token attribute and combine several simple rules into a complex rule for a specific object class. Complex rules are defined as hierarchical combinations of simple rules and may be viewed as defining a volume in a multi-dimensional feature space, which represents the set of joint constraints on the feature set.

Simple Token-Attribute Rules

The degree to which the attribute value of a token satisfies the constraints of a simple rule can be translated into a confidence that the token is associated with an instance of the object. The output of a simple rule can then be viewed as a vote for the assertion that the token represents the object (or, more generally, a concept). This approach was first applied to regions, (61, 118, 149, 155) where the region attributes include color, texture, shape, size, image location, and relative location to other objects. More recently (20, 21), the approach has been extended to line tokens, where the features include length, orientation, contrast, width, and so on.

A simple rule is defined as a piecewise-linear mapping function on a feature. It consists of a central positive voting range (where the response of the rule is 1), surrounded by zero voting ranges, surrounded in turn by veto ranges. The rule response is linearly ramped from values of 1 to 0 on both sides of the central positive range. The veto ranges effectively eliminate the consideration of those tokens with unacceptable attribute values as an instance of the object class; for example, a region can be removed as a "sky" candidate if it is green or at the bottom of the image.

Simple rules are parameterized by six thresholds corresponding to the endpoints of the ranges and typically are formed by examining the relationship of the histogram of an attribute across all tokens in multiple

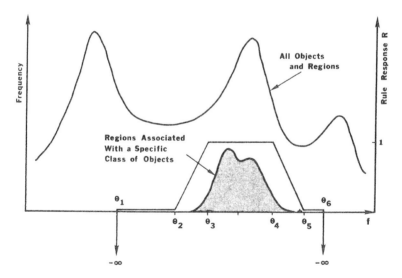

FIGURE 1.10. A simple rule as a constraint on a token attribute. The two histograms obtained from a sample of hand-labeled images show the frequency of feature values of regions for all objects and the frequency of feature values of regions associated with a specific class of objects. The simple rule is shown as a piecewise-linear function mapping feature value f_i into a response R (0–1 range). The object-specific mapping is parameterized by six threshold values and stored in the knowledge network.

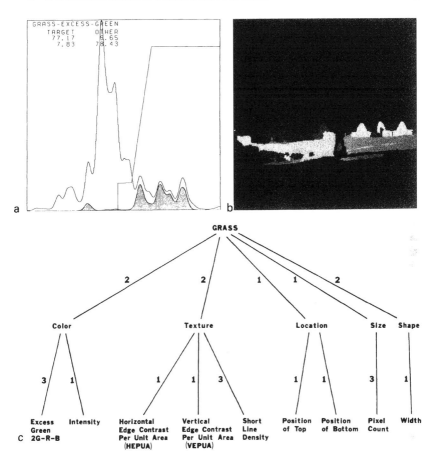

FIGURE 1.11. Example of complex object hypothesis rule for grass. (a) Histograms of color feature called "Excess Green" (defined as 2G-R-B), with a simple rule shown as a superimposed piecewise-linear function; (b) Response of simple rule coded as intensity (high response is bright); (c) Complex rule for grass.

images to the histogram of that attribute extracted from tokens associated with a single object class (the "class-conditional" histogram; see Figure 1.10). For example, the color or texture of grass regions would be compared to the color and texture of all regions. Using the six values, nonsymmetric rules may be formed; the simple rule example shown in Figure 1.11(a) is based on an "excess-green" opponent color feature (2G-R-B) of regions and is part of a complex rule [see Figure 1.1(c)] for hypothesizing "grass." Figure 1.11(b) shows the "grass" object-label hypotheses from this simple rule for one of the standard images; in this figure, brightness encodes the rule response (with a response of 1 as brightest). Note that black regions either evaluated to 0 or were vetoed.

Complex Token-Attribute Rules

A complex rule is a hierarchical collection of other rules, which may be either simple or complex. A typical structure is illustrated in Figure 1.11(c), which shows the complex rule structure for "grass." The top-level rule is organized as a set of five other complex rules (one for color, texture, size, shape, and location), each of which is composed of one or more simple rules. The response of a rule at one level in the hierarchy is determined by mapping the responses from lower level rules through a combination function, in this case a simple weighted average (the weights are shown on the arcs in the figure). Our intention is that rules be weighted with a small integer value (3 to 5 levels) representing strong, medium, and weak contributions. The rules should be robust enough so that a fairly rough specification will suffice without the necessity for "parameter twiddling." Many other rule structures and combination functions are possible. Figure 1.12 shows typical results from the application of the complex rules for "grass," "sky," and "foliage."

It is also worth mentioning here that the token attribute-rules (and the relational rules introduced in the next section) can also be used for filtering and grouping. A rule might be applied to a token set to retain only those tokens that have certain properties. These rules can be applied sequentially, so that the subset of tokens remaining after application of the rule can become the focus of another simple or complex rule. Rules used in this manner provide a form of control where subsets of tokens are narrowed (or filtered) via a sequence of rule applications. In later sections, we will show how these techniques can also be used to form composite tokens, which are aggregates of various token types, thus achieving grouping and fusion capabilities at the same time.

Interactive Environment and Alternative Rule Forms

Knowledge engineering of rules can be greatly facilitated by an interactive environment for rule construction. A user can get an immediate sense of effectiveness of proposed rules by displaying the rating of each symbolic candidate in intensity or color. Thus, rule development becomes a dynamic process with a natural display medium for user feedback.

An interactive environment for generating and testing rules has been developed. A user may create a rule, display its results on a set of test images, edit the rule, and construct one or more complex rules that incoprorate it. When look-up tables on an image display system are available, the user can interactively change the piecewise-linear function that is loaded into the look-up table. By encoding all of the pixels of each image token (e.g., pixels of a region or line) with its value of a particular attribute (e.g., intensity, length, etc.), the look-up table can immediately display the rule vote. Thus, the user can change the rule and see the results in real time (i.e., at video rate).

In addition, a simple language interface has been constructed so that rules can be specified on any feature in terms of five intervals of the

FIGURE 1.12. Examples of applying complex rules to generate object hypothesis rules. Each object has a complex rule which can be used to rank order a type of token in a focus-of-attention process. Each image shows the rule response for regions coded in intensity (high ≡ bright).

dynamic range of a feature: "very low," "low," "medium," "high," "very high" (54, 61). These labels induce a partition on the range of the feature, and for each interval the user specifies whether the rule response is "ON," "OFF," or "VETO." Figure 1.12(c) was obtained using a rule of this type.

There have been several different rule forms employed in our research environment. Rather than the six-point central positive range for the mapping function, any piecewise linear function with multiple veto and positive voting ranges might be used; for example, extracting an orientation image of a line around the origin of the orientation scale will require positive voting ranges at each end of the scale (since the scale is circular).

An alternative rule form has developed from an initial version of an automatic rule development subsystem that has been motivated via a Bayesian viewpoint. The rule structure can be viewed as a discrete approximation to a continuous distribution. It is based upon the ratio of histograms of a token attribute for a particular object to that of all objects, sampled from a labeled set of images. For a single feature and meaningful statistics this is an optimum maximum likelihood decision rule (61). Thus, if a sufficient range of object examples are available to meaningfully represent an object, automatic development of rules should be possible.

Finally, some users have explored different variations of combination functions with simple rules. The version we have presented involves a weighted sum of the output of simple rules whose values range from 0 to 1 (with a veto range). Some experiments in our group have utilized a multiplicative form ranging from 0 (a veto) to some number greater than 1, with 1 as a neutral value.

The Need for Perceptual Grouping Mechanisms and Information Fusion

We have argued in preceding sections that low-level algorithms, which initially do not use any knowledge of the scene or its characteristics, should never be expected to produce symbolic descriptions of image events that are a close match to the object descriptions in the knowledge base. Consequently, there must be additional mechanisms for dealing with the problems of an incomplete and partially incorrect intermediate symbolic representation. In the following subsections we describe both data-driven (bottom-up) and knowledge-based (top-down) processing techniques that can build an intermediate representation with tokens that better match the primitive elements of the object descriptions in the knowledge base. Thus, the emphasis here is on the reorganization of the intermediate representation into new, more abstract collections of tokens.

Perceptual Grouping and the Reorganization of Intermediate-Level Data

There has been surge of interest in data-directed grouping phenomena in computer vision. One general strategy is to form collections of tokens by detecting relations between tokens that are likely to be nonaccidental (e.g., see 151, 152). The relation represents a grouping criterion for organizing the set of tokens to produce a new token. These ideas are much less vague if particular grouping strategies are considered, such as linking fragmented colinear lines with nearby endpoints, grouping sets of parallel and perpendicular lines that have some spatial coherence, merging similar short lines that form a textured area, and grouping regions (possibly nonadjacent) that have similar characteristics of color, texture, size, shape, and/or location.

Grouping algorithms must, of course, contend with the combinatorics of the large number of image tokens (such as the 2,000 to 10,000 lines and the 200–500 regions for some of the algorithms described in the previous sections), the many different attributes of each token and the many possible relationships between tokens. Thus, there must be some technique to focus attention on areas where the grouping processes will most likely be useful. One technique for data-directed grouping is to locally histogram (i.e., via subimages) various attributes of a given token and look for interesting events, such as many parallel lines, or orthogonal lines, or many small textured regions in certain areas of the image. Certain properties, such as orthogonal line groupings, might be of sufficient universal interest that they are always extracted. In each of the cases cited, the strategies can be applied without the application of knowledge, but the computational cost might be rather severe.

Knowledge-driven application of perceptual grouping mechanisms is the obvious alternative to the data-driven control just described. The grouping mechanisms themselves can remain substantially the same; only their invocation need be modified. Thus, specific grouping strategies would be applied to specific areas of the image, often with specific goals. We envision that many grouping strategies will be invoked via the top-down schema processes that will be described in the following section. It should be obvious that if the system focuses upon a particular region, regions that are similar in color, texture, and so on, and that are spatially close (i.e., within a certain distance of each other) can be selected. Thus, if tree foliage is expected to be highly fragmented and have dark homogeneous shadow regions adjacent to lighter green regions, these characteristics can be used to group such regions and form a new region token with very different properties than the individual tokens in the set. If short texture lines were extracted, and a connected components algorithm was applied to their support regions (discussed previously), then textured regions would be extracted rather simply.

Later, we outline new algorithms, as well as specify how some of the algorithms and techniques already described can be used to fill the needs of perceptual organization strategies. Some of these discussions are fairly brief, because the work is recent or has been described elsewhere in this chapter. Note also that the goals and techniques that will be described heavily overlap those of information fusion that are outlined later.

Information Fusion

A major problem confronting vision systems that use multiple sensors or that generate multiple low-level descriptions from image data is the coherent and consistent integration of information contained in the multiple representations. It has also become evident that each low-level process extracts only partial descriptions, and that there is a great deal of redundancy among these descriptions, which can be profitably exploited. Thus, maximum reliability can only be achieved through processes that integrate information represented in widely varying forms. For the reasons discussed earlier in this chapter, we take the view that information fusion can most effectively be accomplished during the interpretation process, rather than at the time that the tokens are first extracted (e.g., by directly integrating region and line algorithms). This approach bears similarity to the philosophy of the CMU approach to sensor fusing in their development of an autonomous vehicle (120). One approach to fusion is illustrated here by extending the rule-based hypothesis system to operate over multiple token types, in this case the regions and lines extracted from the image data (20, 21). The techniques could easily be extended to include fusion of information from lines, regions, corners, surfaces, volumes, and generally, any other token abstracted from the sensory data.

Relational Rules Applied to Multiple Tokens

Up to this point, only rules based on properties associated with a single token (e.g., a region) have been considered; these may be viewed as unary rules, defining a unary relationship between the token and the hypothesis. By defining binary relationships between token pairs, an approach to the problems of both grouping and information fusion is obtained.

It is important to understand that the token-attribute rules are not directly classifying or labeling regions, but rather allowing the system to focus attention. They provide a rank ordering of tokens as candidates for object hypotheses. This rank ordering can be used in various ways to associate object-class hypotheses with the token. Note that some strategies might involve the application of a sequence of different types of rules to a tokenset, each time filtering the tokenset so that less likely candidates are eliminated. For example, a single exemplar region for tree crown might be selected via a complex rule for foliage. Then a distance relational rule could be used to select regions whose centroids or boundaries are nearby (i.e., within some maximum distance). Finally, for those remaining regions, a similarity relational rule on brightness and color might further filter the possible tree regions into a reasonably sized set of candidates.

The rule system that has been developed can be extended in a very simple way to compare and aggregate tokens of the same type. A single attribute of any pair of scalar-valued tokens can be compared by simply taking the difference in their values. (Note that for some nonscalar attributes, such as orientation, which has a circular scale, a somewhat more complex orientation difference must be defined, so that values of $0°$ and $359°$ will be evaluated as a difference of $1°$). The difference of attribute values provides a relational measure of similarity, or attribute difference, between tokens. Given some token, there is now a basis for selecting among all other tokens those that satisfy a set of similarity relations applied to a set of attributes. For example, regions that are of "similar" intensity and "close" in distance can be extracted. Lines that are "parallel" or of "similar" orientation to a given line token can be selected, or those of "orthogonal" orientation with endpoints that are less than some specified distance apart can be extracted.

Of course, the basis for the selection of tokens is an appropriate specification of the similarity or comparison relations. Terms such as *similar, different, near, far, parallel,* and *orthogonal* must all have a computational definition. The rule system can be used to implement comparisons of token attributes by defining a simple rule on the difference between the attribute values of all tokens to the attribute value of a given token (or some other value somehow specified by the user or the system). In effect, the voting function is a computational measure of the degree to which a relation has been satisfied, and therefore, in some sense, defines the value of a "fuzzy" relation.

Information Fusion via Relations
Across Multiple Token Types

Here, the goal is to extend the rule system to include composite tokens, which are aggregations of tokens across the multiple representation that satisfy a specified set of relations. The key-integrating mechanism is the use of relations between tokens of different types. From those aggregate objects satisfying the relation, new features are extracted and used to generate object class hypotheses. To be somewhat more specific, consider the interpretation of a road scene with a view down the road. The formation of a "road" hypothesis should not be based on any single token type (e.g., regions), but rather on an aggregation of lines, regions, and surfaces that have specific relations to each other and that share road attributes. Ideally, one would like to find a homogeneous region of the correct relative brightness and color, bounded by two converging straight lines, and approximately covered by a horizontal planar surface.

The simultaneous use of both region and line information, for example, permits two types of perceptual grouping operations to take place across representations. On the one hand, a region or set of regions can guide the grouping of lines (an example of this is developed in the following section), while on the other hand, a line or set of lines can guide the grouping of regions. In the following discussion the terms *region* and *line* are used to refer either to the tokens obtained from the corresponding segmentation process or to sets of regions and lines already grouped by other processes.

There are many ways to use relations between tokens to form aggregations of tokens. An initial implementation in the VISIONS system utilizes a primary token type (region tokens) through which tokens of other types are selected and filtered via a sequence of simple, complex, and relational rules. Since the region and line tokens stored in the ISR are both pixel-based, intersection turns out to be a convenient mechanism for associating line tokens with a region. Intersection of the support pixels of a line with the pixels in a region allows the definition of various relations in a straightforward manner. Examples include relations such as INTERSECTING (whose value is either TRUE or FALSE depending upon whether a region and line have a nonempty intersection); and BOUNDING and INTERIOR, with a numeric value ranging between 0 and 1 representing the degree to which these relations are satisfied (20, 21).

Some Example Grouping Mechanisms

Grouping via Rule-Based Token Attributes and Relations

Many grouping strategies naturally fit into, and are definable with, the tools that have already been presented. Grouping via relations between different token types, such as line and region groupings, can be achieved in a fairly simple yet general manner. The idea is very similar to that described in the previous section for the object-hypothesis rules (which accepted only a single token type as the argument). Features can be measured from the aggregate structure and used to generate object hypotheses. Perhaps more importantly, a set of relational rules can be applied sequentially to filter the initial set of aggregate tokens in order to select sets with particular properties.

The intersection type of relational rule can be used in some very diverse ways. One example is to use INTERSECTION and INTERIOR relational rules to select only interior lines—lines that are sufficiently or completely interior to any region—and then to use a complex token attribute rule to rank short, high contrast horizontal lines [Figure 1.13(a)]. The line score could then be averaged to form a texture feature on regions. Alternatively, a line-density measure can be formed as a region texture measure by counting the occurrences of lines receiving a high score from the line-attribute rule and then normalizing by the size of the region. Figure 1.13(b) shows this measure mapped onto the re-

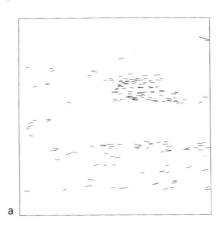

a

FIGURE 1.13. Examples of relational rules and information fusion. (a) A texture measure is formed by extracting short, horizontal lines which are INTERIOR to a region. The resulting set of lines are shown; (b) The density of extracted lines can be used to form a region attribute for rank ordering the regions; the density of shading depicts the region rating; (c) Telephone pole hypotheses can be generated by finding regions that are BOUNDED by pairs of parallel vertical lines; the line pairs formed by extracting vertical lines then selecting BOUNDING vertical lines, and finally PARALLEL pairs of BOUNDING vertical lines are shown; (d) The region scores are shown mapped back to the image (hatched regions have no long vertical lines and are vetoed). Note that further analysis of the regions with high scores will be necessary to fully and accurately extract the telephone poles; (e) Vertical and horizontal BOUNDING lines are extracted; (f) The region-line aggregations provide a focus-of-attention on rectangle hypotheses that form the geometric structure of the shutters/windows of the house.

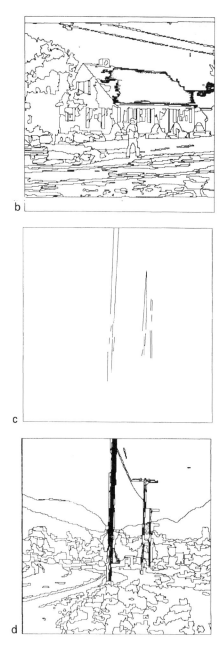

FIGURE 1.13. (*continued*)

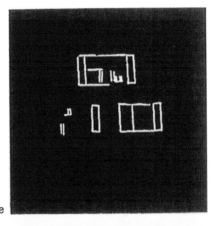

e

f

gions. The texture measure can be used to hypothesize or verify the roof region, which has horizontal-shingle texture. Note that grass is the only other region that has any significant horizontal-texture rating.

A simple shape measure can be computed by determining if a region is bounded by a pair of long vertical lines. The filtering rule for this feature selects only those lines that lie on a region boundary, and the ranking rule assigns high values to overlapping pairs of long vertical lines. Thus, given a region token, those line tokens that INTERSECT the region are selected; then the BOUNDING relation can be used to retain only those lines that are sufficiently on the boundary of the region; next, vertical lines are extracted via a simple rule applied to line orientation; and finally, the PARALLEL relation on the resulting lines would yield an aggregate structure of a region and those parallel vertical lines that bound that region. As shown in Figure 1.12(c,d), this rule is useful for extracting telephone poles. As a last example, horizontal and vertical lines that are on region boundaries can be extracted in an effort to find rectangular structures, such as the regions and lines forming the shutter-window structures of the house; see Figure 1.13(e,f). Note that windows are usually very difficult to extract due to reflections and transparency. Additional details about the structure of the relational-rule system and further experimental results may be found in (20, 21).

Grouping Line Tokens Based on Geometric Relationships

Abstract collections of lines can prove to be very useful in the development of object hypotheses. Certainly once an object has been hypothesized, confirmation of an expected relationship between a set of line tokens can be used as further evidence for the correctness of the hypothesis. There are certain "primary" relations between subsets of straight lines that are sufficiently important that one might be interested in extracting all occurrences prior to attaching semantic significance. A set of parallel lines whose endpoints form straight lines will usually prove to be important (e.g., for geometric structures, such as the shutters in a house, telephone poles along a road, etc.). Similarly, perpendicular lines that have a pair of nearby endpoints can form "corner" structures, which could be grouped into larger geometric objects, such as rectangles. If the orthogonality criterion is dropped, and corners of any orientation are extracted, then they could be grouped into parallelograms and trapezoids by using a parallel-line criterion for the further grouping of corner-line pairs. If an orthogonal intersecting-line grouping was attempted, weak structures, such as the window panes in windows might be extracted and used as the basis of hypothesizing or verifying windows between shutter rectangles.

When large numbers of tokens are present there are some interesting computational, storage, and retrieval issues that must be considered in the search for meaningful structures. A decision must be made regarding those relations that are explicitly represented between pairs of tokens, since there can be a significant cost associated with finding and storing all token pairs (or sets) that satisfy a given relation, such as parallel or "near." Unfocused grouping of tokens also leads to the problem of generating a large number of uninteresting token sets, which would also defeat the purpose of searching for interesting aggregations.

Within our research group, there is an active research effort by Reynolds and Beveridge (114) on the development of line-grouping processes based upon geometric and spatial relations; their initial effort produces rectilinear line groupings using the spatial proximity of lines. Measures for relations between lines have been quantified for spatially proximate orthogonal (SPO), spatially proximate parallel (SPP), and spatially proximate collinear (SPC) lines. We have provided an example of the SPO relation in Figure 1.14(a) that is dependent upon the length, parameterized distance of each line from their intersection, and deviation from orthogonality.

Example line groupings are shown in Figure 1.14(b) as a set of straight lines extracted from the aerial image of Figure 1.1. The three relations can each be applied to four pairs, which satisfy each of the three relations. Groupings of various sorts can now be applied. In Figure 1.14(c), a connected components algorithm was used to form line aggregations; a line is considered "connected" to another if any of the three relations are satisfied. The result is a grouping of lines where local proximity is always satisfied, and rectilinear structures of parallel and orthogonal lines are extracted. In order to do this efficiently the lines in the ISR are stored in 10° orthogonal line buckets; that is to say, the bucket for the 11°–20° range will also contain lines in the 101°–110° range. Some of these could be the basis for further processing, such as the formation of rectangles.

Top-down strategies allow the geometric/spatial relationships to be used in a much more directed manner. In aerial images, at appropriate resolution, one can expect roads to appear as sets of parallel lines as in

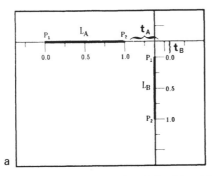

a

FIGURE 1.14. Grouping via geometric relationships. (a) A graphical illustration of spatial proximity for orthogonal lines. Both the degree of proximity defined via parameterized distances t_A and t_B and the degree of deviation from orthogonality will contribute to the SPO measure for a pair of lines; (b) All lines of length ≥ 5 (pixels) extracted from Figure 1.1(h); (c) Four example groupings obtained from a connected components algorithm for all lines which satisfy any of the SPO, SPP, and SPC relations.

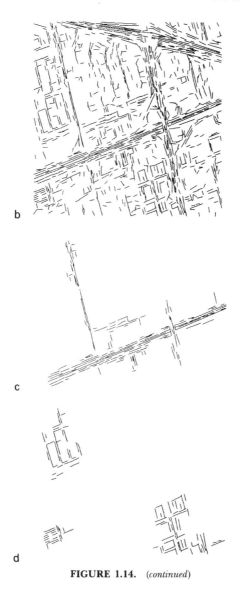

b

c

d

FIGURE 1.14. (*continued*)

Figure 1.14(c), and intersections as perpendicular line groupings of roads. One can expect buildings to appear as rectangles, and thus one might use weak evidence for the fourth side of a rectangle to complete it as in subgraphs of Figure 1.14(c). In another case the geometry of houses and roofs might imply that a parallelogram should be present, and that shingle texture should appear within the parallelogram. If only three sides of a parallelogram were found, a top-down line-linking procedure might be invoked, and a texture-extraction procedure for short horizontal edges might be applied to the area within the parallelogram [see Figure 1.13(a)]. An example of such a knowledge-directed grouping strategy is given in the following section, "Interpretation" and Figure 1.24.

Hierarchical Grouping of Co-Linear Line Segments

One very important property of images is the presence of long straight lines. Unfortunately, most algorithms detect line fragments, which then must be joined into longer lines. In this section we restrict our attention to the grouping of lines into longer, straight lines based on the general notions of collinearity and proximity (139, 140). The algorithm by Boldt and Weiss presented here could be viewed as a straight-line extraction process, beginning with the output of a standard edge-operator, and terminating with a set of straight lines. Consequently, it can be viewed as an alternative to the Burns line-extraction algorithm. However, the relevant point here is the geometric-grouping mechanism that is the basis for combining shorter straight lines (in the limit-edge elements) into longer straight lines. A straight line can be viewed as a sequence of line segments in which consecutive pairs are roughly col-linear and similar in contrast, where each segment is close to its successor, and arranged so that the entire sequence passes a straightness test. Figure 1.15 illustrates the relations that are relevant to grouping lines. These criteria depend on scale; long line fragments, for example, can be separated by a larger gap than small ones and still be close. A sequence of lines not straight at one scale can be part of a longer sequence that passes the same straightness test at a larger scale.

The idea of grouping line segments is not new. Nevatia and Babu (101) developed criteria for grouping edges; however, they only applied them locally and they did not take into account more global context. McKeown et al. (89) have also devised rules similar to those used by Boldt and Weiss and have applied them to the problem of linking elongated regions. They use the criteria that (a) the regions must be close; (b) they must not overlap too much; (c) they must have similar orientations; and (d) the lateral distance must be small. Thus, they implement the rules of collinearity and proximity. A major difference between their approach and ours, however, is that they do not use a hierarchy.

The algorithm, when viewed as a segmentation process, begins with an edge-detection operator (in this case the zero-crossing of a Laplacian), although any operator that produces measurements of the contrast, direction, and location (including start and end points) of the edge could

a)

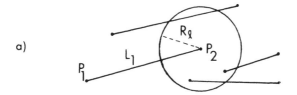

b)

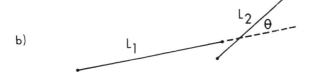

c)

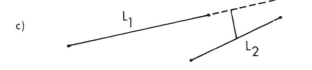

d)

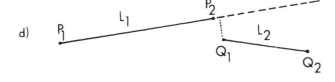

e)

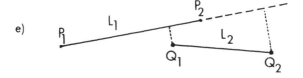

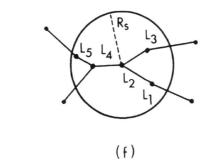

(f)

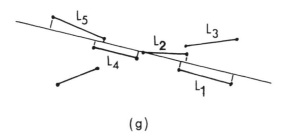

(g)

FIGURE 1.15. Straight line grouping (a–e) Grouping relations; (a) Proximity—lines are candidates for grouping with L_1 if they are within the linking radius R_l from endpoint P_2, where R_l is a function of the length of L_1; (b) Orientation—lines must have similar orientation; (c) Lines must be close in the lateral direction; (d) Endpoints—the endpoint P_2 must be close to the projection of endpoint Q_1; (e) Overlap—the lines must not overlap too much; P_2 must be closer to the projection of Q_1 than to the projection of Q_2; (f) Link Graph—for each line there is a candidate group of lines, which are possible extensions from each endpoint; (g) Straightness test—each sequence of lines is tested and the straightest is selected if it passes a threshold test.

be substituted. The remainder of the algorithm can then be viewed as a line-grouping process which starts with a set of straight lines derived from any process. In fact the grouping process can be applied to the set of lines produced by the Burns algorithm.

Each grouping cycle consists of two steps: linking and merging. In the linking step, pairs of line segments are tentatively connected based on binary relations. In the merging step, sequences of linked line segments are examined and possibly replaced by a single line segment. The linking step improves the efficiency of the merging step by significantly reducing the number of line sequences that would be examined by blind search. The computational complexity is reduced by repeated hierarchical grouping of lines into longer lines. Thus, there is an implicit scale-space hierarchy (151, 152), and the search always remains local with respect to the current scale.

The linking step consists of a search for pairs of lines that satisfy the geometric and nongeometric criteria, which make them candidates for grouping. The geometric criteria are collinearity and proximity (the end points must be close, but the lines must not overlap too much), and the nongeometric criterion is similarity of contrast; these criteria (and others) are shown in Figure 1.15(a–e). The same linking process is performed separately for each endpoint of each line, and can obviously be done in parallel. The result is a directed graph with the line segments as its vertices and the links as its arcs; a portion of the link graph is shown in Figure 1.15(f). In general, a line will be linked with several other lines.

The merging process consists of search and replacement. The merging process will examine paths in the link graph and test them for straightness. The amount of geometric context used is determined by a *search radius,* shown superimposed over a portion of the link graph in Figure 1.15(f), which bounds the length of a sequence of lines that is tested for straightness. Each sequence of lines is approximated by a straight line illustrated in Figure 1.15(g), and if the straightest path for a given line passes a straightness threshold, that sequence is replaced by a single straight line. The algorithm examines each line in the link graph at one scale, and the linking and merging process is repeated at each scale, with the linking and replacement radii increasing by a constant factor from one scale to the next.

The algorithm has been applied effectively to natural scenes and aerial images. Figure 1.16(a) shows the initial edge segments, which are input to the grouping algorithm; these are obtained by associating unit-length edges with selected locations along the Laplacian zero-crossing contours. Figure 1.16(b–d) shows the output of the geometric-grouping algorithm at each stage of the iterative grouping. Figure 1.16(e) shows the final result on the entire image; unit-length lines remaining after completion of the grouping cycles have been removed. Figure 1.16(f) demonstrates the application of a filter on length and contrast to the full set of lines shown in Figure 1.16(e). The full line set can be filtered and

---

FIGURE 1.16.   Hierarchical grouping of colinear segments. (a) Initial line segments in subimage of chimney; (b) After two cycles of grouping; (c) After four cycles; (d) After six cycles; (e) Final results on whole image; lines of length 1 were filtered out; (f) After filtering on length and contrast.

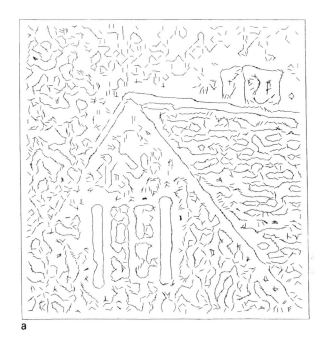

a

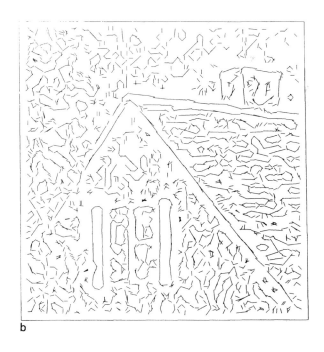

b

63

c

d

FIGURE 1.16. *(continued)*

e

f

FIGURE 1.16. (*continued*)

65

FIGURE 1.17. Additional examples of hierarchical grouping of colinear segments. The algorithm can be applied everywhere as a bottom-up line extraction process or applied in local areas under top-down control.

manipulated in various ways to extract different views of the data in much the same way as that of the output of the Burns' algorithm. Figure 1.17 shows the output of the line grouping algorithm on several full images.

Region Grouping

The segmentation algorithms presented earlier sometimes produce dramatically unexpected results, and at other times, produce expected but fragmented representations. The low-level executive system (72) under construction can coordinate knowledge-based feedback to the segmentation and feature extraction level.

As an example, we briefly note here that the rule-based region-merging algorithm can also be used to perform certain types of grouping. Again, it will be crucial to have some amount of knowledge beyond what was available during the initial application of segmentation algorithms. If object-dependent strategies can be developed that anticipate the manner in which the segmentation algorithms fail, then knowledge-based processing can reinvoke the region merging processes with appropriately different parameter settings. We are only beginning to explore strategies to utilize it in a general manner.

SCHEMAS AND IMAGE INTERPRETATION

A central problem in image understanding is the representation and appropriate use of all available sources of knowledge during the interpretation process. Each of the many different kinds of knowledge that may be relevant at various points during interpretation imposes different kinds of constraints on the underlying representation. In general, the representation must be sensitive enough to capture subtle differences and variations in object classes, yet be robust enough to capture broadly applicable "sketches" of objects and expected scenarios.

In some cases, the knowledge is declarative in form (e.g., "Sky is blue."), and consequently, vision systems must have access to knowledge of the attributes of objects and their parts. In other cases the knowledge is relational in form: the decomposition of objects into parts, the relationships between the parts, and the contextual properties of larger collections of objects. Other kinds of knowledge are more procedural in form, such as knowledge of the perspective transformations mapping from three-dimensional to two-dimensional, or the knowledge encoded in a top-down two-dimensional grouping procedure for extracting tree foliage and shadows. In some form or another, knowledge about individual objects (instances, classes, and descriptions), of events (action, situations, cause and effect), of performance (how-to, skills), and metaknowledge (knowledge about what we know: extent, origins, reliability, etc.) must be encoded in an accessible representation.

In this section we define a general methodology for knowledge-based parallel processing and a development environment to support that work.

Schemas as a Representation
of Knowledge in VISION

In the VISIONS system, scene-independent knowledge is represented in a hierarchical-schema structure organized as a semantic network (30) of schema nodes (55, 58, 106, 148, 149, 150). Each schema defines a highly structured collection of elements in a scene or object and encodes the knowledge of how to recognize that object/scene. It should be noted that a related concept of perceptual and motor schemas has been long advocated by Arbib (9, 10). Our goal is to develop a network of concurrent processes that will cooperatively build an interpretation of the scene. Each object in a scene schema or part in an object schema can have an associated schema that further describes it. One can view the schemas as a vertical structuring of knowledge in that the knowledge is organized across representational levels by the object description. Each schema node has both a declarative description appropriate to the level of detail describing the relations between the parts of the schema, and a procedural component describing object-recognition techniques expressed as a set of hypothesis and verification processed called "interpretation strategies."

Although such a hierarchy provides rich descriptive capabilities, it is also necessary to distinguish between the representation of a specific instance of a visual object (Ed's house) and the general class of objects (a two-story Victorian) to which it belongs. Thus, a further division of knowledge into long term (LTM) and short term memory (STM) across the levels of the hierarchy is necessary for differentiating the system's permanent a priori knowledge base from the representation derived from the sensory data of a specific image during the interpretation process. Figure 1.18 illustrates the idea that both STM and LTM are multi-level representations of two-dimensional symbolic tokens of points (or vertices), lines, and regions, and three-dimensional tokens of surfaces and volumes, and then abstract semantic tokens of objects and scenes. A node in LTM represents the general class of an object and may be related to a node in STM by an instance-of arc, which specifies that the node is an instance or member of the general class.

Under the model that views active schemas as generating a set of concurrent communicating processes, another view of the schema system and the manner in which it is intended to relate to the image understanding architecture (discussed later in the chapter) is illustrated in Figure 1.19. Since schemas are intended to run in parallel wherever possible, a multiprocessor is shown interposed between LTM and STM, with a schema running on each processor (in the limit). STM then becomes a blackboard, with different access functions tuned for efficient retrieval of data from the large volumes of intermediate tokens and for the smaller amounts of object and scene hypotheses. LTM stores the schema classes, and the active schemas are responsible for instantiation of additional schemas.

The set of KSs are processes which can be invoked and applied to

INTERPRETATION SYSTEM

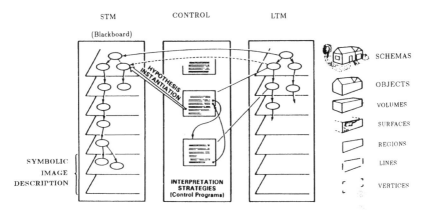

FIGURE 1.18. Short-term memory (STM) and long-term memory (LTM) in the VISIONS System. STM consists of the data structures that form an interpretation of the scene. It is a hierarchical multi-level directed graph representation, where the lower levels are the symbolic tokens extracted from the sensory data and the higher levels are the inferred concepts of object and scene labels, as well as surface and volume hypotheses. LTM consists of stored knowledge about the world. LTM is organized hierarchically via the PART-OF and IS-A relations over the scene and object schemas. The schemas contain interpretation strategies that are responsible for matching the expected structures in the scene to the data in STM and for creating the image-specific instance of the schema.

particular portions of the image and STM under the control of interpretation strategies of the schemas. In particular, the difference between schemas and KSs must be understood. Schemas currently are object- and scene-based, with fairly complex control strategies for recognition. In our system the KSs are processes that are to be applied by interpretation strategies and consequently have relatively simple control strategies. The schemas invoke the KSs and pass parameter information sufficient for the KS to return a result. The KSs vary greatly in form and complexity while the schemas have a uniform representation.

Many of the strategies relating to geometric structures are based on standard or constrained two-dimensional views of an object or scene. The views are not image-specific views but rather projections of expected structure to the image plane for a loosely constrained viewpoint. Only very simple three-dimensional models have been experimented with (however; see [159, 160]); Weymouth (149) employed a simple wire-

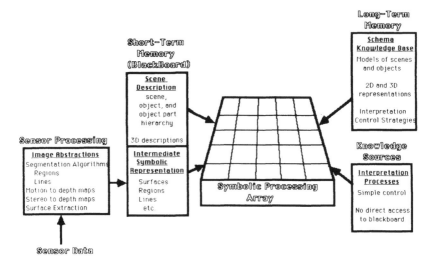

FIGURE 1.19. Overview of VISIONS system components. Sensor processes operate on sensor data producing a symbolic token in the intermediate symbolic representation (ISR). Note that the short-term memory is a blackboard divided into the ISR with a large number of tokens and the inferred scene and object descriptions. Scene and object schemas form long-term memory; associated interpretation strategies can be invoked and executed in parallel on a multiprocessor (called the SPA) with each node accessing the blackboard independently. Knowledge sources are distinguished from schemas by their simplicity of control and that they do not directly access the blackboard.

frame model of a house and simple relationships between the ground plane and house wall. Parma (106) also utilized simple three-dimensional reasoning schemes. However, the major results have been achieved using a network of two-dimensional views (149), where each view represents a canonical viewpoint on the Gaussian sphere of all possible viewpoints. This canonical viewpoint is representative of a particular sector of the Gaussian sphere for which the features of the object (scene) are qualitatively invariant (36). Thus, in some sense we are compiling three-dimensional information into this network in a form that leads to efficient recognition via associated strategies for matching the expected two-dimensional projections of three-dimensional objects with the image.

Example Interpretation Strategies

Schemas may be viewed as (possibly nonoverlapping) partitions of the knowledge base. The procedural knowledge embedded within object-specific (or to be more precise, schema-node-specific) interpretation strategies provides local control information. Once activated, the interpretation strategies are responsible for verifying and rejecting hypotheses, assessing their validity, extending hypotheses by selecting and grouping related data and hypotheses, instantiating the schema node, and activating related schemas. The interpretation strategies may be domain and object dependent, or uniform across domains.

In their initial implementation, the interpretation strategies have been encoded primarily in procedural form. However, it is unlikely that any intermediate-level process would be useful only for a specific object (whether it be matching of expected object attributes with token attributes, geometric grouping, verifications of spatial relations, etc.). As more strategies are implemented and we gain experience with their utility and generality, our goal is to extract some of the components and to represent them as parameterized "knowledge sources." These will then become the building blocks from which interpretation strategies are constructed. Ultimately, each schema-interpretation strategy could become nothing more than a structured series of calls to the knowledge sources.

The contextual verification and extension of hypotheses via consistency with stored knowledge and expectations leads to a variety of interpretation strategies that may be data-directed (bottom-up strategies) or knowledge-directed (top-down strategies) or both. In the next few sections we will present examples of several different classes of interpretation strategies. The first example is a hypothesis generation and extension strategy which uses the object-hypothesis rule system to select "exemplar" regions hypothesized to represent an object, and then extends them to similar regions. The second class of strategies uses geometric information to direct the grouping of intermediate events to better match the expected model (in this case, a house roof). The last example strategy involves the detection and correction of errors in the interpretation strategy (this strategy is discussed in the context of the overall interpretation results).

Exemplar Selection and Extension

Object hypotheses can be obtained by applying the object hypothesis rules (refer to the previous section) to the intermediate symbolic representation in order to select object "exemplars," which capture image-specific characteristics of the object. The rank-ordered set of image tokens for each object can be used to select one or more exemplar candidates. The set of exemplars can be viewed as a largely incomplete kernel interpretation.

Exemplar regions can be used in various ways to select similar regions

(60, 61, 118, 148). In many situations another instance of an object or object part can be expected to have a similar color, size, or shape. For those objects for which the spectral characteristics can be expected to be reasonably uniform over the image, the similarity of region color and texture can be used to extend an object label to other regions, perhaps using the expected spatial location and relative spatial information in various ways to restrict the set of candidate regions examined. This strategy assumes that the image-specific variation of a feature of an object is expected to be much less than the inter-image variation of that feature for the same object.

The similarity criteria might also vary as a function of the object, so that regions would be compared to the exemplar in terms of a particular set of features associated with that object. Thus, a sky exemplar region would be restricted to comparisons with regions above the horizon and that look similar (in terms of color and texture) to the largest, brightest region located near the top of the picture. A house wall showing through foliage can be matched to the unoccluded visible portion based upon color similarity and spatial constraints derived from inferences from the house wall geometry.

One possibility is to utilize the object-specific set of simple token features that were associated with the object hypothesis rules. As shown in the previous section, similarity relational rules can be functions of feature differences of similar tokens. It is also easy to use vetos for large token differences or for spatial constraints to restrict the spatial area over which candidates for exemplar extension will be considered.

The shape and/or size of a region can also be used to detect other instances of multiple objects, as in the case when one shutter of a house has been found (106) or when one tire of a car has been found or when one car on a road has been found. In many situations another instance can be expected to have a similar size and shape in the physical environment, and geometric constraints can be used to determine expected region sizes and locations. This permits reliable hypotheses to be formed even with high degrees of partial occlusion. The presence of a single shutter of a house provides strong spatial constraints on the location of other shutters. If two shutters are found, then perspective distortion can be taken into account when looking for the other shutters, even without a camera model, under an assumption that the tops and bottoms of the set of shutters lie on a straight line on the face of the house.

In Figure 1.20(a) we show the regions forming the highest-ranked object hypotheses as the object exemplars. The region features were used via similarity relational rules to measure the difference between the exemplar region and each candidate region. The rule response was con-

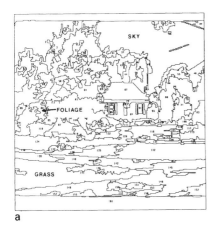

a   b

FIGURE 1.20. Exemplar selection and extension. One of the standard interpretation strategies involves the selection of exemplar tokens, which are then used as an "island of reliability" to extend the interpretation. (a) Exemplar regions for SKY, FOLIAGE, and GRASS, selected as the highest-ranking regions candidates via their object hypothesis rules; (b) The similarity between the exemplar region for grass shown in (a) and all regions; brightness encodes similarity.

verted into a distance metric, and bright regions correspond to small differences. Each of the rules contained location and size components, which enter into the final distance measurement, but in general, there are more intelligent ways of using these features in the interpretation strategy responsible for grouping regions. Figure 1.20(b) shows the similarity rating of regions obtained using the features of the grass rule.

Knowledge-Based Control of Grouping Processes

In this section we briefly motivate the types of additional top-down strategies that will be necessary for properly reorganizing the intermediate tokens to match the object better. The basic idea will be sketched using an example from Weymouth's thesis (149): the problem of grouping and interpreting a house roof from a fragmented intermediate representation. Figure 1.21 shows a number of intermediate stages in the application of a house roof interpretation strategy associated with the house roof schema. Figures 1.21(a,b) portray a pair of region and line segmentations that exhibit the difficulties expected in the output of low-level algorithms; Figure 1.21(a) also shows the initial roof hypothesis. In this example the region-segmentation algorithm was set to extract more detail from the image by producing a larger number of regions. The result, which is typical of a class of segmentation problems, is the fragmentation of the roof; the left portion, which was shadowed by trees, was broken into several regions separate from the main roof region. The set of lines intersecting the roof region are shown in Figure 1.21(c). When examined carefully, the line extraction results show fragmented line segments, multiple parallel lines, and gaps in lines.

The goal is to use these typical segmentation results to produce the trapezoidal region (which is almost a parallelogram) representing the perspective projection of a rectangular roof surface and to determine the orientation in three-dimensional space of that surface. The top-down grouping strategy employed here is organized around evidence of the almost parallel lines forming the two sets of sides of the trapezoid. There are alternate strategies for other typical situations where some of this information is missing. Thus, this roof grouping strategy expects some evidence for each of the four sides, and in particular uses the long lines bounding the hypothesized roof region (Figure 1.21d). By merging similar regions that are partially bounded by the long lines (Figure 1.21e), removing shorter, parallel, almost-adjacent lines, joining colinear line

a   b

FIGURE 1.21.   Steps in the schema directed interpretation of a roof. (a) Region representation with the initial roof hypothesis region marked; note that it is fragmented because of the tree shadow; (b) The set of lines that were filtered on length and contrast to produce initial candidates for the interpretation system; (c) The set of lines intersecting the hypothesized roof region; (d) Long lines bordering the boundary of the roof hypothesis region; (e) New roof hypothesis after merging regions that are partially bounded by the long lines in the previous image; (f) After joining colinear, nearby segments and removing close parallel lines; (g) The completed boundaries forming the hypothesized roof trapezoid.

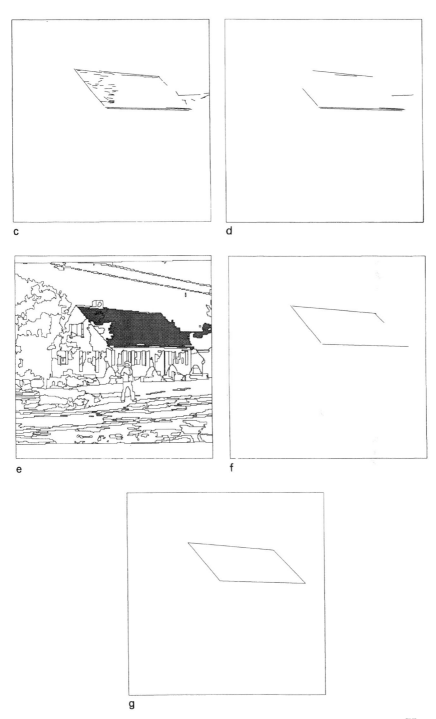

c   d

e   f

g

segments, and then fitting straight lines to the boundaries, a partial approximate parallelogram can be formed as shown in Figure 1.21(f). Finally, Figure 1.21(g) shows the complete hypothesized roof trapezoid. The three-dimensional geometry of the roof can then be computed (up to some possibly nontrivial degree of error) based upon either the location of the pair of vanishing points of the two sets of image lines that are parallel in the physical world or one pair of parallel lines and an assumption of perpendicular angles to a third line (96, 97, 98).

The point of this discussion is that the interpretation process required a flexible strategy for grouping and reorganizing the lines and regions obtained from imperfect segmentation processes. At this point we have developed each such strategy independently, but we are beginning to define some standard intermediate-grouping primitives that will form the basis of a variety of general top-down strategies this area is being actively explored by our research group.

Interpretation

Interpretation experiments are being conducted on a large set of "house scene" images. Thus far, we have been able to extract sky, grass, and foliage (trees and bushes) from many of these images with reasonable effectiveness, and have been successful in identifying shutters (or windows), house walls, roofs, roads, and telephone/power lines in some of them. Object hypothesis and exemplar extension rules as described in previous sections were employed. Additional object-verification rules requiring consistent spatial relationships with other object labels are being developed. The features and knowledge utilized vary across color and texture attributes, shape, size, location in the image, relative location to identified objects, and similarity in color and texture to identified objects. In the following figures, we show isolated intermediate and final results from the overall system.

Figure 1.22 shows selected results from the object-hypothesis rules after exemplar extension and region merging. Some of the interpretation results shown were obtained using a different (somewhat coarser grained) set of initial segmentations than those presented earlier and a different set of object hypothesis and exemplar extension strategies than those presented earlier.

Figure 1.23 illustrates typical interpretations obtained from a house-scene schema-interpretation strategy that utilizes a set of object-hypothesis rules for exemplar selection, extends the partial model from the most reliable of these hypotheses, and employs relational information

FIGURE 1.22. Result of schema interpretation strategies for generating object hypotheses. (a) Roof; (b) Grass; (c) Shutters; (d) Foliage; (e) Sky. Each of the object hypotheses shown here can be applied independently and in parallel. Each object hypothesis generated must be verified and in many cases further refined. Note the shutters in (c) where some regions are incorrectly labeled and others are missing. Nevertheless, these object hypotheses forms a partial interpretation that can be further developed incrementally.

a

b

c

d

e

for verifying hypotheses and predicting image location of object parts and related objects. The image areas shown in white in Figure 1.23 are uninterpreted either because the object did not exist in the knowledge network (and hence no label could be assigned) or because the object varied in some way from the rather constrained set of alternate descriptions of the object stored in the knowledge base.

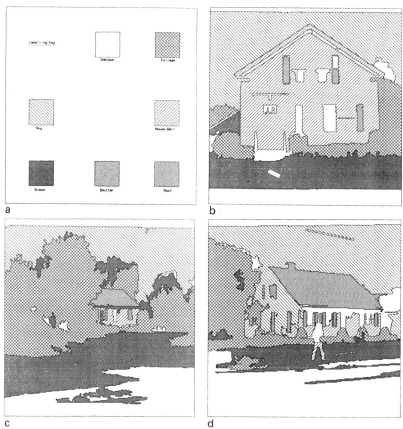

FIGURE 1.23. Example final interpretations. These images show the final results obtained by combining the results of the interpretation strategies under the constraints generated from the knowledge base. (a) Interpretation key; (b–d) interpretation results. In (d), the missing boundary between sky and wall results in a labeling conflict for the side wall (which is labeled as "sky" here). Note: These experiments did not significantly utilize the line information in the interpretation strategies for grouping and information fusion as discussed in the section beginning on p. 40; those capabilities have been more recently developed and are being integrated at a general level.

FIGURE 1.24. Feedback-directed resegmentation and interpretation. (a) There are multiple conflicting hypotheses for the shaded region; (b) The result of a resegmentation process with more sensitive setting; (c) The resulting interpretation when the resegmented regions are added to the initial segmentation and reinterpreted.

The interpretation shown in Figure 1.23 illustrates a problem that may be expected to occur quite frequently. The original interpretation was produced using a fairly coarse segmentation, which is desirable from the standpoint of computational efficiency since fewer regions are involved. However, the sky and house wall are merged into one region as shown more clearly in Figure 1.24(a). An example of the effectiveness of semantically-directed feedback to the segmentation processes is depicted here. The missing boundary between the house wall and sky led to competing object hypotheses (sky and house wall) based upon local interpretation strategies. The region is hypothesized to be sky by the sky strategy; application of the house wall strategy using the roof and shutters as spatial constraints to select a region exemplar for house wall and then extend it via similarity of regions, color, and texture, leads to a wall hypothesis. There is evidence available that some form of error has occurred in this example: (a) conflicting labels are produced for the same region by local interpretation strategies; (b) the house-wall label is associated with regions above the roof (note that while there are houses with a wall above a lower roof, the geometric consistency of the object shape is not satisfied in this example); and (c) the sky extends down the image close to the approximate horizon in only a portion of the image (which is possible, but worthy of closer inspection).

In this case resegmentation of the sky–house-wall region, with segmentation parameters set to extract finer detail, produces a reasonable segmentation of this region (Figure 1.24b). It should be pointed out that in this image there is a barely discernable boundary between the sky and house wall. However, once the merged region is resegmented with an intent of overfragmentation, this boundary can be detected. Now, the same interpretation strategy used earlier produces the quite acceptable results shown in Figure 1.24(c). We note that this capability (of detecting labeling conflicts and resegmentation) was not automatic at the point these results were produced, but is now being implemented as part of Kohl's forthcoming doctoral dissertation on knowledge-directed feedback under the control of a low-level executive (72).

Experience with Knowledge Engineering in the Schema System

Weymouth's (149) design of the schema network was a learning experience from which we were able to distill some observations about design techniques (150). Several generations of investigation and redesign of the schemas and interpretation strategies were required before semirobust results were achieved. A new schema system, based on this experience, is being designed and implemented; it is described in the next section. The integration of interpretation strategies in a schema network provides a mechanism for controlling the interpretation of a scene. Dependencies between and among schemas are expressed in the relational arcs and in the interpretation strategies. These dependencies, together with the results of partial interpretations, provide the basis for control of interpretation. This section outlines some heuristics using that information.

A large range of knowledge has been integrated into a fine-grained representation of interpretation strategies that can successfully cooperate to build a global interpretation. Image interpretation in less-constrained domains requires a large amount of knowledge about the particular domain, and the development of this knowledge bears similarity to the construction of "expert systems": The information must be collected, checked for consistency, experimentally verified, modified, and compiled. The challenge lies in the fact that the domain of vision is not one in which there is a clear understanding of the expert knowledge; it is extremely difficult for anyone to give a description (especially at the level of detail required by an expert system) of the information that we use for visual perception.

Deciding where to place information about object parts was one type of design decision. Decisions had to be rendered on whether to represent object parts as separate schemas or solely within the schema of the whole object. The guiding principle in the early effort came from the number and type of dependencies among the parts. In objects where there were complex relationships among the parts, the interpretation strategy for the object whole created the hypotheses for the parts. Thus, the creation of shutter and shutter-pair hypotheses was the dominion of the shutters schema, and the creation of the hypothesis for each individual wall of the house is the responsibility of the walls schema. On the other hand, for the schema in which there were methods for recognizing the parts that were less dependent on the relations between the parts (i.e., roof as part of house), the parts were constructed as separate schemas.

Our concentration on a modularized procedural representation aided in the development of interpretation strategies. We were often able to test a strategy in isolation before combining it with others. Our methodology was to attempt to construct interpretation strategies with as little interaction as possible with other interpretation strategies, relying on the verification stages to incorporate relational information. The limits of this approach were felt most acutely in the lack of sophistication in the type of communication and "coordination" available to the schema. When schema instances can be linked only to satisfy a goal, and then when they can only interact at a very coarse granularity in their respective strategies, they are necessarily limited in the types of cooperation possible.

Another type of design decision concerned control and communication of information between schemas. When should the activation of schemas be made explicit, and when should activation occur indirectly through STM (37)? When should explicitly activated schemas be activated in parallel, and when should they be activated sequentially? How should interpretation strategies be designed to maximize the amount of overlap in processing? When objects are closely related—such as the house, walls, and roof—the amount of influence they might have on one another suggests that a direct communication link will be helpful (that is, through requesting a goal and communicating through the goal contract). For example, the interpretation of the house depends on the interpretation of its parts (roof and wall), and these were invoked directly. Furthermore, the house strategy suspends processing (by waiting for the parts hypothesis) after making the goal requests. On the other hand, where the dependencies are less critical and more indirect (the objects on the ground-plane, for example), especially when the related objects are not essential for further processing, then the interpretation strategy was structured to do what processing it could and use indirect communication via the blackboard to obtain information about hypotheses. Periodic polling of STM for requested hypotheses can continue while a schema is engaged in other useful processing, and when no other processing remains, it can suspend activity until the requested hypotheses are posted in STM.

Parallel distributed control is being developed and explored in the use of schemas. Allowing schema activity to proceed, whenever feasible, increases the opportunities for parallel execution and encourages (to some extent) the early acquisition of evidence to support primary hypotheses. A simple principle to enhance parallelism is to request all parts and subclasses early in the interpretation, thereby spawning multiple schema processes, which can proceed in parallel.

Implementing Schemas

The development of a prototype schema system confronts many of the same issues that have arisen in other interpretation and control domains, such as speech understanding (80, 81, 158). Among them are questions about the knowledge representation, the communication of information, error recovery, and the selection of knowledge sources. Building upon the experiences of Weymouth (149) with the previous schema system, a new programming shell for research implementation of schemas as a set of concurrent cooperating processes has been developed by Draper (39). The purpose of the shell is to encourage development and testing of schema strategies by optimizing the programming and testing time. A prototype shell is in place and various object schema types are at different stages of development and testing under the current shell. Experience from a set of early experiments will lead to improvements in the shell structure itself. The implementation is in Common LISP on TI Explorers, with image data and low-level processes handled on VAXen.

Inferencing Under Uncertainty

As we have shown, the construction of a semantic representation of a scene involves sources of information and processes whose local view of the data may introduce inherent ambiguities into the interpretation of that data. Sometimes it is not possible to say what the data represents, but rather, what it does not represent (i.e., some interpretations can be ruled out). In many cases, the data obtained from an image, and the partial interpretations obtained from them, can be considered to be partial *evi-*

dence for or against the occurrence of semantically meaningful events. The schema strategies responsible for constructing an interpretation of an image cannot be certain that the available information is complete, accurate, or independent. Thus, major problems facing systems that must perform inferences from this kind of data include the representation of uncertainty within the system, the mechanisms by which uncertain information is combined, and the manner in which uncertain evidence may be extended through inference.

For the past several years, our research group has been examining the use of the Shafer–Dempster theory of evidence (38, 121) as the basis for evidential reasoning in the VISIONS system. Lowrance's thesis (85) showed how the Shafer-Dempster approach could be implemented in *dependency graphs*, which are the formal representations of dependency relations (arcs) between propositions (nodes). In this formalism, the likelihood of a set of propositions is represented by a distribution of a unit mass (similar to a probability distribution) over subintervals of the unit interval. The lower bound of the subinterval represents the degree of support provided to a proposition by a body of evidence, while the upper bound of the subinterval represents the extent to which the proposition remains plausible. The width of the interval represents the uncertainty (e.g., ignorance) in the belief of the proposition.

Lowrance (85) showed how mass distributions could be extended through the dependency graph from the set of propositions the evidence directly supports to those propositions that it indirectly supports. This work has since been extended by Lowrance and Garvey (44, 86) and by Wesley, Lowrance, and Garvey (144). Wesley et al. (142) viewed image interpretation as the process of inferring belief in the presence or absence (in the image) of a subset of visual entities represented in the knowledge base, and implemented LTM as a hierarchical dependency graph suitable for inferencing using the Lowrance model. The results of a limited set of experiments indicated that the inferencing model performed as expected, and that the evidential model was an attractive alternative to traditional Bayesian-based inferencing mechanisms (40, 67, 76).

Reynolds et al. (113, 116) and Lehrer et al. (79) addressed the problems of the automatic generation of mass functions, the computational complexity of Dempster's rule, and the mapping of continuous feature values into initial object hypotheses. They proposed a unified computational framework for generating and combining evidence. This approach, using the concept of a plausibility distribution, is an alternative to the rule-based object hypothesis system introduced in the previous section; a large-scale experiment comparing the two methods is currently underway (79).

Integrating information from multiple sources and propagating the combined information over the knowledge base is only one aspect of image interpretation. Complex domains require incremental extension of partial models, so that the constraints represented in the knowledge network can be exploited at the right time and at the right place. Consequently, a second important problem in image interpretation is the issue of control of the interpretation process: Where should attention be focused? What measurements should be made? How should competing hypotheses be resolved? And, how can the goals of the system be accomplished? Wesley's thesis (146, 147) extends the idea of evidential reasoning to control of knowledge-based systems, in particular to control in the VISIONS image-understanding system (145). In Wesley's system, a second *control* layer is added to the VISIONS system. Control-related information is obtained by control-knowledge sources, which measure the state of the interpretation process. This information is evidential in nature and is used to reason about the best course of action to pursue in order to extend the current partial interpretation.

The Schema Shell

The schema shell defines an object called the "schema." A schema is a software construct that contains all of the system's knowledge about some high-level task. Schema instances are active entities that apply this knowledge to accomplish the task. Schema instances are restricted to communicate through a blackboard to coordinate their actions. Of course this methodology will allow simulation of message passing as a more direct form of communication. When the presence of an object is suspected, a schema instance of the corresponding object class is created; this schema instance runs concurrently with any other active instances. If aspects of its chore can be done independently, it can spawn multiple concurrent *strategies*, which share a common memory, adding another level of parallelism to the system. The instantiated schema determines what further low- and intermediate-level processes to run and incorporates the results in its object-instance model. In this way it provides a vertical structuring of both knowledge and control. This form of schema design is both a simplification and a generalization of the schemas used by Weymouth (149). Major differences include the adoption of a single, general purpose communication mechanism, the separation of local memory from communication, and a simplified method of schema creation. In particular Weymouth chose a strategy of structuring hypothesis and verification strategies, which needed to be successfully executed prior to a schema writing a hypothesis on the blackboard; thus, weak hypotheses were not made visible and kept internal to the schema instance. Draper (39) is now exploring a strategy of allowing weak hypotheses to be posted with associated weak confidences, leaving the responsibility of whether such information should be used to the schemas reading this information, rather than those writing it.

In order to arrive at a coherent global interpretation, schema instances must communicate with each other. This is achieved without violating modularity by means of a central blackboard (BB). All messages are written to, and read off, the blackboard, as opposed to standard object-oriented systems, in which messages are passed directly between the objects (102). This severs the link between the sender and receiver of a message. A schema that produces information is not required to know of all the schemas that use it, nor do any two instances have to be active at the same time to communicate. Similarly, a schema instance does not need to know the possible sources of a message. Another effect of the blackboard is that schemas choose which messages they will receive. Instead of the function/caller semantics associated with most message passing systems, communication in the schema shell is a cooperative venture between two (or more) equal participants.

Posting a message to the blackboard simply requires a message and a blackboard-section name to which it is written. The mechanisms for reading, erasing, and modifying messages, on the other hand, are of necessity more complex. To read a message, a schema instance must specify the section to be read from and some method for selecting among the messages present on that section. The selection criterion is provided in the form of a predicate; all messages evaluating to TRUE under the predicate are returned (in a list) by the read function. A problem occurs when no messages are found. There is then a choice between returning the empty list or suspending the schema instance until a suitable message has been written. Since both are useful in different circumstances, the schema shell provides two basic reading functions: *read-or-nil* and *read-or-wait*. If no messages are found, the former returns nil, while the latter suspends the calling schema instance. A suspended instance is said to be *sleeping*, and we expect it to incur extremely little overhead until a suitable message is written and the instance is awakened. The shell also provides routines for removing messages from the blackboard as they are read (*erase-or-nil* and *erase-or-wait*) and for altering existing messages (*modify-blackboard*). Messages may also be selected according to when they were written (or most recently modified).

The Schema Template

Weymouth (149) developed a set of VISIONS schemas that used five basic types of object recognition (i.e., interpretation) strategies. He provided a limited demonstration of feasibility in a natural domain, carrying out experiments on four house scenes in six images. However, this research only begins to explore the possibilities for object recognition using schemas. Therefore, in order to encourage the development of new and different object- and scene-recognition schemas that can productively cooperate, a set of conventions in the form of a schema template has been developed to guide the knowledge engineer. However, we wish to emphasize that this is a part of ongoing research and has yet to be adequately tested. As our experience with schemas grows and we introduce new domains, these conventions will undoubtedly be altered. Our goal here is only to avoid the development of chaotic systems of schema networks.

The schema template divides the action of a schema into seven concurrent *interpretation strategies,* as in Figure 1.25. The OHM (for *O*bject *H*ypothesis *M*aintenance) strategy is activated when the schema is instantiated. Its task is to monitor the blackboard for information relevant to the object that the schema describes and to activate the other strategies as they become appropriate. Whenever relevant data appears, the OHM forwards it to the corresponding strategy. It is also responsible for the external appearance of the schema. The OHM maintains the object hypothesis on the blackboard, including the confidence measures, and so forth, and any goals that are posted by that schema.

The other six interpretation strategies involve specific recognition subtasks. The categories of interpretation strategies are meant not as a strict taxonomy of visual knowledge, but rather as a useful organization for the types of knowledge we have chosen to exploit so far. The Initial

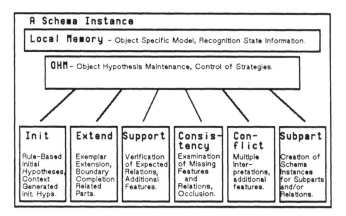

FIGURE 1.25. The schema template. The template provides a skeletal structure to guide the construction of schemas; it incorporates seven concurrent interpretation strategies which support various stages in the life of a hypothesis: creation, extension, integrating support, checking consistency, resolving conflict, and creating other related hypotheses.

Hypothesis strategy provides a focus-of-attention mechanism. Its job is to provide an indication of where in the image the other strategies should expend further effort, usually by generating inexpensive but plausible hypotheses. The other strategies are Extension, which extends the current hypothesis based on partial results; Support, which exploits redundancy by seeking additional evidence for the current hypothesis; Consistency, which must reason about any missing or inconsistent tokens and relations; Conflict, which handles multiple interpretations of the image or three-dimensional world; and Subpart, which activates schemas for expected visual subparts of the object. Obviously, not all strategies are needed or even meaningful for all objects; some objects, for instance, do not have subparts represented in the knowledge base. Furthermore, the boundaries between the strategies are drawn on a pragmatic basis. Subpart reasoning is a special case of Support, but was made a separate strategy to give the OHM more explicit control in expanding the compositional hierarchy. Note that since schemas are independent of their parents, creating a subpart's schema could continue to an unknown depth.

Each interpretation strategy has access to a library of low- and intermediate-level routines, which it uses as knowledge sources (KSs). The job of an interpretation strategy is to select those KSs that will aid it in its task and to run them. It must then integrate these results into the schema instance's current object model. As a result, a strategy is composed of code for object-specific control and object-model maintenance. The exceptions to this rule are the OHM strategies, which are the schema's interface to the global context. As we come to understand schema strategies better, we will provide improved tools for their construction.

As part of its task of monitoring the blackboard, the OHM must support error recovery and data synchronization. Errors emerge when later evidence refutes previously believed hypotheses. One solution to this problem is to maintain a history as hypothesis-dependency graphs (55), depicting for each conclusion the hypotheses upon which it depends. Unfortunately, recalculating the conclusion from scratch in such systems can be expensive. The schema system, therefore, uses a procedural form of this technique that preserves the computational state. The template requires that an OHM never terminate, unless it has removed its object hypothesis from the blackboard. Instead, it waits for messages that might affect its hypothesis. In this way, the OHMs provide a procedural-dependency network. The invalidation of any hypotheses will cause all schema instances dependent on it to wake up and compensate for the loss. This is efficient only to the extent that the schema shell can ensure that any process waiting on a (currently) nonexistent message consumes virtually no resources. While this is true in our current implementation, we are presently running on only a single processor. As we move onto a truly parallel, distributed machine in the near future, this method of error recovery will be tested experimentally for its feasibility and effectiveness.

OHMs are also responsible for data synchronization. Generally, a strategy will read messages of a certain type, processing each in turn. If, however, an OHM reads a message that alleviates the need for a currently executing KS, it can abort or reset the strategy before that KS has completed. Although currently unused, this ability could allow the system to synchronize data if necessary. It must be kept in mind that the ideas just presented here are currently being developed and evaluated in an empirical manner. New experiments are being developed in new domains, and the schema system is being modified and tuned as these domains are explored.

EXTENSIONS TO MOTION AND STEREO DATA

There are two obvious reasons why static-image interpretation must be extended to analysis of multiple images. First, many robotics applications involve a sensor moving through an environment, and information must be temporally integrated so that a dynamic model of the world is constructed. The development of dynamically changing egocentric representations of a world in motion is a challenging problem for computer vision. Second, the image depth of objects and their surface properties are important features for the interpretation of a scene and subsequent interaction with the objects and the environment. Both motion and stereo can provide this kind of information from multiple images. Consequently, a significant secondary focus of our research activity involves efficient recovery of this information and integration with the static image analysis components of the VISIONS system.

Let us briefly consider some of the extensions that are necessary as we bring static-vision interpretation and motion analysis together. First, the current ISR must be augmented to include surface patches derived from depth arrays (sparse or dense) obtained from motion analysis. Second, tokens in the ISR should be enriched with depth and motion attributes: Line and region tokens can have two-dimensional motion attributes, while surface tokens can have three-dimensional depth and motion attributes. The enriched representation provides additional features for interpretation; for example, a car moving on a road might be segmented in an image sequence more reliably and hypothesized to be a vehicle more easily and reliably. Third, motion analysis of the past N frames allows predictive capability for the next sequence of frames (25, 108,

125). Thus, much of the computation can involve monitoring the following frames for expected changes. Attention can then be focused on areas that are different than expectations or where a more accurate analysis is required.

Our research has both an empirical and a scientific component. We will outline the key areas of our motion and stereo research, providing references of our own work, but we will not attempt to survey the extensive literature in these areas. For recent surveys in these areas refer to (4, 7, 22, 69, 71, 135). The scientific goals of our work include the following:

1. *Correspondence of two-dimensional image events occurring in multiple images (5, 6, 7, 47).* This is a key capability that, in some manner, is at the foundation of the computation for any motion, stereo, or registration algorithm (Note: gradient-based methods are an alternative to direct-correspondence methods). Matching of local intensity windows via correlation, or points and lines via symbolic token matching are carried out for either a binocular pair or a motion sequence. The result is a disparity array in stereo analysis or a displacement field in motion analysis. Hierarchical processing, both for correlation matching and gradient-based methods, is an important and effective technique in motion analysis that is actively being explored in our laboratory (7, 46, 153).

2. *Temporal Grouping of two-dimensional image events.* The coherence of an image event across a sequence of images should provide a robustness that is impossible to achieve in a single-static image. Thus, perceptual organization of space-time edges into lines can use both dimensions where neither alone would suffice.

3. *Recovery of relative sensor motion when it is unknown (1, 2, 3, 77, 78).* This requires decomposition of general motion into its translational component and rotational component. In unconstrained general motion five parameters must be recovered, while in cases of constrained sensor motion, fewer parameters specifying the sensor motion must be recovered (e.g., pure translation involves two parameters).

4. *Computation of relative environmental depth from known or recovered sensor motion (1, 2, 3, 25, 77, 78, 125, 126, 154, 155).* Once the axis of translation is available (and the rotational component is removed), then displacements of image features are constrained to move along linear paths radiating from the focus of expansion (FOE), which is the point of intersection between the infinite image plane and the axis of translation (see Figure 1.26(a,b). The rate at which the projection of an environmental point moves between frames is a function of the depth of the environmental point, the

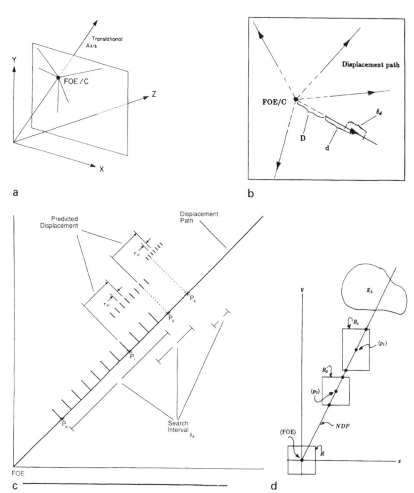

FIGURE 1.26. Multiframe recovery of depth from translational motion.
(a) For pure translational motion, displacements of image features are
constrained to move along linear paths radiating from the focus of expansion (FOE), which is the point of intersection between the infinite image
plane and the axis of translation; (b) An environmental point of approximately known depth D will be displaced a distance d with an uncertainty
interval of δ_d; (c) As depth is refined over multiple frames, future search
windows can be smaller and matched at higher resolution (r_w); (d) The
search window R_2 is actually two-dimensional because there is actually
two-dimensional uncertainty R in the position of the FOE and two-dimensional uncertainty R_0 and R_1 in the position of the feature points $< p_0 >$
and $< p_1 >$ respectively in two previous frames; (e) The two-dimensional
correlation surface at successive temporal matches at higher resolution.

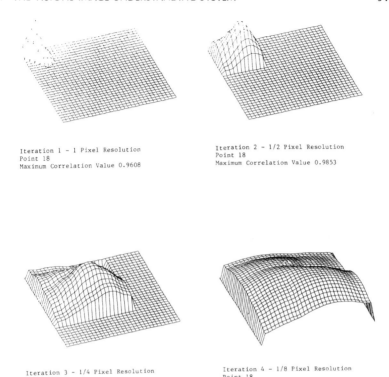

Iteration 1 - 1 Pixel Resolution
Point 18
Maximum Correlation Value 0.9608

Iteration 2 - 1/2 Pixel Resolution
Point 18
Maximum Correlation Value 0.9853

Iteration 3 - 1/4 Pixel Resolution
Point 18
Maximum Correlation Value 0.9437

Iteration 4 - 1/8 Pixel Resolution
Point 18
Maximum Correlation Value 0.9447

e

distance of its image plane projection from the FOE, and the relative rate of motion of the sensor to the environmental point. Given known camera parameters and a displacement field, the depth of environmental surface elements can be computed up to the accuracy of the image measurements.

5. *Detection of independently moving objects (1, 2, 3, 8).* The recovery of motion parameters and environmental depth is complicated when the scene contains independently moving objects. The moving objects must be segmented from the static environment, so that the motion of the object can be recovered. The relative translation between the moving object and the moving sensor can be used to compute the depth of the moving object. This is a very difficult problem and may not be solveable in many situations due to inherent ambiguities in the measurements.

6. *Computation of depth from stereo (7, 153).* This area is well-studied, but still needs to be integrated with motion processing. Processing of stereo and known translational motion have the common problem of obtaining depth from feature point correspondences along constrained match paths, although the problem of ambiguity in the match process is still an issue.

7. *Fusion of stereo and motion processing.* Constraints from binocular motion should allow more effective depth recovery than either by itself. This area is only beginning to receive attention in the field.

8. *Surface recovery from depth arrays.* Once depth is available, then the problem of recovering surface information must be considered. There is growing interest in this area, but there has been limited research in the field up to this point in time (also discussed earlier in this chapter), and one can expect many difficult problems similar to those for intensity and/or color segmentation.

Our current research projects have made significant headway in a number of these areas. The research has a theoretical foundation, but a significant consideration has been the development of robust algorithms tested on synthetic data with ground truth, as well as motion sequences derived from a sensor moving through natural scenes. We believe that we have a robust algorithm (developed by Lawton) for recovery of sensor translation (77, 78, 108), possibly the only algorithm at this time for detection of moving objects under general unknown sensor motion that has been successfully applied to real data (developed by Adiv) (1, 2), a two-dimensional matching algorithm that integrates a hierarchical orientation-dependent confidence measure with a smoothness assumption in the extraction of dense displacement fields (developed by Anandan, 5, 6, 8), and a hierarchical gradient-based relaxation method that is an alternative for achieving local smoothness in a dense displacement field (developed by Glazer, 46, 47). This set of algorithms demonstrates some degree of effectiveness for the recovery of motion parameters, displacement fields, and depth arrays in a variety of situations, although the techniques have not been integrated into a motion system for analyzing natural images.

As a first step in the process of integrating motion analysis with our interpretation system, we have chosen to focus on some well-defined subproblems of the general problem of a dynamic sensor translating through an unknown environment. We are seeking to determine a sparse depth map of environmental points under translational motion that is known up to some limit of experimental accuracy in the motion parameters (25, 125, 126). The local ambiguity in the matching process (often due to the resolution of the discrete matching process) leads to ambiguity in recovering environmental depth. Bharwani has developed an algorithm that uses correlation matching at a coarse image resolution to obtain a coarse estimate of depth from an initial pair of frames. The coarse depth result is used to predict displacements and a search window in a future frame. Additional frames are then used to refine the depth map via a finer resolution search for a match in the localized area (see Figure 1.26c). The technique allows refinement in depth estimates over the sequence of images while maintaining constant computational limits on processing between frames: As the accuracy of the environmental depth increases, the search window gets smaller and the match resolution can be correspondingly increased. Thus, both "start-up" and "updating" strategies follow naturally as part of a hierarchical spatial and temporal processing paradigm.

The inaccuracies actually are not one-dimensional as implied in Figure 1.26(b) due to digitization error (among other sources of error). Snyder (125) provided a thorough quantitative analysis of the effect of uncertainty in the locations of the FOE and image feature points in a pair of digital frames. A reasonable default assumption is that there is some degree of uncertainty due to the digitization process, typically $\pm \frac{1}{2}$ pixel when subpixel interpolation has not been used. Thus, the search window is actually two-dimensional as in Figure 1.26(d). The analysis includes the estimated accuracy in depth from previous frames to form an error range in computed depth, and with the error range in locations of FOE and feature points, a two-dimensional search space can be computed for future frames. Snyder's main conclusions are that uncertainty in the feature points (U_p) dominates uncertainty in the FOE (U_{foe}) unless U_{foe} is much larger than U_p. This theoretical analysis has lead to a modification of the windows to a two-dimensional area as shown in Figure 1.26(e). Note that the best match in successive frames shows the object moving and more accurately estimates the image displacement and hence the depth range.

Finally, there is a similar analysis underway by Snyder related to the relative accuracy of stereo and depth computation for environmental points at different distances and which appear in different locations in the image relative to the FOE. This analysis will also explore the theoretical limit of stereo and motion analyses to discriminating a moving object from the adjacent static background at a similar distance (126).

As these algorithms provide information on the depth of environmental points, they will be used to enrich the ISR so that more effective interpretation can take place. In addition, there is a research project underway to use both efforts to navigate a mobile vehicle in an outdoor environment on the UMass campus (11, 12).

PARALLEL ARCHITECTURES

Architectural Requirements for Vision

Real-time machine vision has turned out to be one of the most computationally intractable domains of artificial intelligence research. It requires
that an interpretation of a changing scene be updated with every new
video frame, once every thirtieth of a second, or no worse than once
every N frames, for some small N (e.g., 3–15). Each color video frame of
reasonably high resolution (512 × 512) contains approximately three-
quarters of a million values. Thus, just performing a single operation on
each data value would require executing about 23 million instructions
per second to keep up at full video rate. However, many researchers
believe that vision requires 2 to 4 orders of magnitude more
computation.

Some of the architectural issues to be addressed for vision stem from
the specific requirements of the problem:

- the ability to process both pixel and symbol data,
- the ability to transform an image into a set of meaningful symbols
  that describe it,
- the ability to select particular subsets of data for varying types of
  processing, and
- the ability to quickly access both low and intermediate data without
  having to move large amounts of information in and out of the
  processor.

A key design goal for an effective architecture is the ability to maintain
the low and intermediate representations simultaneously in the same
machine: sensory data in pixel format and symbolic region, and line and
surface representations. The necessity of transferring an image to an
external processor for evaluation by a sequential program in order to
continue further processing must be avoided. It is time consuming to
transfer the volume of information contained in an image and its derived
descriptions. Even if it took no time to accomplish the transfer, the time
required for serial evaluation would still be too great. Instead, the low-
level vision processor must be able to provide enough feedback to the
controlling processor to allow all of the operations to take place within
the low-level vision machine itself.

There are many types of parallel architectures that have been proposed for use at specific levels of vision processing. At this point in the
development of the field of computer vision there is no consensus
among leading researchers on approaches to real-time vision. However,

as we outlined earlier, there seems to be a growing consensus toward the need for at least two, and probably three forms, of processing. Consequently, there almost certainly needs to be at least two types of processing elements, and possibly three, with different levels of computational granularity.

Thus, we believe that the most significant architectural conclusions derived from an understanding of the full computer vision problem are:

1. the multiple levels of representation and stages of processing require very different types of processing elements, in terms of both granularity of data and the form of algorithms that need to be applied; and

2. the communication pathways between, and within, the processing levels and their bandwidth requirements must be considered an integral part of the architectural structure (83).

Processing Characteristics at Each Level of Vision

We have mapped the three levels of abstractions discussed throughout this chapter into a three-level tightly coupled architecture in which each level has the appropriate structure for the set of tasks at that level. The most well understood stage is the low-level where there is uniform computation at local points, usually at each pixel across the image. At this level we are concerned with pixels, which are numerical image data organized as a spatial array. Operations such as smoothing, edge detection, region segmentation, feature extraction, and feature matching between frames in motion and stereo processing are performed in SIMD fashion. Some of these operations may require processing over larger image distances, and therefore this type of processing may overlap some forms of intermediate-level processing discussed next.

At the intermediate level our concern is with symbolic tokens for lines, regions, and surfaces which specify extracted image events. The types of operations needed at this level are partitioning and merging operations. These tokens are transformed into more useful structures on the basis of information from both the low-level operations and high-level hypotheses about the possible objects in the image. The intermediate level also requires specialized processors. Consider the large numbers of line and region fragments that can be generated by even the most robust low-level algorithms. To perform grouping operations we need a large amount of less-local communication between intermediate processors. We need to match fragments of lines and merge them across potentially large fractions of the image. Similarly, regions need to be merged, and sometimes compared, with others from possibly noncontiguous areas. In order for it to be done quickly, architectural support for both interlevel and intralevel communication, as well as a flexible data manipulation repertoire of instructions is required. The Intermediate Symbolic Representation is a database that must operate as a server for the queries made by both the high-level and intermediate-level processing elements.

At the high level we are concerned with semantic processing involving mechanisms for focus of attention, the formation and verification of object hypotheses, and knowledge-based inference using complex control strategies for fusion of information from multiple knowledge sources. This type of processing involves extensive nonlocal symbolic computation and is most effectively performed on LISP type machines. The computational and communication needs of these processes is provided by a network of high-level processors which provide the third tier of processing power needed to solve the image understanding problem. Knowledge-based processing involves structures such as frames or schemas, with associated rules to be applied to tokens, in order to carry out interpretation using the context of expected objects and their relationships.

Communication Between Processing Levels

Central to vision processing is the flow of communication and control up and down through all representation levels. In the upward direction, the communication consists of image abstractions and segmentation results from multiple algorithms (and possibly from sensory sources). It also involves the computation of a set of attributes of each extracted image token to be stored in a symbolic representation. Summary information and statistics allow processes at the higher levels to evaluate the status of low- and intermediate-level operations.

In the downward direction the communication consists of knowledge-directed control of processing and grouping operations, the selection of subsets of the image, the specification of further processing in particular portions of the image, the modification of parameters of lower level processes, and requests for additional information in terms of the intermediate representation.

Thus, a key problem in selecting the appropriate two or three types of processing elements for the required computation is how the communication between machines can be structured. One cannot simply plug two interesting machines together if they cannot achieve the required communication bandwidth between them. Levitan's recent doctoral dissertation (83) documents research in the UMass architecture group over the last several years to identify and quantify the important aspects of communication in parallel algorithms and architectures.

Motivation of Associative Processing

Because associative computation may not be very familiar to many computer scientists and computer-vision researchers, let us briefly motivate their concepts in a bit of detail (43, 137). There are four processing capabilities that we will consider basic to associative computation:

1. global broadcast/local compare
2. some/none response
3. count responders
4. select first responder

Associative processing is a technique whereby the processors of the array have the ability to compare sets of data broadcast from a central controller to their own local (pixel) data. They can then conditionally process both local data, as well as broadcast data, based on the results of those tests. As a simple example, processors can conditionally store different broadcast tags based on the values of local data and thus *associate* their values with tags to support symbolic processing.

Associative processing can best be understood by an example of a single controller (a teacher) interacting with an associative array (a class of students) (43, 136). A teacher who needs to know if any student in a class has a copy of a particular book can ask each student, in turn, if they have the book. This would correspond to a computer program running sequentially though all the pixels in an array (or all the region tokens in a symbolic representation) looking for a particular intensity value. On the other hand, the teacher can simply state, "If you have the book, raise your hand." The students each make a check, in parallel, and respond appropriately. This corresponds to a broadcast operation from the controller and a local comparison operation at each pixel in an array to check for a particular value. Both operations assume that the local processors have some "intelligence" to perform the comparison. Clearly, the cost of the extra local intelligence is offset by the savings gained in time, which for images is on the order of the number of pixels (i.e., one-quarter of a million).

Query and response is just the first part of associative processing. Thus far, only a scheme for content addressable comparison ("If your hand is up, I'm talking to you.") has been described. To perform associative processing, we must be able to conditionally generate tags based on the value of data and use those tags for further processing. An example of this kind of association would be, "If you have an excuse from your mother or a doctor, then you can consider yourself 'EXCUSED'." A condition of the data has been associated with a label or tag. For region tokens, simple operations could be performed such as: If the intensity, color, and texture attributes are each in a certain range (i.e., rules on token attributes), label yourself POSSIBLE-SKY. The interesting processing comes when the controller starts performing logical operations on tags. Since each pixel or token could have multiple tags based on properties of the data, as well as things like spatial coordinates, operations could be performed like: If you are NOT-TREE and NOT-ROOF and (POSSIBLE-SKY or POSSIBLE-CLOUD) and IN-TOP-OF-IMAGE then label yourself LIKELY-SKY. As processing continues, only subsets of the pixels are involved in any particular operation. Pieces of the image are selectively processed based on their properties, but all pixels with a given set of properties are operated on in parallel.

The ability to associate tags with values is half the battle for high-speed control. Responses must be received back from the array quickly. Forcing the teacher to ask each student if they have their hand up defeats the process. The teacher can see immediately if any of the students have their hands up, and can quickly count how many do. Similarly, a some-response/no-response (some/none) wire running through the pixel array allows the controller to immediately determine properties about the data in the array, and therefore the state of processing in the array *without looking sequentially at the data values themselves.*

Additionally, fast hardware to perform a count of the responders allows the controller to see summary information about the state of the data in the array. Programs that can *conditionally* perform operations based on the state of the computation can then be written. The teacher can see if most students have their books, or not, and plan the lecture accordingly. By using the properties of the radix representation of numeric values in the array, we can use the counting hardware to sum the values in the array. The ability to sum values gives us the power to compute spatially weighted averages such as the center-of-mass of a region.

These examples of students and pixels illustrate the power of associative processing. Associative processing is a paradigm for communication in the upward direction and control in the downward direction between each pair of levels in the hierarchy. Criteria can be broadcast for selecting pixels, or regions, or symbolic tokens for selective processing. In this way higher levels control lower levels. The response that comes after processing data can be tested and/or counted to control conditional branching for the next step of processing in a given algorithm. Thus, the lower levels provide feedback to higher ones.

The associative select operation "select-first-responder" provides one more mechanism for transferring nonsummary information from a lower to a higher level in the vision-processing hierarchy. The higher level may select a single value in a lower level and read it out. This transfer of information is one-to-one: A single value at a lower level is copied to a higher level. The select-first operation is also useful for spreading-activation algorithms, where an initial seed point must be chosen.

Overview of the UMass Associative Image Understanding Architecture (IUA)

The University of Massachusetts (UMass) is developing a three-level tightly-coupled associative architecture to achieve real-time performance at all levels of vision processing (84, 90, 138). The UMass Associative Image Understanding Architecture (the UMass Associative IUA) combines an integrated approach to the three types of computation outlined, including the critical problems of communication between the three levels. The proposed architecture is a synthesis of an associative (or content addressable) processor and a cellular array processor at the bottom level (developed in Weems's doctoral dissertation, 137), interfaced to a network of intermediate communications processors, and a network of high-level symbolic processors at the top level.

The IUA is depicted in Figure 1.27 with the following levels:

- CAAPP (Content Addressable Array Parallel Processor (138).
  A 512 × 512 array of one-bit-serial ALUs and associative processing capability.
- ICAP (Intermediate Communication Associative Processor).
  A 64 × 64 array of 16-bit-parallel ALUs and associative processing capability.
- SPA (Symbolic Processing Array).
  An 8 × 8 array of microprocessors capable of LISP symbolic processing, each of which can serve as a global associative controller to the subarrays that follow.

The associative nature of the UMass IUA (at all levels), combined with the tight coupling between levels, supports the high-bandwidth interlevel communications and control needed to perform both sensory-to-symbolic transformations and high-level symbolic processing. Of particular importance is the ability to store both sensory data and the symbolic representation of lines, regions, and surfaces in the same physical cellular memory at the bottom two levels so that the global associative processing mechanisms can be applied to both, without any movement of data.

The key to associative-parallel processing is that data can be queried and retrieved in parallel extremely quickly. The retrieval mechanism is

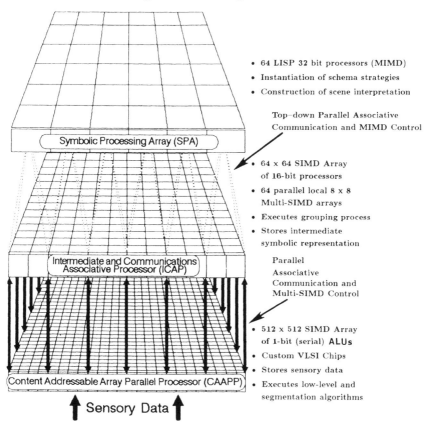

FIGURE 1.27. Associative image understanding architecture (IUA). There are three levels of tightly coupled parallel computing elements with associative communication and control between levels.

based upon accessing data by its content. The machine allows global broadcast from the controller to all cells; an activity bit to be set by each cell for its response; and the global response from the array of cells to the controller in terms of a count, some/none and select-first functions. In particular, a comparand may be broadcast from central control, and cells whose contents fail to match the broadcast comparand will be turned off so that operation of exact match to comparand, greater than (less than) comparand, maximum, and minimum, may each be performed in parallel on all cells of the memory. Thus, in the intermediate symbolic representation, one can set the activity bits for region tokens that are blue and high in the image by properly broadcasting comparison instructions to all cells, and then the number of responders, if any, can be ascertained immediately. If desirable, the find-first capability will allow sequential access by the global controller to all responding cells at approximately the instruction rate of the machine.

The CAAPP array is a 512 × 512 SIMD array of 262,144 simple processing elements, with 64 cells on a chip and 8 × 8 chips on a board. Thus, the design includes a processing element for each pixel at the sensory-processing level with 256 bits of RAM, 5 register bits, and a 1-bit ALU for bit-serial arithmetic and logic functions, and simple data routing circuitry. Information in each cell can be moved North, South, East, or West on the array so that neighboring cells can communicate with each other. It excels at very tightly coupled, very fine-grained parallelism; its architecture is especially oriented toward associative processing with global summary feedback mechanisms.

The ICAP is also a square grid array processor ([N, S, E, W] communication network), intended to perform intermediate-level processing on image events and tokens that are in physical registration with the pixel data. It provides data reduction and a high bandwidth communication channel between the lower-level processors and the SPA, (see the following paragraph) and allows partial results from widely separated image events to be combined quickly. There will be an array of 64 × 64 ICAP elements, one for each chip in the CAAPP array at the lowest level. Each of the 4096 ICAP processors consists of a 16-bit parallel ALU, 64K bytes of RAM, and data-routing hardware.

The Symbolic Processing Array (SPA) is configured as a network of 64 powerful, general-purpose microprocessors intended for performing MIMD high-level symbolic operations and for controlling subarray processing in the ICAP and CAAPP arrays. Each SPA processor is associated with an 8 × 8 array of ICAP processors and 64 × 64 array of CAAPP cells. The communication between processes will primarily be in terms of a "blackboard" architecture with communication managed by the processes themselves. As these processes run and make requests to the ICAP (and sometimes directly to the CAAPP), they extract information about the image and post the results of their analysis on the blackboard for other processes to use. At the beginning of processing, the lower arrays will be controlled by a single global controller and run entirely as a full-scale SIMD processor; at later stages when hypotheses are posted on the blackboard the machine will be multi-SIMD with each of the 64 symbolic processors controlling an ICAP and CAAPP subarray to run independent processing strategies.

During the last 4 years, the architecture and vision research groups at UMass have gone through three designs of the CAAPP, two VLSI layouts of the CAAPP, built a set of simulators, implemented 35 algorithms, analyzed and revised instruction sets, and produced two doctoral dissertations on associative processing and parallel algorithms that form the basis of this work (83, 137). The ICAP and SPA are more recent design stages. A test chip of the 3μ NMOS version of the CAAPP processing element has been received from the MOSIS facility and is undergoing testing. The ICAP is being designed now and in its first implementation may be built with a commercially-available chip. The goal of our research effort is the construction of a $\frac{1}{64}$ processor slice of the proposed hardware architecture with an associated software support environemnt; the implementation and final design effort is being carried out in cooperation with Hughes Research Laboratories, which will be building the initial board(s). The initial prototype will be a board with 4096 CAAPP cells, 64 ICAP cells, and controlled by one LISP processor.

The VISIONS System on the IUA

The VISIONS system on the IUA can be depicted by modifying Figure 1.19 as shown in Figure 1.28. The SPA implements the schema system and communicates object hypotheses through the STM blackboard. The three major differences in the diagrams reflect:

1. the mapping of low-level sensory processing onto the CAAPP array;
2. the embodiment of the ISR (i.e., the intermediate tokens) in the CAAPP and ICAP memory, instead of having the lower half of the STM blackboard as a separate data base; and
3. the parallel and associative nature of communication and retrieval of data between the SPA and the ICAP and CAAPP arrays.

The last point that should be noted is that the ISR can be shared in the CAAPP and ICAP memory. The information in the 64 CAAPP cells (64 × 256 bits = 16k bits) can be copied into the associated ICAP cell (64k bytes × 16 bits = 1024k bits) in a fraction of a frame time, and high-level queries can access information from either at, approximately, instruction rate. The symbolic data in the CAAPP can be structured via a linked list so that any token of sufficient size (i.e., greater than some minimum size threshold of pixels) can use the memory of the CAAPP cells as a linked list, storing an ordered set of token attribute-value pairs across the memory of the cells/pixels in each region.

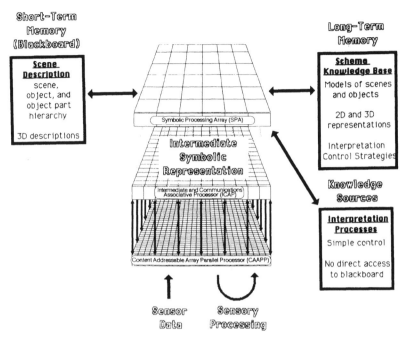

FIGURE 1.28.   The VISIONS system mapped onto the associative IUA. Sensory processing takes place in SIMD mode on the CAAPP, while the intermediate symbolic representation is stored at both the CAAPP and ICAP level. Schemas and knowledge sources are invoked to run in parallel on the SPA, building the interpretation on the distributed or shared memory multiprocessor.

Of course we expect there to be many questions in the reader's mind concerning the implementation of the algorithms that we have described in this paper. Any reasonable level of detail is beyond the scope of the broad presentation of this chapter. Thus, we can only briefly motivate the techniques that underlie the algorithms; in that regard we provide a single algorithm in a bit of detail in the next section.

Implementing the Straight-Line Algorithm on the Associative IUA

The straight-line extraction algorithm described earlier in this chapter was modified to take into account the massive parallelism available on the IUA and will be used to motivate how the structure of the machine might be used. The general idea is to run the line-detection part of the algorithm in a hierarchical fashion using CAAPP cells, one ICAP processor, and one SPA processor. The resulting line support (or gradient orientation) regions extending over the artificial boundaries are merged in a later step. Thus, each pyramid is concerned only with the area of the image underneath it. The timing information included here is an estimate of the execution times of the various portions of the algorithm; it reflects all data movement times as well as algorithm execution times.

The line computation process begins by loading the image into the CAAPP, computing the X and Y directions of the gradient at each cell, and then uses a table look-up technique to generate the gradient direction to a resolution of $1°$. Each cell now has the gradient direction and magnitude. The quantized-orientation bucket for each cell is then determined by broadcasting the bucket boundaries to each cell (in parallel). Since there are two sets of buckets (rotated from each other by $22.5°$), this is done twice. The total execution time up to this point is approximately $\frac{1}{2}$ ms, assuming an 8-bit image. Next, a connected-components algorithm is executed independently in the CAAPP area under each ICAP cell for each of the two partitions generated by the overlapping orientations, and one of these is selected by a voting process using a select-first and response-count scheme. The connected components and voting process takes approximately one ms.

A connected-components algorithm is now executed at the ICAP level over the 8×8 ICAP cells associated with one SPA processor. This involves associatively accessing the line-support region attributes from the CAAPP level and requires approximately 3 ms. Since some regions extend outside the boundaries of one SPA, the whole process is repeated at the SPA layer and requires approximately an additional 5 ms. At this point, all of the attributes of a line-support region are either in the memory of an ICAP or a SPA processor. For each region, the line corresponding to the moment of maximum inertia is found, rather than by intersecting the two planes in the original algorithm. Here, both ICAPs and SPAs are running concurrently. Assuming that each ICAP or SPA is computing for no more than 3 or 4 lines, the maximum time for this step is roughly 3–4 ms.

Finally, the line attributes are broadcast back to the CAAPP level to the endpoints and other attributes (if necessary). This is accomplished at the controller level and involves broadcasting the line label and characteristics. Each pixel in each line-support region then calculates whether it lies on the line. The broadcasting step for the line information is done sequentially for each region and the pixel calculations at the CAAPP level is done in parallel for all regions. The first step requires approximately 3.5 us for each region; assuming 1,000 regions, the time required is on the order of 3.5 ms. The second step requires 1 ms.

At this point, each line is represented by the pixels that belong to it and a line label; total execution time of the algorithm is roughly 17 ms.

CONCLUSION

The VISIONS system has undergone a continuous evolution over the years, driven primarily by a deeper appreciation of the nature of image understanding as both our research and that of the field have progressed. The current version of our system has produced reasonable interpretations of fairly complex outdoor scenes (e.g., house scenes and road scenes), and variations of the system have been applied to aerial images with some success. We view the system as an experimental testbed within which further evolution may be accomplished; we expect that there will be long term but slow improvement in the power and capabilities of the system as particular areas/modules/system components are improved and generalized.

Several areas of research are being vigorously pursued. One of these is the integration of motion into the interpretation process and the concurrent investigation into dynamically changing egocentric-world representations. A second component of the system that needs significant development (and there is some effort underway) is the three-dimensional representation of shape and methods for using three-dimensional information during interpretation. Although the current system has some three-dimensional knowledge of objects and can infer some three-dimensional structure, the capabilities are not adequate for a system expected to exhibit a reasonable degree of generality. There is an effort underway that involves compilation of three-dimensional information into a network of two-dimensional characteristic views associated with objects and scenes (36). A third area of research involves the inferential/evidential reasoning capabilities of the system, particularly methods for inferencing over the knowledge base using partial information from many sources. We have explored Dempster–Shafer mechanisms for evidential reasoning over the past 3–4 years (85, 113, 116, 142, 143, 146), and we now have a version of an object-hypothesis system based on feature evidence that operates in a manner similar to the rule-based object hypotheses presented in this chapter; comparisons of effectiveness are planned. However, the use of Shafer–Dempster evidential approaches to carry out propagation of partial beliefs/evidence in a semantic network has not yet developed to a point where it is clear how and whether to integrate it into our system. Mechanisms for propagating confidences/probabilities/beliefs will continue to be a primary research issue. Fourth, the knowledge base of the system needs to be expanded to more objects and more interpretation strategies, and the system needs to be exercised on a wider variety of images. We have a series of experiments planned for the near future which will exercise both our entire system and test our research group's ability to build a knowledge base for new task domains relatively quickly. Finally, in the UMass Image Understanding Architecture, we are actively exploring computational architectures suited to the types of processing inherent in image understanding, explicitly taking into account the set of algorithms presented in this chapter and the bandwidth requirements of the communication channels between the different levels. When a physical slice of the architecture is constructed it will be used to run real-time vision interpretation experiments.

ACKNOWLEDGEMENTS

The authors wish to thank the members of the VISIONS research group, both past and present, for their contributions to a long-term dream. Since the beginning, there have been moments where particular individuals have provided significant leadership in the maturation of the ideas.

We wish to specifically acknowledge several individuals who have made major contributions to our 12-year effort. Tom Williams was there at the inception of the VISIONS project and contributed greatly to the design of the system through the first 6 years. Ralf Kohler designed the VISION software development environment that has supported empirical development in a flexible manner for many years. Joey Griffith has had his fingers in almost every aspect of the project for the last 6 years. George Reynolds has taken on a significant leadership role in the development of many aspects of intermediate processing. We also wish to acknowledge the leadership provided by Daryl Lawton and P. Anandan in developing our motion group.

In addition, a number of other people have made their presence felt including Terry Weymouth, John Lowrance, Frank Glazer, Paul Nagin, Bryant York, Gilad Adiv, Charlie Kohl, Len Wesley, Cesare Parma, and current members Bruce Draper, Rob Belknap, Bob Collins, Michael Boldt, Brian Burns, Ross Beveridge, Nancy Lehrer, Seraj Bharwani, Val Cohen, Jim Burrill, Bob Heller, Mark Snyder, Igor Pavlin, Rich Weiss, Les Kitchen, Chip Weems, and Steve Levitan.

We also wish to thank Janet Turnbull for her continuing support over the years, and Laurie Waskiewicz for her perserverance and good humor during the production of this chapter.

This work has been supported by the Air Force Office of Scientific Research under grant F49620-83-C-0099, by the Defense Advanced Research Projects Agency under contracts N00014-82-K-0464 and DACA76-85-C-0008, and by the National Science Foundation under grant DCR-8318776.

REFERENCES

1. G. Adiv, "Determining 3-D motion and structure from optical flow generated by several moving objects. *IEEE transactions on pattern analysis and machine intelligence,* Vol. PAMI-7, July 1985, pp. 384–401.
2. G. Adiv, "Interpreting optical flow." Ph.D. Dissertation, Computer and Information Science Department, University of Massachusetts at Amherst, September 1985.
3. G. Adiv, "Inherent ambiguities in recovering 3-D motion and structure from a noisy flow field." *Proceedings of the Computer Vision and Pattern Recognition Conference,* San Francisco, CA, June 1985, pp. 7077.
4. J. Aliomonos & A. Basu, "Shape and 3D Motion from Contour without Point-to-Point Correspondence: General Principles." *Proceedings of the Computer Vision and Pattern Recognition Conference,* 1986, pp. 518–527.
5. P. Anandan, "Computing dense displacement fields with confidence measures in scenes containing occlusion." *SPIE Intelligent Robots and Computer Vision Conference,* Vol. 521, 1084, pp. 184–194; also *DARPA IU Workshop Proceedings,* 1984; and COINS Technical Report 84-32, University of Massachusetts at Amherst, December 1984.
6. P. Anandan & R. Weiss, "Introducing a smoothness constraint in a matching approach for the computation of optical flow fields." *Proceedings of the Third Workshop on Computer Vision: Representation and Control,* October 1985, pp. 186–196.
7. P. Anandan, "Motion and stereopsis." COINS Technical Report 85-52, University of Massachusetts at Amherst, December 1985.
8. P. Anandan, "Measuring visual motion from image sequences." Ph.D. Dissertation, University of Massachusetts at Amherst, January 1987.
9. M. A. Arbib, "Segmentation, schemas, and cooperative computation." In *Studies in mathematical biology, part 1,* S. Leven (Ed.). MAA Studies in Mathematics, Vol. 15, 1978, pp. 118–155.
10. M. A. Arbib, "Perceptual structures and distributed motor control." In *Handbook of physiology: The nervous system, II Motor control,* V. B. Brooks (Ed.). American Physiological Society: Bethesda, MD, pp. 1449–1480.
11. R. Arkin, "Path planning and execution for a mobile robot: A review of representation and control strategies." COINS Technical Report 86-47, University of Massachusetts at Amherst, October 1986.
12. R. Arkin, "Path planning for a vision-based autonomous robot." COINS Technical Report 86-48, University of Massachusetts at Amherst, October 1986.
13. R. Bajcsy, & M. Tavakoli, "Computer recognition of roads from satellite pictures." *IEEE transactions on systems, man, and cybernetics, SMC-6,* September 1976, pp. 623–637.
14. H. H. Baker, "Depth from edge and intensity based stereo." Report No. STAN-CS-82-930, Department of Computer Science, Stanford University: CA, September 1982.
15. D. Ballard, C. Brown, & J. Feldman, "An approach to knowledge-directed image analysis." In *Computer vision systems,* A. Hanson & E. Riseman (Eds.). Academic Press: New York, 1978, pp. 271–281.
16. D. Ballard, & C. Brown, *Computer vision,* Prentice-Hall, Inc.: Englewood Cliffs, NJ, 1982.
17. H. G. Barrow, & J. M. Tenenbaum, "Computational Vision." *IEEE Transactions on Pattern Analysis and Machine Intelligence,* Institute for Electrical & Electronic Engineers, May 1981, pp. 572–595.
18. H. G. Barrow & R. J. Popplestone, "Relational Descriptions in Picture Processing." In *Machine Intelligence 6.* B. Meltzer & D. Michie (Eds.). Edinburgh University Press: Edinburgh, 1971, pp. 377–396.

19. H. Barrow, & J. Tenenbaum, "MSYS: A system for reasoning about scenes," Technical Note 121. April 1976, AI Center, Stanford Research Institute.

20. R. Belknap, E. Riseman, & A. Hanson, "The information fusion problem and rule-based hypotheses applied to complex aggregations of image events," COINS Technical Report. University of Massachusetts at Amherst, in preparation, 1987.

21. R. Belknap, E. Riseman, & A. Hanson, "The information fusion problem and rule-based hypotheses applied to complex aggregations of image events." *Proceedings DARPA IU Workshop*, Miami Beach, FL, December 1985.

22. S. T. Barnard, & M. A. Fischler, "Computational stereo." *Computing Surveys, 14*(4), December 1982, pp. 553–572.

23. P. J. Besl, & R. C. Jain, "Range image understanding." In *Proceedings IEEE Conference on Computer Vision and Pattern Recognition*, San Francisco, CA, June 9–13, 1985, New York, pp. 430–451.

24. R. Beveridge, A. Hanson, & E. Riseman, "Segmenting images using localized histograms," COINS Technical Report, University of Massachusetts at Amherst, 1986.

25. S. Bharwani, A. Hanson, & R. Riseman, "Refinement of environmental depth maps over multiple frames." *Proceedings DARPA IU Workshop*, Miami Beach, FL, December 1985.

26. I. Biederman, A. Glass, & E. W. Stacy, "Searching for objects in real-world scenes." *Journal of Experimental Psychology, 97*, 1973, 22–27.

27. I. Biederman, "On the semantics of a glance at a scene." In *Perceptual organization*, M. Kubovy & J. R. Pomerants (Eds.). Lawrence Erlbaum Associates: Hillsdale, NJ, 1981, pp. 213–255.

28. I. Biederman, "Scene perception: A failure to find benefit from prior expectancy or familiarity." *Journal of Experimental Psychology: Learning, Memory, and Cognition, 9*, 1983, 411–429.

29. T. Binford, "Survey of model-based image analysis systems," *International Journal of Robotics Research, 1*, 1982, 18–64.

30. R. Brachman, "What's in a concept: Structural foundations for semantic networks." BBN Report 3433, 1976.

31. M. Brady, "Computational approaches to image understanding." *Computing Surveys, 14*, March 1982, pp. 3–71.

32. R. Brooks, "Symbolic reasoning among 3-D models and 2-D images." *STAN-CS-81-861*, and AIM-343, June 1981, Department of Computer Science, Stanford University.

33. J. B. Burns, A. Hanson, & E. Riseman, "Extracting linear features," *Proceedings of the 7th ICPR*, Montreal, 1984. Also COINS Technical Report 84-29, University of Massachusetts at Amherst, August 1984.

34. J. B. Burns, A. R. Hanson, & E. M. Riseman, "Extracting straight lines." *IEEE Transactions on Pattern Analysis and Machine Intelligence 8*, (4), July 1986, 425–455.

35. J. Burrill, "Speeding up the Weymouth-Overton smoothing operator." COINS Technical Report, University of Massachusetts at Amherst, in preparation, 1986.

36. J. Callahan & R. Weiss, "A model for describing surface shape". *Proceedings of Computer Vision and Pattern Recognition*, San Francisco, June 1985, pp. 240–245.

37. D. D. Corkill & V. R. Lesser, "A goal-directed hearsay-II architecture: Unifying data- and goal-directed control." COINS Technical Report 81-15, University of Massachusetts at Amherst, June 1981.

38. A. P. Dempster, "A Generalization of Bayesian Inference." *Journal of the Royal Statistical Society*, Series B, *30*, 1968, pp. 205–247.

39. B. Draper, A. Hanson, & E. Riseman, "A software environment for high level vision." COINS Technical Report, University of Massachusetts at Amherst, in preparation, 1986.

40. R. Duda, P. Hart, & N. Nilsson, "Subjective Bayesian methods for rule-based inference systems." National Computer Conference, *AFIPS Conference Proceedings, 45,* 1976, pp. 1075–1082.

41. L. Erman, F. Hayes-Roth, V. R. Lesser, & D. Raj Reddy. "The hearsay-II speech-understanding system: Integrating knowledge to resolve uncertainty." *Computing Surveys, 12*(2), June 1980, pp. 213–253.

42. O. Faugeras & K. Price, "Semantic descriptions of aerial images using stochastic labeling." *IEEE Transactions on Pattern Analysis and Machine Intelligence 3,* November 1981, pp. 638–642.

43. C. C. Foster, "Content addressable parallel processors." Van Nostrand Reinhold: New York, 1976.

44. T. Garvey, J. Lowrance, & M. Fischler, "An inference technique for integrating knowledge from disparate sources." *Proceedings of the 7th IJCAI,* 1981, pp. 319–325.

45. D. B. Gennery, "Modelling the environment of an exploring vehicle by stereo vision." Ph.D. thesis, Stanford AI Laboratory, June 1980.

46. F. Glazer, G. Reynolds, & P. Anandan, "Scene matching by hierarchical correlation," *Proceedings of the IEEE Conference on Computer Vision and Pattern Recognition,* June 1983, pp. 432–440.

47. F. Glazer, "Hierarchical motion detection." forthcoming Ph.D. Dissertation, Computer and Information Science Department, University of Massachusetts, Amherst, 1986.

48. J. Glicksman, "A cooperative scheme for image understanding using multiple sources of information." Ph.D. Dissertation, University of British Columbia, November 1982.

49. J. Griffith, A. Hanson, E. Riseman, & R. Kohler, "A rule-based image segmentation system." COINS Technical Report, University of Massachusetts at Amherst, in preparation, 1987.

50. W. E. L. Grimson, "On the reconstruction of visible surfaces." In *Image understanding 1984,* S. Ullman & W. Richards (Eds.). Ablex: NJ, 1984, pp. 195–223.

51. A. R. Hanson, & E. M. Riseman, "Preprocessing cones: A computational structure for scene analysis," COINS Technical Report 74C-7, University of Massachusetts at Amherst, September 1974.

52. A. R. Hanson, & E. M. Riseman, "The design of a semantically directed vision processor (Revised and Updated)." COINS Technical Report 75-C1, University of Massachusetts at Amherst, September 1975.

53. A. R. Hanson, & E. M. Riseman, "Design of VISIONS: Segmentation and interpretation of images." *Conference Record of 1976 Joint Workshop on PR and AI,* Hyannis, MA, June 1976, pp. 135–144.

54. A. R. Hanson, & E. M. Riseman (Eds.). *Computer Vision Systems,* Academic Press: New York, 1978.

55. A. R. Hanson, & E. M. Riseman, "VISIONS: A computer system for interpreting scenes. In *Computer Vision Systems,* A. Hanson & E. Riseman (Eds.). Academic Press: New York: 1978, pp. 303–333.

56. A. R. Hanson, & E. M. Riseman, "Segmentation of natural scenes." In *Computer Vision Systems,* A. Hanson & E. Riseman (Eds.), Academic Press: New York, 1978, pp. 129–163.

57. A. R. Hanson, & E. M. Riseman, "Processing cones: A computational structure for image analysis." In *Structured Computer Vision,* S. Tanimoto & A. Klinger (Eds.). Academic Press: New York, 1980, pp. 101–131.

58. A. R. Hanson & E. M. Riseman, "A summary of image understanding research at the university of Massachusetts." COINS Technical Report 83-35, University of Massachusetts at Amherst, October 1983.

59. A. R. Hanson, E. M. Riseman, & P. A. Nagin, Authors Reply to "Image segmentation:

A comment on 'Studies in global and local histogram-guided relaxation algorithms'." *PAMI 6*, No. 2, March 1984.

60. A. R. Hanson, E. M. Riseman, J. S. Griffith, & T. E. Weymouth, "A methodology for the development of general knowledge-based vision systems." *Procedings of IEEE Workshop on Principles of Knowledge-Based Systems*, Denver, CO, December 1984, pp. 159–170.

61. A. R. Hanson, & E. M. Riseman, "A methodology for the development of general knowledge-based vision systems." In *Vision, brain, and cooperative computation*, M. Arbib & A. Hanson (Eds.). MIT Press: Cambridge, MA, 1986, pp. 285–328.

62. R. M. Haralick, "Ridges and valleys on digital images." *Computer vision, graphics and image processing, 22*(1), 1983, pp. 28–39.

63. M. Herman, & T. Kanade, "The 3D mosaic scene understanding system: Incremental reconstruction of 3D scenes from complex images." *Proceedings of the DARPA IU Workshop*, October 1984, pp. 137–148.

64. B. K. P. Horn, "Obtaining shape from shading information." In *The psychology of computer vision*, P. H. Winston (Ed.), McGraw-Hill: New York, 1975, pp. 115–155.

65. B. K. P. Horn, "Understanding image intensitities." *Artificial intelligence*, Vol. 8, 1977, pp. 201–231.

66. B. K. P. Horn, & B. A. Schunck, "Determining Optical Flow." *Artificial intelligence*, Vol. 17, 1981, pp. 185–203.

67. R. A. Hummel, & M. Landy, "A statistical viewpoint on the theory of evidence." New York University, Courant Institute of Mathematical Sciences (Tech. Rep. 194), December 1985.

68. K. Ikeuchi, "Numerical shape for shading and occluding contours in a single view." AI Memo 566, AI Lab, MIT Press: Cambridge, MA, February 1980.

69. M. Jenkin, "The stereopsis of time varying imagery." RBVC Technical Report, RBVC-TR-84-3, Department of Computer Science, University of Toronto: Toronto, 1984.

70. T. Kanade, "Model representation and control structures in image understanding." *Proceedings of IJCAI-5*, August 1977.

71. J. R. Kender, "Shape from texture." Ph.D. Dissertation, Computer Science Department, Carnegie-Mellon University: Pittsburgh, PA 1980.

72. C. Kohl, Ph.D. Dissertation, Department of Computer and Information Science, University of Massachusetts at Amherst, in preparation, 1987.

73. R. R. Kohler, "A segmentation system based on thresholding." *Computer graphics and image processing, 15*, 1981, pp. 319–338.

74. R. R. Kohler, & A. R. Hanson, "The VISIONS image operating system." *Proceedings of 6th International Conference on Pattern Recognition*, Munich, Germany, October, 1982.

75. R. R. Kohler, "Integrating non-semantic knowledge into image segmentation processes." COINS Technical Report 84-04, University of Massachusetts at Amherst, March 14.

76. H. E. Kyberg, "Bayesian and non-bayesian evidential updating." Department of Computer Science (Tech. Rep. 139), University of Rochester: New York, July 1984.

77. D. T. Lawson, "Processing translational motion sequences." *Computer graphics and image processing, 22*, 1983, pp. 116–144.

78. D. T. Lawton, "Processing dynamic image sequences from a moving sensor." Ph.D. Dissertation (COINS Technical Report 84-05), Computer and Information Science Department, University of Massachusetts, 1984.

79. N. Lehrer, G. Reynolds, & J. Griffith, "A method for initial hypothesis formation in image understanding." COINS Technical Report, University of Massachusetts at Amherst, in preparation, 1987.

80. V. R. Lesser, R. D. Fennell, L. D. Erman, & D. R. Reddy, "Organization of the hearsay-II speech understanding system." *IEEE Transactions on ASSP 23*, 1975, pp. 11–23.

81. V. R. Lesser, & L. D. Erman, "A retrospective view of the hearsay-II architecture." *Proceedings of IJCAI-5,* Cambridge, MA, 1977, pp. 790–800.
82. M. Levine, & S. Shaheen, "A modular computer vision system for picture segmentation and interpretation," *IEEE Transactions on Pattern Analysis and Machine Intelligence, 3,* September 1981, pp. 540–556.
83. S. P. Levitan, "Parallel algorithms and architectures: A programmers perspective." Ph.D. Dissertation, Computer and Information Science Department, also, COINS Technical Report 84-11, University of Massachusetts at Amherst, May 1984.
84. S. P. Levitan, C. Weems, A. R. Hanson, & E. M. Riseman, "The UMass image understanding architecture." In *"Pyramid multi-computers."* Leonard Uhr (Ed.), Academic Press: New York, 1987.
85. J. Lowrance, "Dependency graph models of evidential support." COINS Technical Report 82-26, University of Massachusetts at Amherst, 1982.
86. J. Lowrance, & T. Garvey, "Evidential reasoning: A developing concept." *Proceedings of the International Conference on Cybernetics and Society,* October, 1982.
87. D. Marr, & E. Hildreth, "Theory of edge detection." *Proceedings of the Royal Society of London, B., 207,* 1980, pp. 187–217.
88. D. Marr, *VISION.* W. H. Freeman and Company, San Francisco, 1982.
89. D. M. McKeown, W. A. Harvey, & J. McDermott, "Rule based interpretation of aerial imagery." Department of Computer Science, Carnegie-Mellon University, September 1984.
90. D. I. Moldovan, J. G. Wu, S. Levitan, & C. Weems, "Parallel processing of iconic to symbolic transformation of images." *Proceeding of the IEEE Conference on Computer Vision and Pattern Recognition,* 1985, pp. 257–264.
91. H. P. Moravec, "Obstacle avoidance and navigation in the real world by a seeing robot rover." Ph.D. Thesis, Stanford University AI Laboratory, CA, September 1980.
92. M. Nagao, & T. Matsuyama, "Edge preserving smoothing." *Proceedings of the Fourth International Joint Conference on Pattern Recognition,* pp. 518–520, November 1978.
93. M. Nagao, & T. Matsuyama, "A structural analysis of complex aerial photographs." Plenum Press: NY, 1980.
94. P. A. Nagin, "Studies in image segmentation algorithms based on histogram clustering an relaxation." COINS Technical Report 79-15, University of Massachusetts at Amherst, September 1979.
95. P. A. Nagin, A. R. Hanson, & E. M. Riseman, "Studies in global and local histogram-guided relaxation algorithms." *IEEE Transactions on Pattern Analysis and Machine Intelligence, 3,* May 1982, pp. 263–277.
96. H. Nakatani, S. Kimura, O. Saito, and T. Kitahashi, "Extraction of vanishing point and its application to scene analysis based on image sequence." *Fifth International Conference on Pattern Recognition,* pp. 360–372, 1980.
97. H. Nakatani, T. Kitahashi, "Inferring 3-d shape from line drawings using vanishing points." *First International Conference on Computers and Applications,* 1984.
98. H. Nakatani, R. Weiss, & E. Riseman, "Application of vanishing points to 3D measurement." *Proceedings of SPIE, 507,* 1984, pp. 164–169.
99. A. M. Nazif, & M. D. Levine, "Low level segmentation: An expert system," (Tech. Rep. 83-4), Electrical Engineering, McGill University: Montreal, April 1983.
100. A. M. Nazif, "A rule-based expert system for image segmentation," Ph.D. Dissertation, Electrical Engineering Department, McGill University: Montreal, 1983.
101. R. Nevatia, & K. R. Babu, "Linear feature extraction and description." *Computer graphics and image processing, 13,* 1980, pp. 257–269.
102. H. Penny Nii, "Blackboard systems: The blackboard model of problem solving and the evolution of blackboard architectures." In *AI magazine, 7,*(2), Summer 1986, pp. 38–53.

103. R. Ohlander, K. Price, & D. R. Reddy, "Picture segmentation using a recursive region splitting method." *Computer graphics and image processing 8, 3,* 1979.

104. Y. Ohta, "A region-oriented image-analysis system by computer." Ph.D. Thesis, Computer Information Science Department, Kyoto University: Kyoto, Japan, 1980.

105. K. Overton, & T. E. Weymouth, "A noise reducing preprocessing algorithm." *Proceedings of the IEEE Conference on Pattern Recognition and Image Processing,* Chicago, IL, 1979, pp. 498–507.

106. C. C. Parma, A. R. Hanson, & E. M. Riseman, "Experiments in schema-driven interpretation of a natural science." COINS Technical Report 80-10, University of Massachusetts at Amherst, April 1980.

107. J. L. Paul, "An image interpretation system." Ph.D. Dissertation, University of Sussex, England, June 1977.

108. I. Pavlin, A. Hanson, and E. Riseman, "Analysis of an algorithm for detection of translational motion." *Proceedings of DARPA IU Workshop,* Miami Beach, FL, December 1985.

109. J. M. Prager, "Segmentation of static and dynamic scenes." Ph.D. Thesis, Computer and Information Science Department, University of Massachusetts at Amherst, 1979.

110. K. E. Price, "Change detection and analysis in multispectral images." Ph.D. Thesis, Carnegie-Mellon University: Pittsburgh, PA, December 1976.

111. K. E. Price, & R. Reddy, "Matching segments of images." *IEEE Transactions on Pattern Analysis and Machine Intelligence, 1,* June 1979.

112. K. E. Price, "Image segmentation: A comment on 'Studies in global and local histogram-guided relaxation algorithms.'" *IEEE Transactions on Pattern Analysis and Machine Intelligence 6, 2,* March 1984.

113. G. Reynolds, D. Strahman, N. Lehrer, & L. Kitchen, "Plausible reasoning and the theory of evidence." COINS Technical Report 86-11, University of Massachusetts at Amherst, April 1986.

114. G. Reynolds, J. Ross Beveridge, "Geometric line organization using spatial relations and a connected components algorithm." COINS Technical Report, University of Massachusetts at Amherst, in preparation.

115. G. Reynolds, N. Irwin, A. Hanson, & E. Riseman, "Hierarchical knowledge-directed object extraction using a combined region and line representation." *Proceedings of the Workshop on Computer Vision: Representation and Control,* Annapolis, MA, April 30–May 2, 1984, pp. 238–247.

116. G. Reynolds, D. Strahman, & N. Lehrer, "Converting feature values to evidence." Proceedings DARPA IU Workshop, Miami Beach, FL, 1985.

117. E. Riseman, & A. Hanson, "The design of a semantically directed vision processor." COINS Technical Report 74C-1, University of Massachusetts, February 1975, Revised version COINS Technical Report 75C-1.

118. E. M. Riseman, & A. R. Hanson, "A methodology for the development of general knowledge-based vision systems." *IEEE Proceedings of the Workshop on Computer Vision: Representation and Control,* 1984, pp. 159–170.

119. L. G. Roberts, "Machine perception of three-dimensional solids." *Symposium of Optical and Electro-optical Information Processing Technology,* Boston, 1964, pp. 159–197.

120. Steven A. Shafer, Antohony Stentz, & Charles E. Thorpe, "An architecture for sensor fusion in a mobile Robot." *International Conference on Robotics and Automation,* San Francisco, CA, 1986, pp. 2202–2011.

121. G. Shafer, "A mathematical theory of evidence." Princeton University Press: Princeton, NJ, 1976.

122. Y. Shirai, "Recognition of man-made objects using edge cues." In *Computer Vision*

Systems, A. Hanson & E. Riseman (Eds.). Academic Press: New York, 1976, pp. 353–362.

123. K. Sloan, "World model driven recognition of natural scenes." Ph.D. Dissertation, Moore School of Electrical Engineering, University of Pennsylvania, 1977.

124. R. Southwick, "FEATSYS—An intermediate-level representation of image feature data." Master's Thesis, Computer and Information Science Department, University of Massachusetts at Amherst, February 1986.

125. M. Snyder, "The accuracy of 3D parameters in correspondence-based techniques." COINS Technical Report 86-28, University of Massachusetts at Amherst, July 1986, pp. 53–59.

126. M. Snyder, "A comparison of the accuracy of depth recovery from motion and stereo." In progress.

127. S. Tanimoto, & A. Klinger, *Structured computer vision.* Academic Press: New York, 1980.

128. J. M. Tenenbaum, & H. Barrow, "Experiments in interpretation-guided segmentation," *Artificial Intelligence Journal, 8,*(3), 1977, 241–274.

129. J. M. Tenenbaum, & H. G. Barrow, "Recovering intrinsic scene characteristics from images." In *Computer vision systems,* A. Hanson & E. Riseman (Eds.). Academic Press: New York 1978, pp. 3–26.

130. D. Terzopolous, "Multi-level reconstruction of visual surfaces." AI Memo, 6712, MIT AI Lab, Cambridge, MA.

131. A. Triesman, "Features and objects in visual processing." Scientific American, November 1986, pp. 114–125.

132. A. Triesman, "Properties, parts, and objects." In *Handbook of perception and performance,* K. Boff, L. Kaufman, & J. Thompson (Eds.). John Wiley: New York, 1986.

133. J. Tsotsos, "Knowledge of the visual process: Content, form and use." *Proceedings of the 6th International Conference on Pattern Recognition,* October 1982, pp. 654–669.

134. J. K. Tsotsos, "Representational axes and temporal cooperative processes" (Tech. Rep. RCVB-TR-84-2). University of Toronto, April 1984.

135. S. Ullman, "The interpretation of visual motion." The MIT Press: Cambridge, MA, 1979.

136. C. Weems, S. Levitan, D. Lawton, & C. Foster, "A content addressable array parallel processor and some applications." *Proceedings of DARPA IU Workshop,* Arlington, VA, June 1983.

137. C. Weems, "Image processing on a content addressable array parallel processor." Ph.D. Dissertation and COINS Technical Report 84-14, University of Massachusetts at Amherst, September 1984.

138. C. Weems, S. Levitan, C. Foster, E. Riseman, D. Lawton, & A. Hanson, "Development and Construction of a content addressable array parallel processor (CAAPP) for knowledge-based image interpretation." *Proceedings of the Workshop on Algorithm-Guided Parallel Architectures for Automatic Target Recognition,* Leesburg, VA, July 16–18, 1984, pp. 329–359.

139. R. Weiss, & M. Boldt, "Geometric grouping applied to straight lines." *Proceedings on the IEEE Computer Society Conference on Computer Vision and Pattern Recognition,* Miami, FL, June, 1986, pp. 489–495.

140. R. Weiss, A. Hanson, and E. Riseman, "Geometric Grouping of Straight Lines," *Proceedings 1985, DARPA IU Workshop,* Miami Beach, FL, 1985.

141. J. S. Weska, "A survey of threshold selection techniques." *Computer graphics and image processing,* 7, pp. 259–265, 1978.

142. L. Wesley, & A. Hanson, "The use of evidential-based model for representing knowl-

edge and reasoning and images in the VISIONS System." *Proceedings of the Workshop on Computer Vision,* Rindge, NH, August 23–25, 1982.

143. L. Wesley, "Reasoning about control: The investigation of an evidential approach." *Proceedings of the 8th IJCAI,* Karlsrube, West Germany, August 1983, pp. 203–210.

144. L. Wesley, J. Lowrance, & T. Garvey, "Reasoning about control: An evidential approach." SPI Technical Note #324, Artificial Intelligence Center, SRI International, Menlo Park, CA, 1984.

145. L. Wesley, "Evidential knowledge-based computer vision." *Optical engineering, 25*(3), March 1986, pp. 363–379.

146. L. Wesley, "The application of an evidential based technology to a high-level knowledge-based image interpretation Systems." Ph.D. Dissertation, University of Massachusetts, in preparation.

147. L. Wesley, & A. Hanson, "Evidential-reasoning: Its application to a high-level knowledge-based image interpretation system." COINS Technical Report, University of Massachusetts at Amherst, in preparation.

148. T. E. Weymouth, J. S. Griffith, A. R. Hanson, & E. M. Riseman, "Rule based strategies for image interpretation." *Proceedings of AAAI-83,* August 1983, pp. 429–432, Washington DC. A longer version of this paper appears in *Proceedings of the DARPA Image Understanding Workshop,* June 1983, Arlington, VA, pp. 193–202.

149. T. E. Weymouth, "Using object descriptions in a schema network for machine vision." Ph.D. Dissertation, Computer and Information Science Department, University of Massachusetts at Amherst.

150. T. E. Weymouth, A. Hanson, & E. Riseman, "Schema-based image understanding: Interpretation strategies for natural scenes." Forthcoming Department of Computer and Information Science Technical Report.

151. A. P. Witkin, & J. M. Tenenbaum, "On the role of structure in vision." In *Human and machine vision,* J. Beck, B. Hope, & A. Rosenfeld (Eds.), Academic Press: New York, 1982.

152. A. P. Witkin, & J. M. Tenenbaum, "What is perceptual organization for?" International Joint Conference on Artificial Intelligence, 1983, pp. 1023–1026.

153. Lance R. Williams, & P. Anandan, "A coarse-to-fine control strategy for stereo and motion on a mesh-connected computer." COINS Technical Report 86-19, University of Massachusetts at Amherst, May 1986.

154. T. D. Williams, "Depth from camera motion in a real world scene." *IEEE Transactions on Pattern Analysis and Machine Intelligence 2, 6,* November 1980, pp. 511–516.

155. T. D. Williams, "Computer interpretation of a dynamic image from a moving vehicle." Ph.D. Thesis and COINS Technical Report 81-22, University of Massachusetts at Amherst, May 1981.

156. R. J. Woodham, "Photometric stereo: A reflectance map technique for determining surface orientation from image intensity." *Proceedings of the 22nd Annual SPIE Conference,* San Diego, CA, August 1978, pp. 136–143.

157. R. J. Woodham, "Photometric method for determining shape from shading." In *Image understanding 1984,* S. Ullman W. Richards (Eds.). Ablex: New Jersey, pp. 97–126.

158. W. A. Woods, "Theory formation and control in a speech understanding system with extrapolation towards vision." In *Computer vision systems,* A. Hanson & Riseman (Eds.), Academic Press: NY, 1978.

159. B. York, A. Hanson, & E. Riseman, "3D object representation and matching with B-splines and surface patches." *Proceedings IJCAI-7,* August 1980, pp. 648–651.

160. B. York, "Shape representation in computer vision." COINS Technical Report 81-13, University of Massachusetts at Amherst, May 1981.

2 ROBUST COMPUTATION OF INTRINSIC IMAGES FROM MULTIPLE CUES

JOHN (YIANNIS) ALOIMONOS
University of Maryland

CHRISTOPHER M. BROWN
University of Rochester

THE CENTRAL GOAL OF MACHINE VISION

The central problem of computer vision may be stated as follows:

> From one or a sequence of images of a moving or stationary object or a scene, taken by a monocular (one eyed) or polynocular (many eyed) moving or stationary observer, to understand the object or the scene and its three-dimensional properties.

All the terms in the above definition are well defined, with the exception of the term *understand*. What is really the meaning of *understand* with respect to this problem? There have basically been two approaches to this question in computer vision: *reconstruction* and *recognition* (Figure 2.1). The reconstruction school attempts to reconstruct the physical parameters of the visual world, such as the depth or orientation of surfaces, the boundaries of objects, the direction of light sources and the like. The recognition school aims for the recognition or description of objects, and studies processes whose end product is some piece of behavior like a decision or a motion. Both schools have strong ties with psychology and neuroscience, and it seems likely that both schools will merge into a new one that may find an answer to the vision problem.

Physical parameters derived from vision can basically be classified in two categories: *retinotopic* and *nonretinotopic*. Nonretinotopic ones can be divided into global features (such as ego motion or light source direction) and objects and relations (Ballard, 1984). Retinotopic parameters are spatially indexed at every image point. Retinotopic parameters (shape,

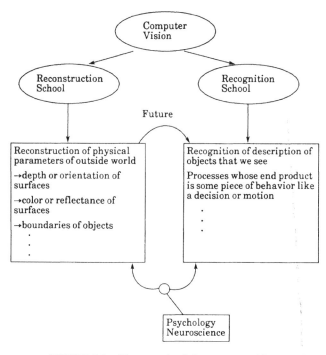

FIGURE 2.1. The two schools in computer vision.

depth, etc.) are the ones of most interest in this chapter. They are global features and are the broad subject of the reconstruction school. Non-retinotopic parameters (features) are the basic subject of the recognition school.

SOME HISTORY

Even as late as 1975, computer vision's purview was very different from its current scope. Much research had been devoted to the blocks micro-world of scenes of polyhedra. Huffman (1971) and Clowes (1971) noted the advantage of making the image-formation process explicit. They realized that image lines and junctions were the images of three-dimensional scene edges and vertices, and they made an extensive catalog of those interpretations of lines and junctions that were possible, given assumptions of planarity and the restriction that at most, three surfaces were allowed to meet at a vertex. These interpretations amounted to local constraints on the volume occupied by a vertex. The local constraints propagated along picture lines since planar polyhedral edges cannot change their nature between two vertices; the constraints and their propagation could explain why some "line" drawings were nonsensical and suggested algorithms for understanding drawings.

Waltz's (1975) work introduced the inherently global constraint afforded by shadows cast from a single distant source and showed that the multiple ambiguities possible without shadows were often resolved to a unique interpretation with shadows. More importantly, the process by which the unique interpretation was discovered naturally lends itself to parallel processing of a particular sort. If each vertex has an associated processor, and each processor changes its state according to the state of those directly connected to it, a stable configuration will be reached with the final states giving locally consistent labelings. Rosenfeld, Hummel and Zucker (1976) noted the connection between this scheme and relaxation processes in numerical analysis.

Huffman (1971) showed further that the local vertex constraints were not enough to capture the important restriction that picture regions were the images of planar surfaces. Mackworth's (1973) algorithm using gradient space was intended to repair this deficit.

A second strand in the development of computer vision concerns what was referred to as "low-level" processing. It consisted largely of methods for the extraction of the intensity changes in an image. The approach mostly consisted of convolving images with local operators to estimate the position, contrast, and orientation of the important intensity changes. Operators were tuned to particular applications and often failed badly outside their domain in the presence of noise. Little serious analysis of actual intensity changes including the signal to noise characteristics of real images had been carried out. Other work in low-level vision consisted largely of the design and construction of region finders. Region finding aimed at isolating those regions of an image that were the images of perceptual surface patches. It was thought that such regions might be isolated by defining some descriptor with respect to which they were uniform and distinguishable from surrounding regions. It was soon clear that even if such descriptors existed, they were not defined simply in terms of color or grey-level intensity values (Barrow & Popplestone, 1971; Brice & Fennema 1970).

By the early 1970s, the consensus was that low-level vision was inherently incapable of producing rich, useful descriptions. It was observed, by analogy to the apparent need for semantics in parsing English sentences, that downward-flowing knowledge of the scene could provide additional constraints. This in turn could inform local decision making. A number of program structures were proposed to effect this interaction between top-down and bottom-up processing of information (Freuder,

1974; Minsky & Papert, 1972; Shirai, 1973; Tenenbaum & Barrow, 1977; Winston, 1972). Similar ideas were advanced about natural language understanding and speech perception. This influenced the design of, for example, Hearsay2 (Lesser & Erman, 1977). To experiment with these ideas, entire systems were constructed that mobilized knowledge at all levels of the visual system as well as information specific to some domain of application. In order to complete the construction of all these systems, it was inevitable that oversimplified assumptions were made. By and large, the performance of these systems did not give grounds for unbridled celebration. The idea of vision modules, especially those computing intrinsic scene parameters, emerged in answer to some of these widely perceived deficiencies.

VISION MODULES

Perhaps the most fundamental difference between computer vision now and a decade ago stems from the current concentration on topics corresponding to identifiable modules in a visual system. The focus of research today is more narrowly defined in terms of a domain, and the depth of analysis is correspondingly greater.

If we want to study the animal visual system or construct seeing machines, the first step is to divide the whole system into functional components that break the overall task into loosely-coupled parts. Then, we should choose the representation of information within the subsystems and the languages of communication among them. After this, the details of the subsystems are tested individually and in combination.

We currently believe that cues such as shading, motion, texture, contours and stereopsis are very important for the perception of the three-dimensional world. For this reason, almost every computer-vision research paper published in that last few years has to do with the perception of shape from shading, shape from texture, shape from contour, shape from motion, depth from stereo, illuminant direction from shading, three-dimensional motion from retinal motion, and so forth.

Not all modules operate directly on the image. Indeed, it seems that few do. Instead they operate on representations of the information computed or made explicit by other processes. In the case of stereopsis, Marr and Poggio (1979) argued against correlating the intensity information in the left and right views. Instead, they suggested that so-called zero-crossings are matched (Marr & Hildreth, 1980). In any case, a great deal of attention has centered on the isolation and study of individual modules, and in each case, on the development of the representations on which they operate, and on those that they produce.

MODULES OPERATING DIRECTLY ON THE IMAGE

A great deal of effort has been devoted to understanding how the important intensity changes in an image can be extracted. Marr (1976) coined the term *primal sketch* to describe such a representation. His work with Poggio led to the use of zero-crossings of the second derivative of the filtered image. This idea was developed in turn by Marr and Hildreth (1980) who proposed that an image is first filtered by four Gaussians having different band-pass characteristics. One of the novel features (as far as computer-vision work is concerned) of the Marr–Hildreth account is the increased size of the operators, which implied increased image resolution.

Horn and his colleagues (Horn, 1970, 1975, 1977, 1979; Ikeuchi & Horn 1981; Strat 1979; Woodham 1979) have studied the perception of surface shape from shading. In brief outline, Horn (1970) formulated a second-order differential equation that he called the "image irradiance equation," which relates the orientation of the local-surface normal of a visible surface, the surface-reflectance characteristics, and the lighting to the intensity value recorded at the corresponding point in the image. The output of shape from shading is a representation that makes explicit the orientation of visible surfaces and may make other information, such as depth and surface discontinuities, explicit also. Several representations have been proposed that make, substantially, the same information explicit. Marr (1978) used the name $2\frac{1}{2}$-D sketch, Barrow and Tenenbaum (1978) discussed intrinsic images, and Horn (1975) mentions needle maps.

Finally, many methods for computing optic flow (image motion) from spatio-temporal derivatives of image intensity have been published recently.

INTRINSIC IMAGE COMPUTATION

Most modern computer vision concentrates on visual modules. We assume that there should exist modules that compute three-dimensional parameters from specific cues, such as shading, motion, stereo, contours, and texture. When we say three-dimensional parameters, we mean intrinsic images, such as shape, depth, reflectance, three-dimensional motion, illuminant direction and the like. So, one could say that much of today's research is: compute Y from X, where Y is an intrinsic property (shape, depth, retinal and three-dimensional motion, etc.) and X is a cue in the image or a property of the observer (shading, texture, stereopsis, etc.).

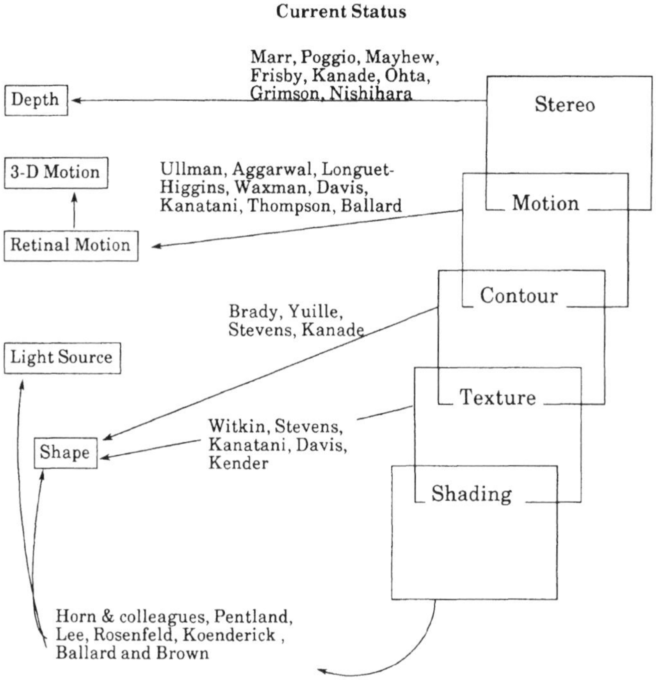

FIGURE 2.2.   Current research status.

Figure 2.2 broadly summarizes the status of contemporary recon-
structionist computer vision. On the right, we see the various cues, and
on the left the intrinsic parameters. Research uses results from physics
and geometry to derive algorithms that use any of the cues on the right
to reconstruct some of the intrinsic properties on the left. An arrow from
box 1 to box 2 indicates that the property in box 2 is recovered from the
cue in box 1. The names along the arrows represent some of the researchers who have worked on this specific recovery.

INFORMATION FROM COOPERATIVE SOURCES YIELDS
UNIQUE AND RELIABLE SOLUTIONS

From Figure 2.2, we see that from a particular cue a particular intrinsic
property can be computed. That is, no cues are combined, in most of the
published work, to recover an intrinsic image. As a result, several of the
computations do not have uniqueness properties (and so additional as-

sumptions are needed about the world to get a unique answer), and several computations that have uniqueness properties under ideal conditions break down in the presence of small amounts of noise. In order to take care of these problems, more information is needed. In particular, if we combine information from the different image cues, the extra constraints could yield uniqueness and robustness. The proposed strategy for the computation of intrinsic images is given in Figure 2.3.

Researchers recently have realized the need for combination of information from different image cues for better estimation of intrinsic parameters. In particular, see Waxman (chapter 3 of this volume) for combining stereo and motion; Grimson (1984) for combining shading and stereo; Richards (1986), Huang & Blonstein (1985), and the work of Milenkovic and Kanade (1985). This chapter continues work in that tradition. That is, we consider each individual problem separately, analyze it, see that a solution without additional assumptions or stability is impossible, and then combine different cues to obtain unique or robust results.

The basic structure of the results in (Aloimonos, 1986) is depicted in Figure 2.4. In the ellipses (top) are the different image cues. By cue we mean a source of information, either coming from the image(s) or from the particular set up or condition of the visual system (stereo-motion). In the squares are the results we obtain (in terms of propositions) when we combine information from two different cues. This chapter explores

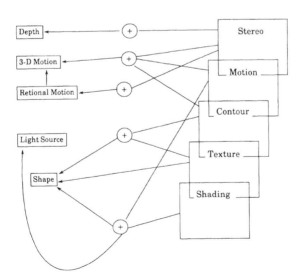

FIGURE 2.3. Strategy of combining inputs.

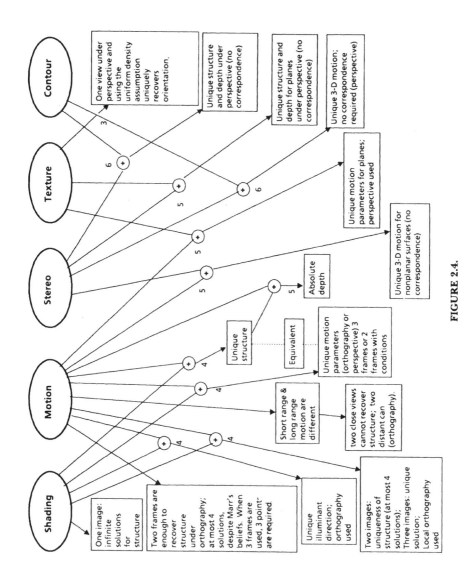

FIGURE 2.4.

122

only two of the results: the combination of shading and motion and the computation of stereo using aggregate methods that do not require a solution to the correspondence problem.

TECHNICAL PREREQUISITES:
IMAGE FORMATION AND INTRINSIC IMAGES

It is necessary to know how an image is formed in order to analyze it. First, we need to find the geometric correspondence between points in the scene and points in the image, and second, we must find out what determines the brightness at a particular point in the image. The next section addresses the first issue.

Perspective Projection

We approximate an optical imaging system with an ideal pinhole at a fixed distance in front of an image plane. Assume that only light coming through the pinhole can reach the image plane. Given that light travels along straight lines, each point in the image corresponds to a particular direction defined by a ray from that point through the pinhole. This is what we know as *perspective projection*.

In the sequel, in order to simplify the resulting equations, we consider the nodal point of the eye, or the point of projection, to be behind the image plane. The geometry is the same except for a sign change. The system we use is depicted in Figure 2.5. We define the optical axis in this case to be the perpendicular from the pinhole to the image plane. We introduce a cartesian coordinate system with the origin at the nodal point and the z-axis aligned with the optical axis and pointing toward the image (Figure 2.5). We should like to compute where the image A' of the point A on some object in front of the camera will appear. Let $\mathbf{V} = (X, Y, Z)$, the vector connecting O to A and $\mathbf{V'} = (x, y, f)$, the vector connecting O to A', with f the focal length, that is, the distance of the image plane from the nodal point O; and, (x, y) are the coordinates of the point A' on the image plane in the naturally induced coordinate system with origin at the point of the intersection of the image plane with the optical axis, and axes x and y parallel to the axis of the camera coordinate system OX and OY. By similar triangles,

$$x = \frac{fX}{Z}, \, y = \frac{fY}{Z} \tag{1}$$

The equations (1) relate the image coordinates to the world coordinates of a point. Very often, to simplify the equations further, we assume $f = 1$, without loss of generality.

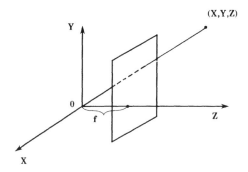

FIGURE 2.5. Perspective projection simplified.

Orthographic Projection

The orthographic-projection model, which is parallel projection with the viewpoint at infinite distance, perhaps seems unrealistic so we shall motivate its use. If, in the perspective-projection model, we have a plane that lies parallel to the image plane at $Z = Z_0$, then we define magnification m as the ratio of the distance between two points measured in the image to the distance between the corresponding points on the plane. So, if we have a small interval on the plane $(dX, dY, 0)$ and the corresponding small interval $(dx, dy, 0)$ in the image, then:

$$m = \frac{(dx)^2 + (dy)^2}{(dX)^2 + (dY)^2} = \frac{f}{Z_0} < 1$$

So a small object at an average distance Z_0 will produce an image that is magnified by m. The magnification is approximately constant when the depth range of the scene is small relative to the average distance of the surfaces from the camera. In this case we can simply write for the projection (perspective) equations, that:

$$x = mX, \text{ and } y = mY \tag{2}$$

with $m = f/Z_0$ and Z_0 the average value of the depth Z. For our convenience, we can set $m = 1$. Then the equations (2) are further simplified to the form:

$$x = X \text{ and } y = Y \tag{3}$$

The equations (3) model the orthographic-projection model, where the rays are parallel to the optical axis or the focal length is infinite (see Figure 2.6). So, the difference between orthography and perspective is small when the distance to the scene is much larger than the variation in

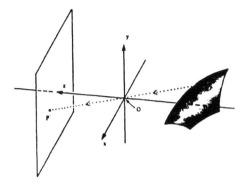

FIGURE 2.6. Orthographic projection.

distance among objects in the scene. A rough rule of thumb is that perspective effects are significant when a wide angle lens is used, while images taken by telephoto lenses tend to approximate orthographic projection, but, of course, this is not exact (Horn, 1986).

Intrinsic Images

Surface orientation is usually represented as the surface normal vector. In intrinsic images, *shape* means the local surface orientation, not some global property of the surface. If the surface is expressed as $Z(X, Y)$ it can be reconstructed from the local surface orientation. If the surface is expressed as $Z(X, Y)$, then $\partial Z/\partial X$, $\partial Z/\partial Y$ are quantities related to the surface normal; they tell how fast the surface slopes off in the X and Y directions.

Under orthographic projection, the image coordinates of a point are equal to the corresponding three-dimensional coordinates, that is $(x, y) = (X, Y)$. So

$$\left(\frac{\partial Z}{\partial X} , \frac{\partial Z}{\partial Y} \right) = \left(\frac{\partial Z}{\partial x} , \frac{\partial Z}{\partial y} \right) .$$

If we know the shape $(\partial Z/\partial X, \partial Z/\partial Y)$ and we know that

$$Z(x + dx, y + dy) - Z(x, y) = \frac{\partial Z}{\partial x} \, dx + \frac{\partial Z}{\partial y} \, dy + (h.o.t.),$$

we see that the depth function $Z(x, y)$ can be computed up to constant additive term. So, if we know shape under orthography, we know the exact surface, but we do not know its *depth*.

Thus,

$$(p, q) = \left(\frac{\partial Z}{\partial X}, \frac{\partial Z}{\partial Y}\right)$$

is one representation for local shape. The surface normal is another. It is given by

$$\frac{(p, q, -1)}{(p^2 + q^2 + 1)^{1/2}}$$

In fact, local shape is nothing but a direction in three-dimensional space, and so there are many representations for it.

1. Coordinates (a, b, c) on the Gaussian (unit) sphere.
2. Latitude and longitude angles, say, (θ, ρ).
3. Slant and tilt. Slant is the tangent of the latitude angle and tilt is the longitude angle. The notation for *slant, tilt* is σ, τ. The slant and tilt are polar versions of the p, q coordinates.

The relationship among these different representations is given by the following equations:

$$\sigma = \tan \theta = \sqrt{(p^2 + q^2)}$$

$$p/q = \tan \phi = \tan \tau$$

Finally, if a, b, c are the coordinates on the Gaussian sphere, then:

$$(a, b, c) = \left(\frac{p}{k}, \frac{q}{k}, \frac{-1}{k}\right) \text{ with } k = (p^2 + q^2 + 1)^{1/2}$$

Structure is the three-dimensional geometrical relationship between scene points and is related to shape.

If the object in view is moving with a general motion, or if the camera is moving, or if both move, then the image is moving too. Let the *retinal velocity* at an image point be (u, v). The resulting vector field (the velocity of every image point) is called the "retinal motion field" or "optic flow field." This flow field is an intrinsic retinal motion image.

Intrinsic parameters exist that do not correspond to every point in the image. These are global properties, and every point in the image is in some relation to them. Examples of these parameters are three-dimensional object- and ego-motion parameters and lighting direction parameters.

If an object moves in front of a camera with a general motion, then this motion can be considered as the sum of an instantaneous translation (U, V, W) and a rotation (A, B, C). These six parameters are called "motion parameters."

If a surface in front of a camera is illuminated by a point light source in the direction (l_x, l_y, l_z), with respect to the camera coordinate system, the direction (l_x, l_y, l_z) is called the "lighting," or "illuminant direction."

REFLECTANCE

The amount of light reflected by a surface element depends on its micro-structure, on its optical properties, and on the distribution and state of polarization of the incident illumination. For several types of surfaces, the fraction of incident illumination reflected in a particular direction depends only on the surface orientation. The characteristics of the re-flectance of such a surface can be represented as a function $f(i, g, e)$ of the angles i = incident, g = phase and e = emergent, as they are defined in Figure 2.7.

The reflectance function $f(i, g, e)$ determines the ratio of surface radi-ance to irradiance measured per unit surface area and per unit solid angle in the direction of the viewer (Horn, 1986). If we want to be precise, we should specify the quantities and units used to define the required ratio. Here, it is sufficient to point out the role that surface orientation plays in the determination of the angles i and g.

Consider the example of perfect specular (mirror-like) reflection. In this case, the incident angle equals the emergent angle and the incident, emergent, and normal vectors lie on the same plane ($g = i + e$). So, the reflectance function is

$$f(i, e, g) = \begin{vmatrix} 1 & \text{if } i = e \text{ and } i + e = g \\ 0, & \text{otherwise} \end{vmatrix}$$

The interaction of light with surfaces of varying roughness and composi-tion of material leads to a more complicated distribution of reflected light. Surface reflectance characteristics can be determined empirically, derived from models of surface microstructure or derived from phe-

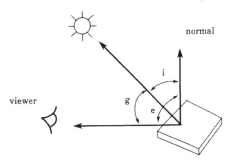

FIGURE 2.7. Reflectance model.

nomenological models of surface reflectance. A common and simple model of surface reflectance is given by the function $f(i, e, g) = \rho$ *cosine i*, where ρ is a constant depending on the specific surface. This reflectance function corresponds to that of a perfectly diffuse (Lambertian) surface, which appears equally bright from all viewing directions; the cosine of the incident angle accounts for the foreshortening of the surface as seen from the source.

The surface normal vector relates surface geometry to image irradiance because it determines the angles i and e appearing in the surface reflectance function $f(i, e, g)$. In orthographic projection, the viewing direction, and so the phase angle g, is constant for all surface elements. So, for a fixed light source and viewer geometry and fixed material, the ratio of scene radiance to scene irradiance depends only on the surface normal vector. Furthermore, suppose that each surface element receives the same irradiance. Then, the scene radiance and, hence, image intensity depends only on the surface normal vector. A reflectance map $R(p, q)$ determines image intensity as a function of p and q (recall $p, q, -1)/\sqrt{(p^2 + q^2 + 1)}$ is the surface normal vector). Using a reflectance map, an image-irradiance equation can be written as $I(x, y) = R(p, q)$, where $I(x, y)$ is the intensity at the image point (x, y) and $R(p, q)$ is the corresponding reflectance map.

A reflectance map provides a uniform representation for specifying the surface reflectance of a surface material for a particular light source, object surface, and viewer geometry. A comprehensive survey of reflectance maps derived for a variety of surface and light source conditions has been given by Horn (1979). A unified approach to the specification of surface reflectance maps has been given in (Horn & Sjoberg, 1981).

Under orthographic projection, expressions for $\cos i$, $\cos e$ and $\cos g$ can be easily derived from the surface normal vector $(p, q, -1)$ and the light source vector $(p_s, q_s, -1)$ and the vector $(0, 0, -1)$, which points in the direction of the viewer. For a Lambertian reflectance function with albedo ρ we get

$$R(p, q) = \frac{-\rho(1 + p\,p_s + q\,q_s)}{\sqrt{(1 + p^2 + q^2)}\,\sqrt{(1 + p_s^2 + q_s^2))}} = I(x, y).$$

Under perspective projection, expression depends on several other factors, including system focal length and off-axis angle of the imaged point.

VISUAL MOTION ANALYSIS

The perception of motion and structure from a temporally varying two-dimensional retinal stimulus is important to computer vision as well as the cognitive and perceptual sciences. For the purpose of this chapter, the input (stimulus) to this process is a two-dimensional line or video image of the intensity of reflected illumination from the moving scene. The first step in the computation, according to most of the existing theories, involves the estimation of two-dimensional motion in the image plane. The second stage involves the computation of the three-dimensional intrinsic parameters like *structure* and *motion parameters* from the two-dimensional image motion. Despite much research on the estimation of image motion, the problem has proven to be extremely hard. The subsequent analysis is based on the following imaging conditions and assumptions:

1. The image is greyscale.
2. The imaged surface moves rigidly and is not accelerated.
3. The image has been segmented—i.e., regions that correspond to scene features have reliably been found.

The problem of estimating image motion from time-varying image intensity distributions is by no means a simple one. There are essentially *two ways* in which this problem has been tackled.

1. The first assumes the dynamic image to be a three-dimensional function of two spatial arguments and a temporal argument. Then, if this function is locally well behaved and its spatio-temporal gradients are computable, the *image velocity* or *optical flow* may be computed (Bandopadhay 1986; Davis, Wu, & Sun, 1983; Haralick & Lee, 1983; Horn & Schunck, 1981; Nagel, 1983; Ullman & Hildreth, 1982). From now on, we will call this kind of retinal motion "differential," or "continuous," or "short range," or "small motion."

2. The second method for measuring image motion considers the cases when the motion is "large" and the first technique is not applicable. In these instances the measurement technique relies upon isolating and tracking highlights and feature points in the image through time. This entails tackling the correspondence problem that can be difficult in many situations. From now on, we will call this kind of motion "discrete," or "long range," or "large motion."

The mathematical relations that hold between the image motion and the three-dimensional scene parameters are quite different for small and large motions (Aloimonos, 1986). Furthermore, due to the difference in the computational theory underlying these two motion types, perceptual processes for motion analysis must also be organized in cognizance of this dichotomy. The input to the perceptual process is a two-dimensional image-intensity function that changes with time. The image contains two kinds of information, photometric and geometric.

MOTION EQUATIONS UNDER PERSPECTIVE AND ORTHOGRAPHY

Here we analyze the relation between the retinal motion and the corresponding three-dimensional motion for the case of perspective, under both small and large motion.

Consider the perspective projection model (Figure 1.5, Equation 1). The focal length f is assumed to be unity in the following analysis.

Now if a rigid surface moves with a translational velocity $V_T = (U, V, W)$ and a rotational velocity $\Omega = (\alpha, \beta, \gamma)$, then from kinematics, the three-dimensional velocity of any portion on the surface can be written as

$$\left(\frac{dX}{dt}, \frac{dY}{dt}, \frac{dZ}{dt}\right) = V_T + \Omega \times (X, Y, Z) \tag{2}$$

where t is the time variable and $\times$ denotes vector product.

In the differential-motion case the image motion or optical flow at the point (x, y) is denoted by $(u, v) = (dx/dt, dy/dt)$. Differentiating equation (1) and substituting from equation (2) we have the following relations

$$u = \frac{U - xW}{Z} - \alpha xy + \beta(x^2 + 1) - \gamma y \tag{3}$$

$$v = \frac{V - yW}{Z} - \alpha(y^2 + 1) + \beta xy + \gamma x \tag{4}$$

Eliminating the unknown depth variable from the above we get

$$\frac{u + \alpha xy - \beta(x^2 + 1) + \gamma y}{v + \alpha(y^2 + 1) - \beta xy - \gamma x} = \frac{U - xW}{V - yW} \tag{5}$$

The preceding equation describes the constraint imposed by the measured value of the optical flow (u, v) at an image point (x, y) on the six motion parameters $(U, V, W, \alpha, \beta, \gamma)$.

The discrete analogs of equations (3), (4), and (5) are more complex in form, and they follow in the rest of this section.

Consider one point $P = (X, Y, Z)$ before the motion with image (x, y). Suppose that the point moves with a general motion, and goes to the position $P' = (X', Y', Z')$ with image (x', y'). Any three-dimensional rigid body motion is equivalent to a rotation by an angle θ around an axis through the origin with directional cosines n_1, n_2, n_3, followed by a translation $T = (\Delta X, \Delta Y, \Delta Z)^\mathrm{T}$. The relation between the coordinates of the point before and after the transformation is given by:

$$(X', Y', Z')^\mathrm{T} = R(X, Y, Z)^\mathrm{T} + T,$$

where R is a 3×3 orthonormal matrix of the first kind (i.e., $det(R) = 1$)

$$R = \begin{bmatrix} r_1 & r_2 & r_3 \\ r_4 & r_5 & r_6 \\ r_7 & r_8 & r_9 \end{bmatrix} \text{ with}$$

$r_1 = n_1^2 + (1 - n_1^2)\cos\theta$, $r_2 = n_1 n_2(1 - \cos\theta) - n_3 \sin\theta$, $r_3 = n_1 n_3 (1 - \cos\theta) + n_2 \sin\theta$
$r_4 = n_1 n_2(1 - \cos\theta) + n_3 \sin\theta$, $r_5 = n_2^2 + (1 - n_2^2)\cos\theta$, $r_6 = n_1 n_3(1 - \cos\theta) - n_1 \sin\theta$
$r_7 = n_1 n_3(1 - \cos\theta) - n_2 \sin\theta$, $r_8 = n_2 n_3(1 - \cos\theta) + n_1 \sin\theta$, $r_9 = n_3^2 + (1 - n_3^2)\cos\theta$

Although the elements of R $r_1, r_2, \ldots r_9$ are complicated functions of the rotation parameters n_1, n_2, n_3, θ, the latter can be easily determined without ambiguity from the former (Tsai & Huang, 1984). Therefore, we can freely talk about the uniqueness and computation of the matrix R, rather than n_1, n_2, n_3, θ.

Taking now into account the perspective projection equations that relate the coordinates X, Y, Z to x, y and the coordinates X', Y', Z' to x', y', we get (assuming that the focal length is unity):

$$x' = \frac{(r_1 x + r_2 y + r_3)Z + \Delta X}{(r_7 x + r_8 y + r_9)Z + \Delta Z}$$

and

$$y' = \frac{(r_4 x + r_5 y + r_6)Z + \Delta X}{(r_7 x + r_8 y + r_9)Z + \Delta Z}$$

By eliminating the depth Z from the above two equations, we get:

$$[x', y', 1] = E \begin{bmatrix} x \\ y \\ 1 \end{bmatrix} \tag{6}$$

where

$$E = \begin{bmatrix} e_1 & e_2 & e_3 \\ e_4 & e_5 & e_6 \\ e_7 & e_8 & e_9 \end{bmatrix} \text{ with}$$

$e_1 = \Delta Z r_4 - \Delta Y r_7$, $e_2 = \Delta Z r_5 - \Delta Y r_8$, $e_3 = \Delta Z r_6 - \Delta Y r_9$
$e_4 = \Delta X r_7 - \Delta Z r_1$, $e_5 = \Delta X r_8 - \Delta Z r_2$, $e_6 = \Delta X r_9 - \Delta Z r_3$
$e_7 = \Delta Y r_1 - \Delta X r_4$, $e_8 = \Delta Y r_2 - \Delta X r_5$, $e_9 = \Delta Y r_3 - \Delta X r_6$

Equation 6 describes the constraint between retinal and three-dimensional motion in the discrete case, and it represents all the information we can get from the motion of one point. We now develop the same equations for the case of orthographic projection.

The projection equation for the case of the orthographic projection, becomes:

$$(x, y) = (X, Y) \tag{7}$$

Again, following the same method as in the previous section, we get that the optical flow field is given by the following equations:

$$u = U + \beta Z - \gamma y \tag{8}$$

$$v = V - \alpha Z + \gamma x \tag{9}$$

It is obvious that the translation in depth does not affect at all the image motion in this case. The equations for the discrete case, if developed, basically solve the problem of structure from motion (Aloimonos, 1986).

PREVIOUS WORK IN MOTION

The problem of *Motion Analysis* concerns the *recovery* of the *structure* of the scene (or objects) in view and the *rigid motion parameters* (of the moving viewed object or of the moving sensor) from the perceived changing retinal image. The problem has been studied for both the cases of *differential-retinal motion* or *short-range motion* (optical flow) and *long-range motion* (discrete displacements), under both *orthography* and *perspective*.

In the case of *discrete* motion under orthography the pioneering work of Ullman (1979a,b) stands out for being highly precise. In his classical paper on the interpretation of structure from motion, Ullman showed how structure was determined uniquely (up to a reflection) from the orthographically projected locations of four non-coplanar points, obtained at three different instances of time. The problem of the interpretation of nonrigid motion (Johansson's "biological motion", 1973) was analysed by Hoffman and Flinchbaugh (1982), Hoffman (1982a), and Webb & Aggarwal (1982). Their analysis is, again, for orthographic projection and discrete motion, with the additional assumption that the axis of rotation is fixed for the entire period of observation (i.e., equivalently, the motion is planar).

In the case of differential motion (optical flow) under orthography, published research is confined to Hoffman (1982b) and Sugihara and Sugie (1984). Hoffman developed a relationship between optical flow derivatives and local surface orientation and illustrated that if the acceleration of the optical flow field is known, then the computation of shape is feasible. On the other hand, Sugihara presented an involved proof that optical flow under orthography cannot recover local surface orientation, and he developed a method that using two optical flow fields, the structure of the object in view can be recovered (at most, four solutions). Sugihara observed that despite the fact that his theoretical analysis predicted four solutions for the structure, given two optical flow fields, in his experiments the solution recovered was unique. So, he developed a conjecture, which states that: two optic flow fields uniquely define structure. In (Aloimonos, 1986), we prove that optical flow cannot recover local surface orientation in a much simpler way, and we give an explanation of Sugihara's conjecture for the discrete case (i.e., we prove that three frames (two optical flow fields means at least three frames) of three points uniquely recover the structure, except some degenerate cases whose set is of measure zero).

In the case of differential motion under perspective the relation between the motion parameters and the retinal motion (Equations 3 and 4) is a nonlinear equation in the direction of the translation and the rotational parameters. The effort of almost all researchers in this area has concentrated on how to solve this nonlinear equation or to formulate the problem in such a way that it becomes tractable. In this case (differential motion under perspective projection), which is a case of great interest, there is much recent work concerning the recovery of the structure and motion parameters of a moving object from its changing retinal image (optical flow). In this area, there is the work of Longuet-Higgins and Prazdny (1980) that developed the relation between the optical flow and the motion parameters as well as the relationship between the gradient of the surface in view and the derivatives of the optical flow. Their method does not guarantee uniqueness of the motion parameters, and the algorithm relies on the solution of a nonlinear system whose coefficients involve second-order derivatives of the optical flow. Furthermore, their method is local, and every local method is bound to be unstable, because a small patch of optic flow under noisy situations will resemble ambiguous flow fields.

Soon researchers in the area realized that Equations 3 and 4 (relation of flow to motion parameters) are bilinear in the *direction of translation* and the *rotational parameters;* this means that the equations are nonlinear in the motion parameters, but if the direction of translation is known, they become linear with respect to the rotational parameters, and vice versa. So, efforts have been made to separate the optical flow in its rotational and translational component and make the problem of the determination of the motion parameters easy. The work of Prazdny (1983) and Lawton and Rieger (1983) are examples of this type of effort.

Both these papers are based essentially on the property of a translational field, that all the flow vectors pass through the same point on the image plane (focus of expansion or focus of contraction). Based on that, they developed statistical methods for the computation of the motion parameters. But there are cases where the optical-flow field vectors pass through the same point, with the motion consisting of both translation and rotation (Bandopadhay, 1986). The work of Bruss and Horn (1983) considers the cases of only translational or only rotational motion and developed algorithms for the determination of the direction of translation or the rotational parameters.

The work of Huang, Tsai, and Fang (Fang & Huang (1984), Huang & Tsai (1981), Tsai & Huang (1984) stands out for being mathematically precise and for being the first to address the uniqueness problem in this area, that is to say, how many values for the motion parameters are compatible with a flow field—or two discrete frames. Despite the fact that this work is done in the discrete case under perspective, the results are not far from the differential case under perspective, because they made the assumption that the rotation used is very small. (If small rotation is considered, then the equations that relate the displacements to the motion parameters, are very similar to the analog ones for the differential case.)

Fang and Huang (1984) proved that the nonlinear system developed using five points has a unique solution, which may be found using iterative methods. They also presented a nine points method, but the condition that has to be satisfied for this method to work, cannot be tested from the image data. Also, Tsai and Huang (1984) studied the problem for the case of a moving plane, and they concluded that the number of solutions is either one or two depending on the multiplicities of the singular values of a matrix that contains eight essential parameters. Finally, Tsai and Huang (1984) proved that three views, in the case where the moving surface is planar, guarantee the uniqueness of the motion parameters. Also, in this area there is the work of Kanade (1985) who developed a method using line correspondences in three frames (small rotation) that can uniquely find the motion parameters. Experimental results, not known to us at this point, will determine how immune to noise the method is or how well the employed assumptions fit practical situations.

Waxman (1983) and Waxman & Sinha (1984), motivated by important psychological and neurobiological experiments by Regan and Beverley (1979), presented a method termed *Dynamic Stereo*. This method is based on the comparison of image flow fields obtained from two cameras in known relative motion. For stationary objects this technique reduces to conventional motion stereo. Finally, in the case of discrete motion under perspective, there is little work (arbitrary rotation)—only that of Ullman (1979a,b) and Tsai and Huang (1984). Ullman studied the problem when the rotation is around the z-axis and, using two views of three points, he developed a *polar equation* (a fourth-degree equation on the sine of the rotation angle) from which he could determine the motion and structure, but the solution was not unique.

Tsai and Huang (1984) developed a method for the determination of motion parameters in the case of curved surfaces. Using seven points, they proved that the five motion parameters can be uniquely recovered (from the other eight essential parameters), provided that the seven points do not belong on two planes with one passing through the origin or one a cone containing the origin. The condition on which their method is based cannot be tested from the image data. After the eight essential parameters have been computed, the five motion parameters can be uniquely computed using the singular value decomposition technique (Stewart, 1973).

THE CORRESPONDENCE PROBLEM

The two models of motion (small-scale and large-scale) assume that two difficult and related problems have been solved.

1. The first assumes the dynamic image to be a three-dimensional function of two spatial arguments and a temporal argument. Then if this function is locally well-behaved and its spatiotemporal derivatives are computable, the image velocity or optical flow may be computed.
2. The second considers the cases where the motion is "large" and the previous technique is not applicable, since the image function is not differentiable. In these instances the measurement technique relies upon isolating and tracking highlights or feature points in the image through time. In other words, operators are applied on both dynamic frames that output a set of points in both images, and then the correspondence problem between these two sets of points has to be solved (i.e., finding which points on both dynamic frames are due to the projection of the same world point).

Both of the preceding approaches need solutions to "the correspondence problem" to compute the optical flow field or the discrete displacements field. Then algorithms are constructed to use them. However, the correspondence problem has proven highly intractable. The same problem occurs in the context of stereo fusion, where a disparities field must

TABLE 2.1
Error of Motion Parameters for
8-Point Correspondence for 2.5%
Error in Point Correspondence

Error of E (essential parameters)	73.91%
Error of rotation parameters	38.70%
Error of translations	103.60%

Note: From Tsai and Huang, 1984.

be computed. Despite much serious work, there currently are no satisfying solutions to the correspondence problem. Modern motion algorithms can be extremely sensitive to errors in correspondence (Tables 2.1, 2.2).

The algorithm in Tsai and Huang, 1984 solves linear equations, but the sensitivity to error in point correspondences is not improved with respect to algorithms that solve nonlinear equations. The same behavior is present in the algorithms that compute three-dimensional motion in the case of planar surfaces.

So, as the motion problem has been formulated (monocular observer), it seems to have a great deal of difficulty because of the correspondence problem. Actually, research in progress demonstrates that the structure from motion problem using one camera cannot be solved reliably when there exists a small uncertainly in the displacements (Aloimonos, in preparation). The work in (Aloimonos, 1986) offers several ways to combat the problem. What follows is a useful technique that uses aggregate region properties to avoid the correspondence problem. This work assumes that another difficult problem has been solved—that of segmenting the scene into regions corresponding to stable object features.
Aloimonos (1986) addressed the problem of finding motion without correspondence, in the case of discrete motion, for both planar and nonplanar surfaces. The core of the method is given here, first applied to the stereo problem. For a full treatment and extension to nonplanar surfaces (see Aloimonos, 1986).

TABLE 2.2
Error of Motion Parameters for
20-Point Correspondence for 2.5%
Error in Point Correspondence

Error of E (essential parameters)	19.49%
Error of rotation parameters	2.40%
Error of translations	29.66%

Note: From Tsai and Huang, 1984.

STEREO WITHOUT CORRESPONDENCE FOR PLANAR SURFACES

In this section we present a method for the recovery of the three-dimensional parameters for the set of three-dimensional planar points from their left and right images without using any point-to-point correspondence; instead we consider all point correspondences at once and so there is no need to solve the difficult correspondence problem in the case of the static stereo.

Let an orthogonal cartesian coordinate system $OXYZ$ be fixed with respect to the left camera, with O at the origin (O being also the nodal point of the left eye) and the z-axis pointing along the optical axis.

Let the image plane of the left camera be perpendicular to the z-axis at the point $(0, 0, f)$, (focal length $= f$).

Let the nodal point of the right camera be at the point $(d, 0, 0)$ and its image plane be identical to the left one; the optical axis of the right camera (eye) points also along the z-axis and passes through point $(d, 0, 0)$.

Consider a set of three-dimensional points $A = \{(X_i, Y_i, Z_i) \mid i = 1, 2, 3 \ldots n\}$ lying on the same plane, the latter being described by the equation:

$$Z = pX + qY + c$$

Let O_1, O_r be the origins of the two-dimensional orthogonal coordinate systems on each image plane; these origins are located on the left and right optical axes while the corresponding coordinate systems have their y-axes parallel to the axis OY, and their x-axes parallel to OX. Finally let $\{(x_{li}, y_{li}) \mid i = 1, 2, 3 \ldots n\}$ and $\{(x_{ri}, y_{ri}) \mid i = 1, 2, 3 \ldots n\}$ be the projections of the points of set A on the left and right retinae, respectively, that is,

$$x_{li} = \frac{fX_i}{Z_i} \qquad y_{li} = \frac{fY_i}{Z_i} \qquad \mid i = 1, 2, 3 \ldots n$$

$$x_{ri} = \frac{f(X_i - d)}{Z_i} \qquad y_{ri} = \frac{fY_i}{Z_i} \qquad \mid i = 1, 2, 3 \ldots n$$

Let (x_{li}, y_{li}) and (x_{ri}, y_{ri}) be corresponding points in the two frames. Then we have the relations

$$x_{li} - x_{ri} = \frac{fd}{Z_i} \tag{10}$$

$$y_{li} = y_{ri} \tag{11}$$

where Z_i is the depth of the three-dimensional point having those projections.

In the sequel, we prove that the quantity

$$\sum_{i=1}^{n} \frac{y_{li}^k}{Z_i}$$

is directly computable without using any point correspondence between the left and right frames. We proceed with the following propositions:

Proposition. Using the aforementioned nomenclature, the quantity

$$\sum_{i=1}^{n} \frac{y_{li}^k}{Z_i}$$

where

$$k \geq 0 \wedge k \neq \frac{m}{2n}, \ m, n \in Z - \{0\},$$

is directly computable.

Proof. We have that

$$\sum_{i=1}^{n} \frac{y_{li}^k}{Z_i} = [\textit{from equation (10)}] = \sum_{i=1}^{n} y_{li}^k \frac{(x_{li} - x_{ri})}{f \, d} =$$

$$= \sum_{i=1}^{n} \frac{x_{li} \, y_{li}^k}{f \, d} - \sum_{i=1}^{n} \frac{x_{ri} \, y_{li}^k}{f \, d} = [\textit{from equation (11)}] =$$

$$= \sum_{i=1}^{n} \frac{x_{li} \, y_{li}^k}{f \, d} - \sum_{i=1}^{n} \frac{x_{ri} \, y_{ri}^k}{f \, d}$$

Thus,

$$\sum_{i=1}^{n} \frac{y_{li}^k}{Z_i} = \sum_{i=1}^{n} \frac{x_{li} \, y_{li}^k}{f \, d} - \sum_{i=1}^{n} \frac{x_{ri} \, y_{ri}^k}{f \, d} \tag{12}$$

from which the claim is obvious.

Proposition. Using the aforementioned nomenclature, the parameters p, q, and c of the plane in view are directly computable without using any point-to-point correspondence between the two frames.

Proof. The equation of the world plane when expressed in terms of the coordinates of the left frame, becomes:

$$\frac{1}{Z} = (f - px_l - qy_l)\frac{1}{cf}$$

So, for all points on the planar surface,

$$\frac{1}{Z_i} = (f - px_{li} - qy_{li})\frac{1}{cf} \qquad i = 1, 2, 3 \ldots n$$

Now, we have:

$$\sum_{i=1}^{n} \frac{y_{li}^k}{Z_i} = \sum_{i=1}^{n} (f - px_{li} - qy_{li})\frac{y_{li}^k}{cf}$$

or

$$\sum_{i=1}^{n} \frac{y_{li}^k}{Z_i} = \frac{1}{c}\sum_{i=1}^{n} y_{li}^k - \frac{1}{cf}\left[\sum_{i=1}^{n} px_{li}\,y_{li}^k + \sum_{i=1}^{n} qy_{li}y_{li}^k\right] \qquad (13)$$

The left-hand side of Equation 13 has been shown to be computable without using any point-to-point correspondence.

If we write Equation 13 for three different values of k, we obtain the following *linear* system in the unknowns p, q, c, which in general has a unique solution (except for the case where the projection of all points of set A, have the same y-coordinate in both frames):

$$\sum_{i=1}^{n} \frac{x_{li}\,y_{li}^{k1}}{f\,d} - \sum_{i=1}^{n} \frac{x_{ri}\,y_{ri}^{k1}}{f\,d} = \frac{1}{c}\sum_{i=1}^{n} y_{li}^{k1} - \frac{1}{cf}\left[\sum_{i=1}^{n} px_{li}y_{li}^{k1} + \sum_{i=1}^{n} qy_{li}y_{li}^{k1}\right]$$

$$\sum_{i=1}^{n} \frac{x_{li}\,y_{li}^{k2}}{f\,d} - \sum_{i=1}^{n} \frac{x_{ri}\,y_{ri}^{k2}}{f\,d} = \frac{1}{c}\sum_{i=1}^{n} y_{li}^{k2} - \frac{1}{c*f}\left[\sum_{i=1}^{n} px_{li}y_{li}^{k2} + \sum_{i=1}^{n} qy_{li}y_{li}^{k2}\right]$$

$$\sum_{i=1}^{n} \frac{x_{li}\,y_{li}^{k3}}{f\,d} - \sum_{i=1}^{n} \frac{x_{ri}\,y_{ri}^{k3}}{f\,d} = \frac{1}{c}\sum_{i=1}^{n} y_{li}^{k3} - \frac{1}{c*f}\left[\sum_{i=1}^{n} px_{li}y_{li}^{k3} + \sum_{i=1}^{n} qy_{li}y_{li}^{k3}\right]$$

where we used Equation 12 to the left hand sides.

The solution of the aforementioned system recovers the structure and the depth of the points of set A without any correspondence, and this is the conclusion of the previously stated proposition.

We have implemented the method shown in the aforementioned equations for different values of k_1, k_2, k_3 and especially for the cases:

1. $k_1 = 0$ $\qquad k_2 = \frac{1}{3}$ $\qquad k_3 = \frac{2}{3}$
2. $k_1 = 0$ $\qquad k_2 = \frac{1}{3}$ $\qquad k_3 = \frac{1}{5}$

The noiseless cases give extremely accurate results.

Before we proceed, we must explain what we mean by noise introduced in the images. When we say that one frame (left or right) has noise of $a\%$, we mean that if the plane contains N projection points we added $[(Na)/100]$ randomly distributed points. (*Note:* [] denotes the integer part of its argument).

When the noise in both frames is kept below 2%, the results are still very satisfactory. When the noise exceeds 5%, only the value of p gets corrupted, but the values of q and c remain very satisfactory. In particular, some of our experiments gave the following results (Aloimonos, 1986): When the three-dimensional plane had parameters $p = 0$, $q = 0$, and $C = 10,000$, the computed parameters in a noiseless case were $p = 0$, $q = 0$, and $C = 10.000$ when the number of points was equal to 1000. In a case where the three-dimensional plane had parameters $p = 1.0$, $q = 1.0$, and $C = 10,000$ and we included 5% noise in the right frame, the computed parameters were $p = 1.7$, $q = 1.2$, and $C = 10,266.7$ when the number of three-dimensional points was equal to 1000. To correct this and get satisfactory results for high noise percentages, we devised the following method, which uses three cameras.

We consider the three-camera configuration system as in Figure 2.8, where the top camera has only vertical displacement with respect to the left one. If all three images are corrupted by noise (ranging from 5% to

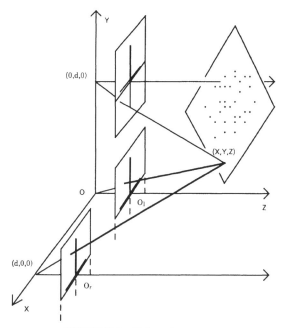

FIGURE 2.8. Trinocular system.

20%), then application of the algorithm to the left and top frames will give very reasonable values for p and c and corrupt q. However, q and c are accurately computed from the application of the same algorithm to the right and left frames. Applying this algorithm to a case where the total number of three-dimensional points was equal to 2,000 and the parameters of the three-dimensional plane were $p = 0$, $q = 0$, $C = 10,000$, with 5% noise in the left frame and 7% in the right and top frame, we got $p = 0.10$, $q = 0.05$, and $C = 10,197$ (Aloimonos, 1986).

So, by applying our stereo (without correspondence) algorithm to the three-camera configuration vision system, we obtained accurate results for the parameters describing the three-dimensional planar patch, even for noise percentages of 20% or slightly more and for different amounts of noise in the different frames.

RECOVERING THE DIRECTION OF TRANSLATION

Here we treat the case where the points of set A just rigidly translate, and we wish to recover the direction of the translation. In this case, the depth is not needed but the orientation of the plane is required. The general case is treated in the next section.

Using our usual perspective model, let us consider a point $P = (X_1, Y_1, Z_1)$ in the world, with perspective image (x_1, y_1), where $x_1 = (fX_1)/Z$ and $y_1 = (fY_1)/Z$. If the point P moves to the position $P' = (X_2, Y_2, Z_2)$ with

$$X_2 = X_1 + \Delta X$$

$$Y_2 = Y_1 + \Delta Y$$

$$Z_2 = Z_1 + \Delta Z$$

then we desire to find the direction of the translation ($\Delta X/\Delta Z$, $\Delta Y/\Delta Z$) (see Figure 2.9).

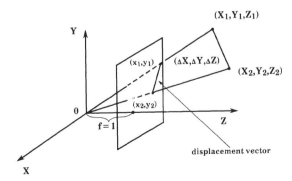

FIGURE 2.9. Motion of a point.

If the perspective image of P' is (x_2, y_2), then the observed motion-of-the-world point in the image plane is given by the displacement vector: $(x_2 - x_1, y_2 - y_1)$ (which in the case of very small motion is also known as "optical flow").

We can easily prove that:

$$x_2 - x_1 = \frac{f\,\Delta X - x_1\,\Delta Z}{Z_1 + \Delta Z}$$

$$y_2 - y_1 = \frac{f\,\Delta Y - y_1\,\Delta Z}{Z_1 + \Delta Z}$$

Under the assumption that the motion in depth is small with respect to the depth, the aforementioned equations become:

$$x_2 - x_1 = \frac{f\,\Delta X - x_1\,\Delta Z}{Z_1}$$

$$y_2 - y_1 = \frac{f\,\Delta Y - y_1\,\Delta Z}{Z_1}$$

These equations relate the retinal motion (left-hand sides) to the world motion ΔX, ΔY, ΔZ.

Detecting 3-D Direction of Translation Without Correspondence

In our usual perspective model-coordinate system, let $A = \{(X_i, Y_i, Z_i)/i = 1, 2, 3 \ldots n\}$, such that

$$Z_i = p X_i + q Y_i + c, \qquad i = 1, 2, 3 \ldots n$$

that is the points are planar. Let the points translate rigidly with translation $(\Delta X, \Delta Y, \Delta Z)$, and let $\{(x_i, y_i) \mid i = 1, 2, 3 \ldots n\}$ and $\{(x_i', y_i') \mid i = 1, 2, 3, \ldots n\}$ be the projections of the set A before and after the translation, respectively.

Consider a point (x_i, y_i) in the first frame which has a corresponding one (x_i', y_i') in the second (dynamic) frame.

For the moment we do not worry about where the point (x_i', y_i') is, but we do know that the following relations hold between these two points

$$x_i' - x_i = \frac{f\,\Delta X - x_i\,\Delta Z}{Z_i}$$

$$y_i' - y_i = \frac{f\,\Delta Y - y_i\,\Delta Z}{Z_i}$$

where Z_i is the depth of the three-dimensional point whose projection (on the first dynamic frame) is the point (x_i, y_i). Taking now into account that

$$\frac{1}{Z_i} = \frac{f - px_i - qy_i}{cf}$$

the above equations become:

$$x_i' - x_i = (f \, \Delta X - x_i \, \Delta Z) \frac{f - px_i - qy_i}{cf} \tag{14}$$

$$y_i' - y_i = (f \, \Delta Y - y_i \, \Delta Z) \frac{f - px_i - qy_i}{cf} \tag{15}$$

If we now write Equation 14 for all the points in the two dynamic frames and sum the resulting equations up, we take:

$$\sum_{i=1}^{n} (x_i' - x_i) = \sum_{i=1}^{n} \left[(f \, \Delta X - x_i \, \Delta Z) \frac{f - px_i - qy_i}{cf} \right]$$

or

$$\sum_{i=1}^{n} (x_i' - x_i) = \sum_{i=1}^{n} \left[\frac{f(f - px_i - qy_i) \, \Delta X - x_i \, (f - px_i - qy_i) \, \Delta Z}{cf} \right] \tag{16}$$

Similarly, if we do the same for Equation 15, we get:

$$\sum_{i=1}^{n} (y_i' - y_i) = \sum_{i=1}^{n} \left[(f \, \Delta Y - y_i \, \Delta Z) \frac{f - px_i - qy_i}{cf} \right]$$

or

$$\sum_{i=1}^{n} (y_i' - y_i) = \sum_{i=1}^{n} \left[\frac{f(f - px_i - qy_i) \, \Delta Y - y_i \, (f - px_i - qy_i) \, \Delta Z}{cf} \right] \tag{17}$$

At this point it has to be understood that Equations 16 and 17 do not require our finding of any correspondence.

By dividing Equation 16 by Equation 17, we get:

$$\frac{\displaystyle\sum_{i=1}^{n} x_i' - \sum_{i=1}^{n} x_i}{\displaystyle\sum_{i=1}^{n} y_i' - \sum_{i=1}^{n} y_i} = \frac{\displaystyle\sum_{i=1}^{n} \left[\frac{\Delta X}{\Delta Z} f \, (f - px_{li} - qy_{li}) - (f - px_{li} - qy_{li}) \, x_{li} \right]}{\displaystyle\sum_{i=1}^{n} \left[\frac{\Delta Y}{\Delta Z} f \, (f - px_{li} - qy_{li}) - (f - px_{li} - qy_{li}) \, y_{li} \right]} \tag{18}$$

Equation 18 is a linear equation in the unknowns $\Delta X/\Delta Z$, $\Delta Y/\Delta Z$ and the coefficients consist of expressions involving summations of point coordinates in both dynamic frames; for the computation of the latter, no establishment of any point correspondences is required.

So, if we consider a binocular observer applying this procedure in both left and right "eyes," we get two linear equations (of the form of Equation 18) in the two unknowns $\Delta X/\Delta Z$, $\Delta Y/\Delta Z$, which constitute a linear system that in general has a unique solution.

If one is not careful when analyzing the previous method, then he might think that all the method does is to correspond the center of mass of the image points before the motion with the center of mass of the image points after the motion, and then based on that retinal motion to recover three-dimensional motion. But this is wrong, because perspective projection does not preserve simple ratios, and so the center of mass of the image points before the motion does not correspond to the center of mass of the image points after the motion. This method aggregates the motion constraints; it does not place centers of mass into correspondence. This method needs the set of the world planar points to be visible by both eyes; otherwise, the mathematics is not valid. But, on the other hand, this method would work with a region of temporally varying texture for which corresponding interest points in multiple views might not exist.

We have implemented this method with a variety of planes as well as displacements; noiseless cases give extremely accurate results, while cases with noise percentages up to 20% (even with different amounts of noise in all four frames—first left and right; second left and right) give very satisfactory results (an error of 5%, at most). A particular experiment follows: When the number of three-dimensional points was equal to 1,000, the noise percentage in all frames 10%, and the actual direction of translation $\Delta X/\Delta Z = -2.00$, $\Delta Y/\Delta Z = 2.00$, the computed translation was $\Delta X/\Delta Z = -1.80$, $\Delta Y/\Delta Z = 2.05$. We now proceed to consider the general case.

Consider again the imaging system (binocular) of Figure 2.10, as well as the set $A = \{(X_i, Y_i, Z_i) \mid i = 1, 2, 3 \ldots n\}$ such that:

$$Z_i = pX_i + qY_i + c, \qquad i = 1, 2, 3 \ldots n$$

(i.e., the points are planar). Let B be the plane on which they lie. Suppose the points of set A move rigidly in space (translation plus rotation), and they become members of a set $A' = \{(X_i', Y_i', Z_i') \mid i = 1, 2, 3 \ldots n\}$. Since all of the points of set A move rigidly, it follows that the points of set A' are also planar; let B' be the (new) plane on which these points lie.

In other words the set A becomes A' after the rigid motion transformation. We wish to recover the parameters of this transformation. From the projection of sets A and A' on the left- and right-image planes and

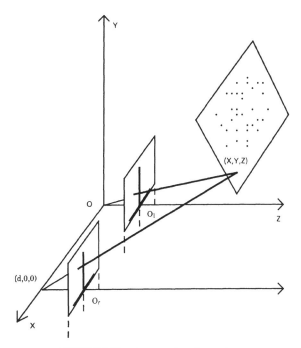

FIGURE 2.10. A stereo imaging system.

using the previous method, sets A and A' can be computed. In other words, we know exactly the positions in three-dimensional of all the points of sets A and A' (and this has been found without using any point correspondences).

So, the problem of recovering the three-dimensional motion has been transformed to the following: "Given the set A of planar points in 3D and the set A' of new planar points, which has been produced by applying to the points of set A a rigid motion transformation, recover that transformation." Any rigid body motion can be reduced to a rotation plus a translation; the rotation axis can be considered as passing through any point in the space, but after this point is chosen, everything else is fixed.

If we consider the rotation axis as passing through the center of mass (CM) of the points of set A, then the vector which has as its two endpoints the centers of mass M_A and $M_{A'}$ of sets A and A' respectively, represents the *exact* three-dimensional translation.

So, for the translation we can write

$$\text{translation} \equiv T = (X, Y, Z) = \mathbf{M_{A'}} - \mathbf{M_A}$$

It remains to recover the rotation matrix.

Let, therefore, $\mathbf{n}_1$ and $\mathbf{n}_2$ be the surface normals of the planes B and B'. Then, the angle θ between $\mathbf{n}_1$ and $\mathbf{n}_2$, where

$$\cos \theta = \frac{\mathbf{n}_1 \cdot \mathbf{n}_2}{\| \mathbf{n}_1 \| \| \mathbf{n}_2 \|} ,$$

(with '$\cdot$' the inner-product operator) represents the rotation around an axis $\mathbf{O}_1\mathbf{O}_2$ perpendicular to the plane defined by $\mathbf{n}_1$ and $\mathbf{n}_2$, where

$$\mathbf{O}_1\mathbf{O}_2 = \frac{\mathbf{n}_1 \times \mathbf{n}_2}{\| \mathbf{n}_1 \times \mathbf{n}_2 \|} ,$$

(with "$\times$" the cross-product operator). From the axis $\mathbf{O}_1\mathbf{O}_2$ and the angle θ we, develop a rotation matrix R_1. The matrix R_1 does not represent the final rotation matrix since we are still missing the rotation around the surface normal. Indeed, if we apply the rotation matrix R_1 and the translation T to the set A, we will get a set A'' of points, which is different than A', because the rotation matrix R_1 does not include the rotation around the surface normal n_2.

So we now have a matching problem: On the plane B' we have two sets of points A' and A'', respectively, and we want to recover the angle Φ by which we must rotate the points of set A'' (with respect to the surface normal $\mathbf{n}_2$) in order to coincide with those of set A'. The problem can be solved by any number of methods. See (Aloimonos, 1986) for one solution. Experiments with this method demonstrated a great deal of stability. The parameters of a particular experiment follow (Aloimonos, 1986): When the number of three-dimensional points was equal to 35 and the noise in the left frames (before and after the motion) was 5% and the noise in the right frames 7% with actual motion: translation = (100, 100, −100) and rotation axis and angle = (0.578, 0.578, 0.578) and 0.15 respectively, the computed motion was translation = (98.2, 103.5, −101.4), rotation axis = (0.53, 0.60, 0.59), rotation angle = 0.17.

COMBINING INFORMATION FROM SHADING AND MOTION

In this section we prove that if we combine shading with motion, we can uniquely compute the direction of the light source and the shape of the object in view. In particular:

1. We develop a constraint between retinal-motion displacements, local shape, and the direction of the light source. This constraint does not involve the albedo of the imaged surface. This constraint is of importance in itself, and can be used in related research in computer or human vision.

2. We develop a constraint between retinal displacements and local shape. Again, this constraint is important on its own, and it is the heart of the algorithms presented later in this chapter.
3. We present algorithms for the unique computation of the lighting direction and the shape of the object in view.
4. We present experimental results that test the theory.

The basic assumption is that the retinal motion is computed everywhere in the image—in the case of a moving observer and a stationary scene, or a stationary observer and a moving object. If several objects are moving in the scene, then a segmentation is required first, that is, the algorithms developed here can be applied to one rigidly moving object.

Shading is important for the estimation of three-dimensional shape from two-dimensional images, for instance, for distinguishing between the smooth occluding contour generated by the edge of a sphere and the sharp occluding contour generated by the edge of a disc. In order to use shading successfully, one must know the reflectance map $R(p, q)$, which can be determined by a calibration object or from knowledge of the surface's reflectance function and the illumination geometry (Horn, 1986). This is because variations in image intensity (shading) are caused by changes in surface orientation relative to the illuminant. This chapter reviews previous approaches to the solution of the determination of the illuminant direction problem and presents a new method for the unambiguous determination of the single-point lighting direction, and from that of the shape information. In particular, we show that if we combine information from shading and motion, we can uniquely compute shape and the illuminant direction. Finally, in this section we make the assumption of orthographic projection, since tractable reflectance equation models under perspective projection are not known. We use the mathematical model for the image formation shown in Figure 2.7.

Assuming orthographic projection, if **n** is the surface normal at a point on the imaged surface, **l** is the illuminant direction and f is the flux emitted toward the surface, and we assume a Lambertian reflectance function for the surface, the image intensity is given by:

$$I = \rho f (\mathbf{n} \cdot \mathbf{l})$$

where ρ is the albedo of the surface, a constant depending on the surface.

Most of the work in shape from shading (Horn, 1975; Ikeuchi & Horn, 1981; Strat, 1979) is based on the assumption that the albedo of the surface in view and the illuminant direction are known a priori; in other words, this work assumes that the reflectance map specifies how the brightness of a surface patch depends on its orientation, under given circumstances. It therefore encodes information about the reflecting properties of the surface and information about the distribution and intensity of the light sources. In fact, the reflectance map can be computed from the bidirectional reflectance-distribution function and the light source arrangement, as shown by Horn and Sjoberg (1979).

When encountering a new scene, we usually do not have the information required to determine the reflectance map. Yet, without this information, we are unable to solve the shape from shading problem.

The dilemma may be resolved if a calibration object of known shape appears in the scene, since the reflectance map can be computed from its image. But what happens when we are not that fortunate? One helpful fact would be the knowledge of the illuminant direction. The only work done for the illuminant direction determination is due to Pentland (1982), Brooks and Horn (1985), Brown, Ballard and Kimball (1983). Pentland's method is based on the assumption that surface orientation, when considered as random variable over all possible scenes, is isotropically distributed. A consequence of this assumption is that the change of surface normals is also isotropically distributed. Pentland's method, which uses the same model of image formation that we do, is valid for some objects. Under his assumptions, Pentland solves the problem uniquely, but his assumptions are restrictive.

Brooks and Horn (1985) presented a method in the general framework of the ill-posed problems and regularization in early vision. Their theory proposes to solve the shape from shading problem, and at the same time, to compute the illuminant direction by minimization of an appropriate functional. They did not present any uniqueness or convergence proofs of their iterative methods, but their experimental results for synthetic images were reasonable. Brown, Ballard and Kimball's (1983) method, based on Lambertian reflectance and a Hough transform technique, recovered the direction of the light source. Finally, Lee and Rosenfeld (1985) used Pentland's idea with a new statistical method.

In the sequel, we proved that the illuminant direction cannot be recovered from only one intensity image of a Lambertian surface. After this, we will prove that two intensity images (moving object or moving observer) with the correspondence between them established can uniquely recover the illuminant direction, and from that the shape. This approach relies on a solution to the correspondence problem, which we have seen to be difficult.

TECHNICAL PRELIMINARIES

Theorem 1.   Given an image (i.e., an intensity fucntion $I[x, y]$), there are an infinite number of surfaces and an infinite number of positions of the light source, that will produce the same image, under the process of image formation described earlier in this chapter.

Proof. Suppose that for a shape $\mathbf{n}_i$ (x, y), $(x, y) \in \Omega$ (Ω is the domain where the image function is defined) and a light source position $\mathbf{s}_1$ we have:

$$I(x, y) = \rho\, \mathbf{n}_1(x, y)\, \mathbf{s}_1$$

where ρ is the albedo of the surface in view (considered constant everywhere).

Define a shape $\mathbf{n}_2(x, y)$ over Ω and a light source position $\mathbf{s}_2$, as follows:

$$\mathbf{n}_2(x, y) = 2\mathbf{m}(\mathbf{n}_1(x, y) \cdot \mathbf{m}) - \mathbf{n}_1(x, y),\ \mathbf{s}_2 = 2\mathbf{m}(\mathbf{s}_1 \cdot \mathbf{m}) - \mathbf{s}_1$$

for any vector $\mathbf{m}$, with $\|\mathbf{m}\| = 1$.

Then, considering a surface with the same albedo as before and with shape $\mathbf{n}_2(x, y)$ and illuminated from a point source in the direction $\mathbf{s}_2$, we have:

$$
\begin{aligned}
\rho\, \mathbf{n}_2(x, y) \cdot \mathbf{s}_2 &= \rho(2\mathbf{m}\,(\mathbf{n}_2(x, y) \cdot \mathbf{m}) - \mathbf{n}_1(x, y)) \cdot (2\mathbf{m}\,(\mathbf{s}_1\, \mathbf{m}) - \mathbf{s}_1) \\
&= \rho\,[4\,(\mathbf{m} \cdot \mathbf{m})(\mathbf{n}_1(x, y) \cdot \mathbf{m})(\mathbf{s}_1 \cdot \mathbf{m}) - 2\,(\mathbf{n}_1(x, y) \cdot \mathbf{m}) \cdot (\mathbf{s}_1 - \mathbf{m}) \\
&\quad - 2\,(\mathbf{s}_1 \cdot \mathbf{m}) + \mathbf{n}_1(x, y) \cdot \mathbf{s}_1] = \rho\, \mathbf{n}_1(x, y) \cdot \mathbf{s}_1
\end{aligned}
$$

So, $I(x, y) = \rho\, \mathbf{n}_2(x, y) \cdot \mathbf{s}_2$.

This means that the image $I(x, y)$ could be due to an infinite number of surfaces illuminated from the one of an infinite number of light sources, since the vector $\mathbf{m}$ can be arbitrary.

The importance of the aforementioned theorem is that no correct and robust method can exist that will find the illuminant direction from one intensity image of a Lambertian surface illuminated from a point source.

The result we are developing is that given two images of a moving object (or two images of the same object taken by a moving observer), with the correspondence between the two images established, the position of the light source can be uniquely determined. But before that, we need to lay some groundwork concerning the relationship between shape, intensity, displacements and the lighting direction, and also between the parameters of a small motion (small rotation) with the shape. We proceed with the following theorem.

Theorem 2. Suppose that two views (rigid motion) of the same (Lambertian) surface (locally planar) are given and let I_1 and I_2 be the two intensity functions. Suppose also that the displacement vector field $(u(x, y), v(x, y)), (x, y) \in \Omega$ is known, where Ω is the domain of the image, that is, a point (x, y) in the first image will move to the point $(x + u(x, y), y + v(x, y))$ in the second image. If the lighting direction is $\mathbf{l} = (l_1, l_2, l_3)$ and the gradient of a surface point whose image is the point (x, y) is (p, q), then the following relation holds:

$$0 = p^2[(l_2\Delta^y u - l_1(1 + \Delta^y v))^2 - r^2 l_1{}^2]$$

$$+ 2pq[(l_1(\Delta^x v - l_2(1 + \Delta^x u))(l_1(1 + \Delta^y u) - l_2\,\Delta^y u) - 2r^2 l_1 l_2]$$

$$+ q^2[(l_1\Delta^x v - l_2(1 + \Delta^x u))^2 - r^2 l_2{}^2]$$

$$- 2pl_1 l_3 r(r - ((1 + \Delta^x u)(1 + \Delta^y v) - \Delta^x u\,\Delta^x v))$$

$$- 2ql_2 l_3 r(r - ((1 + \Delta^x u)(1 + \Delta^y v) - (\Delta^y u\,\Delta^x v))$$

$$- ((1 + \Delta^x u)(1 + \Delta^y v) - \Delta^y u\,\Delta^x v)^2$$

$$+ l_1{}^2((\Delta^x v)^2 + (1 + \Delta^y v)^2) + l_2{}^2((\Delta^y u)^2 + (1 + \Delta^x u)^2)$$

$$+ l_1 l_2((1 + \Delta^x u)\Delta^x v + \Delta^y u(1 + \Delta^y v))$$

$$- r^2 l_3{}^2 - 2rl_3{}^2((1 + \Delta^x u)(1 + \Delta^y v) - \Delta^y u\,\Delta^x v) \qquad (19)$$

where,

$$r = \frac{I_2(x + u(x, y), y + u(x, y))}{I_1(x, y)}$$

and

$$\Delta^x u = u(x + 1, y) - u(x, y)$$

$$\Delta^y u = u(x, y + 1) - u(x, y)$$

$$\Delta^x v = v(x + 1, y) - v(x, y)$$

$$\Delta^y v = v(x, y + 1) - v(x, y)$$

Equation 19 is local, that is, it involves the gradient at a point (x, y), the displacements around the point (x, y) along with the global direction of lighting.

Proof. To exploit the rigid motion assumption, we represent the surface normal by two vectors and note that their length, angular separation, and hence, their dot and cross product are preserved by rigid motion. Consider the surface S, a point A on S, the vector $\mathbf{n} = p\mathbf{i} + q\mathbf{j} + \mathbf{k}$ perpendicular to S at the point A, and the plane Π that is tangent to the surface S at the point A (see Figure 2.11). The vectors $\mathbf{a} = (1, 0, -p)$ and $\mathbf{b} = (0, 1, -q)$ lie in Π and:

$$\mathbf{a} \times \mathbf{b} = p\mathbf{i} + q\mathbf{j} + \mathbf{k} = \mathbf{n}$$

We shall use vectors $\mathbf{a}$ and $\mathbf{b}$ as the shape (surface normal) representation. We use our standard camera model.

Consider a point $A(x, y)$ on the surface S at time t whose shape vectors are $\mathbf{a} = \text{vec}(AB) = \mathbf{i} - p\mathbf{k}$ and $\mathbf{b} = \text{vec}(AC) = \mathbf{j} - q\mathbf{k}$ ($\text{vec}(AB)$ means the vector from the point A to the point B). Since the projection of $\mathbf{a} =$

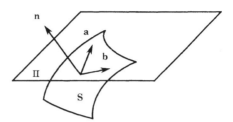

FIGURE 2.11.   Shape vectors.

vec(AB) on the image plane is i, we conclude that if $I_A = (x, y)$ is the projection of A then the projection of B will be $I_B = (x + 1, y)$. Similarly, the projection of C will be the point $I_C = (x, y + 1)$ on the image plane. Consider now the object at the next frame where the point A will become A', with shape vectors $\mathbf{a}' = A'B'$ and $\mathbf{b}' = A'C'$ (Figure 2.12).

Let $I_{A'}$ be the projection of A'. I_A' is the position to which I_A moves, which can be determined from the displacements. Thus, $I_A' = (x + u(x, y), y + v(x, y))$. Similarly, if $I_{B'}$ and $I_{C'}$ are the projections of B' and C', then $I_{B'}$ is the position to which I_B will move. Of course, displacement at I_B is due to the motion of the surface's point that has the same x, y coordinates as B (orthography), but because of the assumed local planarity, this point is the same as B. (The planarity constraint of course fails at boundaries). So, we have: $I_{B'} = (x + 1 + u(x + 1, y), y + v(x + 1, y))$, and for the same reasons $I_{C'} = (x + u(x, y + 1), y + 1 + v(x, y + 1))$. The projection of $\mathbf{a}' = \text{vec}(A'B')$ on the image plane is thus:

$$I_{A'}I_{B'} = [1 + u(x + 1, y) - u(x, y)]\mathbf{i} + [v(x + 1, y) - v(x, y)]\mathbf{j}$$

But according to our hypotheses, the above relation can be written:

$$I_{A'}I_{B'} = (1 + \Delta^x u)\mathbf{i} + \Delta^x v\mathbf{j}$$

Similarly, we get:

$$I_{A'}I_{C'} = \Delta^y u\mathbf{i} + (1 + \Delta^y v)\mathbf{j}$$

The above two equations give us the expressions for $I_{A'}I_{B'}$ and $I_{A'}I_{C'}$, which are the projections of the shape vectors $\mathbf{a}'$ and $\mathbf{b}'$, respectively. But then,

$$\mathbf{a}' = (1 + \Delta^x u)\mathbf{i} + \Delta^x v\mathbf{j} + \lambda\mathbf{k} \text{ and}$$

$$\mathbf{b}' = \Delta^y u\mathbf{i} + (1 + \Delta^y v)\mathbf{j} + \mu\mathbf{k}$$

where λ, μ are to be determined.

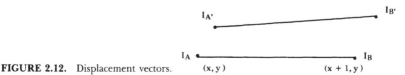

FIGURE 2.12.   Displacement vectors.

But since rigid body motion preserves the vector length, we have that

$$\|\mathbf{a}'\|^2 = \|\mathbf{a}\|^2 \text{ or}$$

$$\lambda = \pm (p^2 - \Delta^x u - \Delta^x v - 2\Delta^x u)^{1/2}$$

Similarly, we get

$$\mu = \pm (q^2 - \Delta^y u - \Delta^y v - 2\Delta^y u)^{1/2}$$

Assuming that neither region is in shadow, we have that:

$$I_1(x, y) = \rho_1 \, \mathbf{n}_A \mathbf{l} \tag{20}$$

and

$$I_2(x + u(x, y), y + v(x, y)) = \rho_2 \, \mathbf{n}_A \mathbf{l} \tag{21}$$

Equation 20 gives the intensity of the point $A(x, y)$ in the first frame. $\mathbf{n}_A$ is the surface normal at the point A (in the first view). Equation 21 gives the intensity at the point $A'(x + u(x, y), y + v(x, y))$ in the second frame. $\mathbf{n}_{A'}$ is the surface normal at the new position of the point A.

Dividing Equations 20 and 21, and setting $I_2(A')/I_1(A) = r$ and taking into account that $\rho_1 = \rho_2$ (surface markings do not change), we get:

$$r\mathbf{n}_A \cdot \mathbf{l} = \mathbf{n}_{A'} \cdot \mathbf{l} \tag{22}$$

But

$$\mathbf{n}_A = \frac{\mathbf{a} \times \mathbf{b}}{\| \mathbf{a} \times \mathbf{b} \|}$$

and from the rigidity of the motion it follows that:

$$\mathbf{n}_{A'} = \pm \frac{\mathbf{a'} \times \mathbf{b'}}{\| \mathbf{a'} \times \mathbf{b'} \|}$$

where the sign is chosen such that $\mathbf{n}_{A'} \cdot \mathbf{k} > 0$.
But since

$$\|\mathbf{a}'\| = \|\mathbf{a}\|, \|\mathbf{b}'\| = \|\mathbf{b}\| \text{ and } \mathbf{a} \cdot \mathbf{b} = \mathbf{a}' \cdot \mathbf{b}', \text{ it follows that}$$
$$\|\mathbf{a} \times \mathbf{b}\| = \|\mathbf{a}' \times \mathbf{b}'\| \tag{23}$$

Using equation (23), equation (22) becomes:

$$r[\mathbf{a}, \mathbf{b}, \mathbf{l}] = \pm [\mathbf{a}', \mathbf{b}', \mathbf{l}'] \tag{24}$$

where the sign chosen is the sign of $[\mathbf{a}', \mathbf{b}', \mathbf{k}]$, and $[,,]$ is the triple scalar product of vectors. But $[\mathbf{a}', \mathbf{b}', \mathbf{k}] = (1 + \Delta^x u)(1 + \Delta^y v) - \Delta^y u \, \Delta^x v$. It is obvious that $[\mathbf{a}, \mathbf{b}, \mathbf{k}] > 0$; if $[\mathbf{a}', \mathbf{b}', \mathbf{k}] < 0$, then we don't have a valid motion, because $[\mathbf{a}', \mathbf{b}', \mathbf{k}] < 0$ means that we have reversed orientation so that the texture in the image is viewed as if seen in a mirror.

So, $[\mathbf{a}', \mathbf{b}', \mathbf{k}] > 0$, and substituting in Equation 24 the values of $\mathbf{a}$, $\mathbf{b}$, $\mathbf{a}'$, $\mathbf{b}'$ after algebraic manipulations and using the fact that:

$$\lambda^2 = p^2 + 1 - (1 + \Delta^x u)^2 - (\Delta^x v)^2$$

$$\mu^2 = q^2 + 1 - (1 + \Delta^y v)^2 - (\Delta^y u)^2$$

$$\lambda\mu = pq - (1 + \Delta^x u)\Delta^y u - (1 + \Delta^y v)(\Delta^x v)$$

we get Equation 19.

Equation 19 involves the lighting direction, but it also involves the shape (p, q). We would like to find the direction $\mathbf{l}$ without knowing the shape (p, q). Theorem 2 has established a constraint between lighting direction, shape, and displacement vectors. We now proceed with the following theorem.

Theorem 3. Suppose that the surface S (locally planar) is moving with a rigid motion, and we use our standard camera model. Let the gradient of the surface (with respect to the first frame) be $(p(x, y), q(x, y))$ and the displacement vector field be $(u(x, y), v(x, y))$. It is known that this motion can be considered as a translation (dx, dy, dz) plus a rotation of an angle θ about an axis (n_1, n_2, n_3) passing through the origin $(n^2_1 + n^2_2 + n^2_3 = 1)$. If the rotation angle θ is small, then the following relations hold:
(a) The displacement vector field $(u(x, y), v(x, y))$ is given by:

$$u(x, y) = dx + Bz(x, y) - Cy$$

$$v(x, y) = dy + Cx - Az(x, y),$$

where $A = n_1\theta$, $B = n_2\theta$, $C = n_3\theta$, and $z(x, y)$, the depth of the surface point whose projection is the image point (x, y).

(b)
$$p(x, y) = \frac{1}{B} \Delta^x u$$

$$q(x, y) = \frac{1}{A} \Delta^y_v$$

$$\frac{A}{B} = \frac{\Delta^y v}{\Delta^x u} \cdot \frac{\dfrac{\Delta^x v - \Delta^y u + \sqrt{(\Delta^y u + \Delta^x v)^2 - 4\Delta^x u \Delta^y v}}{2} - \Delta^x v}{\Delta^y v}$$

Proof.
(a) Trivial.
(b) Using the two equations in (a) and the assumption about local planarity, we get:

$$\Delta^x u = Bp$$

$$\Delta^x v = C - Ap$$

$$\Delta^y u = Bq - A$$

$$\Delta^y v = -Aq$$

where the p and q are considered at the point (x, y). From the above equations we get:

$$p(x, y) = \frac{1}{B} \Delta^x u$$

$$q(x, y) = \frac{1}{A} \Delta^y v$$

$$\frac{A}{B} = \frac{\Delta^y v}{\Delta^x u} \cdot \frac{\dfrac{\Delta^x v - \Delta^y u + \sqrt{(\Delta^y u + \Delta^x v)^2 - 4\Delta^x u \Delta^y v}}{2} - \Delta^x v}{\Delta^y v}$$

THE LIGHTING DIRECTION CONSTRAINT

In this section we develop the constraint that will be used as the heart of the algorithm that will solve the problem of the determination of the illuminant direction.

If we let $1/A = \alpha$, $1/B = \beta$, $B/A = K$, and use part (b) of Theorem 3 to substitute in equation (19) for p and q, we get the following equation.

$$0 = (\Delta^x u)^2 \, \beta^2 \, [(l_2 \Delta^y u - l_1(1 + \Delta^y v))^2 - r^2 l_1^2]$$

$$+ 2\Delta^x u \Delta^y v K \beta^2 \, [(l_1(\Delta^x u - l_2)(1 + \Delta^x u))(l_1(1 + \Delta^y v) - l_2 \Delta^y u) - 2\,r^2 l_1 l_2]$$

$$+ (\Delta^y v)^2 \, K^2 \beta^2 \, [(l_1 \Delta^x v - l_2(1 + \Delta^x u))^2 - r^2 l_2^2]$$

$$- 2(\Delta^x u)\beta l_1 l_3 r(r - (1 + \Delta^x u + \Delta^y v + \Delta^x u \, \Delta^y v - \Delta^y u \, \Delta^x v))$$

$$- 2(\Delta^y v) \, K\beta l_2 l_3 r(r - (1 + \Delta^x u + \Delta^y v + \Delta^x u \, \Delta^y v - \Delta^y u \, \Delta^x v))$$

$$- (1 + \Delta^x u \, \Delta^y v + \Delta^x u + \Delta^y v - \Delta^y u \, \Delta^x v))$$

$$+ l_1^2((\Delta^x v)^2 + (1 + \Delta^y u)^2) + l_2^2((\Delta^x u)^2 + (1 + \Delta^x u)^2)$$

$$+ l_2 l_1((1 + \Delta^x u) \, \Delta^x v + \Delta^y u(1 + \Delta^y v)) - r^2 l_3^2$$

$$+ 2r l_3^2(1 + \Delta^x u + \Delta^y v + \Delta^x u \, \Delta^y v - \Delta^y u \, \Delta^x v) \qquad (25)$$

This equation is a polynomial in l_1, l_2, l_3, β.

Considering Equation 25 in four points we get a polynomial system of four equations in four unknowns. A simple but tedious calculation of the Jacobian of this system gives us the fact that the Jacobian has rank four (except for the degenerate cases whose set has measure zero). The inverse-function theorem implies that the function defined by the equations of the system is locally an isomorphism, which means that its zeros are isolated. But, from Whitney's theorem, the set of the zeros of this algebraic system is an algebraic set, and it has finite components.

The conclusion of this is that the solutions of the system are finite. If we now consider Equation 25 in five points, then we get a system of five equations in four unknowns which, barring degeneracy, will have at most one solution.

It is clear from the previous discussion that two intensity images of a Lambertian surface, with the correspondence between them established, gives the lighting direction uniquely. In the next section, we present a practical way to recover the lighting direction based on the constraint developed in this section.

THE ALGORITHM FOR FINDING ILLUMINANT DIRECTION

First, we choose an azimuth-elevation parameterization to represent the vector that denotes the lighting direction. More specifically, we set:

$$l_1 = \cos \Phi \cos \theta$$

$$l_2 = \sin \theta$$

$$l_3 = \cos \Phi \cos \theta$$

where θ and Φ are the azimuth and elevation (See Figure 2.13).

Now we consider Equation 25 in n points in the images, and we get n equations eq1, eq2, . . . , eq$n$ in the three unknowns β, θ, Φ. Then, the following algorithm solves the problem:

```
for all θ
for all Φ
        {   get n quadratic equations in β
            Check if they have a common solution
            If yes, output (θ, Φ).
        }
```

Although it is difficult to compute the displacement field for every point in the image, one can sometimes compute the parameters of the correspondence of small regions. If we can establish region correspondences and have a small planar region S_1 in the first image that corre-

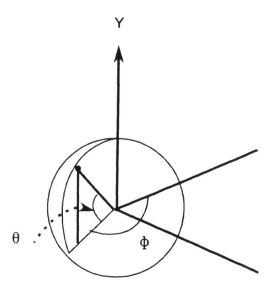

FIGURE 2.13. Gaussian sphere.

sponds to a small region S_2 in the second image, then the parameters of an affine transformation $f(x, y) = (ax + by + c, dx + cy + f)$ between the two patterns can be computed using a variation of a least-squares method introduced by Lucas and Kanade that is described in Webb (1981). In that case, the essential constraint (Equation 25) has a similar form and the whole analysis proceeds as previously.

We have implemented the aforementioned algorithm, and it works successfully for synthetic images. Figure 2.14 represents the displacements vector field that was obtained from the motion (rotational with $\omega_x = 1$, $\omega_y = 2$, $\omega_z = 3$) of a sphere. Figure 2.15 represents the image of the sphere before the motion. The surface of the sphere is supposed to be Lambertian, the albedo $\rho = 1$ and the lighting direction with gradient (ps, qs) = (0.7, 0.3), (i.e., to the right and a little above the horizon. The computed lighting direction was (0.65, 0.33). The observed inaccuracy is due to discretization effects. In our synthetic experiment, we did not compute the displacements; instead, we calculated them since we knew the motion and the exact position of the sphere.

Theorem 4. With the assumptions and notation of Theorem 2, the gradient (p, q) of a surface point whose image is the point (x, y), with displacement vector (u, v), satisfies the constraint:

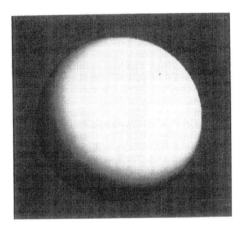

FIGURE 2.14. Intensity image.

$Ap_2 + Bq_2 - 2Cpq + D = 0$, with

$A = (\Delta^y u(x, y))^2 + (\Delta^y v(x, y))^2 + 2\Delta^y v(x, y)$

$B = (\Delta^x u(x, y))^2 + (\Delta^x v(x, y))^2 + 2\Delta^x u(x, y)$

$C = \Delta^y u(x, y) + \Delta^y u(x, y)\Delta^x u(x, y) + \Delta^x v(x, y) + \Delta^x v(x, y)\Delta^y v(x, y)$

$D = C^2 - AB,$

where the coefficients $\Delta^x u$, $\Delta^y u$, $\Delta^x v$, $\Delta^y v$ are defined in Theorem 2.

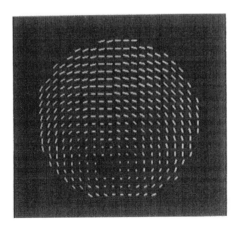

FIGURE 2.15. Displacements field.

Proof. From the proof of Theorem 2, because of the rigid motion assumption, we have the preservation of the dot product. So,

$$\mathbf{a.b} = \mathbf{a'.b'}$$

or

$$Ap_2 + Bq_2 - 2Cpq + D = 0 \tag{26}$$

where (p, q) is the gradient at the point (x, y), and

$A = (\Delta^y u(x, y))^2 + (\Delta^y v(x, y))^2 + 2\Delta^y v(x, y)$

$B = (\Delta^x u(x, y))^2 + (\Delta^x v(x, y))^2 + 2\Delta^x u(x, y)$

$C = \Delta^y u(x, y) + \Delta^y u(x, y)\Delta^x u(x, y) + \Delta^x v(x, y) + \Delta^x v(x, y)\Delta^y v(x, y)$

$D = C^2 - AB$

Equation 26 gives the constraint between displacements and shape, and represents a conic section in p-q space. This conic section is a hyperbola or parabola depending on the values of the coefficients A, B, C. Equation 26 is a constraint between shape, displacements, and the lighting direction. We will refer to Equation 19 as the *lighting constraint*, and to Equation 26 as the *shape-motion* constraint.

So far, we have developed two constraints on shape that also involve retinal motion displacements and the lighting direction. The lighting constraint is a conic on p, q, with coefficients that depend on intensities (relative), displacements and lighting direction. The shape-motion con-

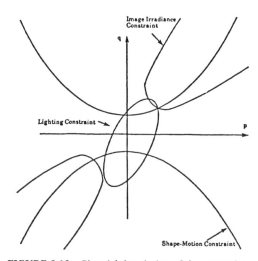

FIGURE 2.16. Pictorial description of the constraint.

straint is again a conic on p and q, with coefficients that depend on the displacement vectors. Finally, we have the image irradiance equation:

$$I = \rho f(\mathbf{n \cdot l})$$

which determines the intensity $I(x, y)$ at a point $(x\ y)$ of the image as a function of the shape n of the world point whose image is the point (x, y) and the lighting direction $\mathbf{l}$, is another constraint on p and q that is also a conic. We will call this the *image-irradiance* constraint. Figure 2.16 gives a geometrical description of the constraints.

COMPUTING SHAPE WHEN THE ALBEDO IS KNOWN

When the albedo is known, then we have at our disposal three constraints at every image point for the computation of shape. The lighting constraint, (let it be $F_1(p, q) = 0$), the shape-motion constraint, (let it be $F_2(p, q) = 0$), and the image-irradiance constraint, (let it be $F_3(p, q) = 0$). These three equations are all of degree two, and their system, barring degeneracy, will have at most one solution. Several algebraic or geometrical techniques exist for solving a system of algebraic equations each of degree two. Direct methods result in solving equations of a high degree, and so we prefer to use an iterative technique; and even though we do not have theoretical results about the convergence of the technique, in practice it has shown to converge very fast, to the right solution.

The function $E(p, q) = \lambda_1(F_1(p, q))^2 + \lambda_2(F_2(p, q))^2 + \lambda_3(F_3(p, q))^2$ should be minimized everywhere in the image, where $\lambda_1, \lambda_2, \lambda_3$ constants with their sum equal to one. By setting the partial derivatives of $E(p, q)$ equal to zero and solving for p and q, we get equations of the following form:

$$p = G_1(p, q, p_{av}), q = G_2(p, q, q_{av}),$$

where G_1 and G_2 are polynomials of p, q, p_{av} and p, q, q_{av}, respectively. These equations can be solved iteratively, provided that we have an approximate initial solution. If the values of p and q at the boundaries are known, then p, q are propagated throughout the image using a general smoothness criterion, by an algorithm similar to the Gauss-Seidel algorithm of Ikeuchi and Horn (1981).

If the albedo is not known, then we cannot utilize the image-irradiance constraint, because it contains the albedo as a coefficient. We have to use the lighting constraint and the shape-motion constraint, which are two conics in p and q. The Jacobian of the system that they form is nonzero. So the function defined by the system is locally an isomorphism (from the inverse function theorem), which means that its zeros are isolated. But from Whitney's theorem, the set of zeros of this algebraic system is an algebraic set and it has finite components. This means that the system has *finite solutions*. In this case, the solutions can be restricted to a unique solution if a local smoothness constraint is used.

In a minimization scheme based on the Lagrange multiplier technique, the solution is obtained without propagating the boundary conditions. If $F_1(p, q) = 0$ is the lighting constraint and $F_2(p, q) = 0$ the shape motion constraint, the error function $E(p, q) = (F_1(p, q))^2$ is to be minimized subject to the constraint $F_2(p, q) = 0$. The Lagrange multiplier scheme says that the p, q that minimize E are one of the solutions of the following system:

$$\nabla E = \lambda \nabla F_2, F_2 = 0$$

where λ is the Lagrange multiplier.

From the input shown in Figures 2.14 and 2.15, our algorithm recovered the shape shown in Figure 2.17. A local smoothing scheme has been used at the end of the program to smooth out the results. The error in the resulting shape is very low, basically due to discretization effects. If we introduce noise in the input, then the results get very much corrupted with no local smoothing, because of the locality of the method. If a local smoothness constraint is utilized, then the results are very good.

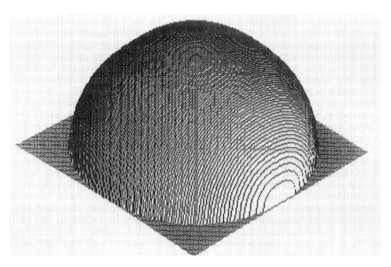

FIGURE 2.17. Reconstructed shape.

CONCLUSION

In our effort to compute intrinsic images in a unique and robust way, we have combined information from different sources. In this chapter we discussed how to combine retinal motion with stereo to compute three-dimensional motion without using any correspondences and how to combine shading with retinal motion to compute shape and illuminate direction.

REFERENCES

Aloimonos, J., "Computing intrinsic images." Ph.D. thesis, Department of Computer Science, University of Rochester: New York, September, 1986.

Ballard, D. H., "Parameter networks." *Artificial Intelligence, 22,* 235–267, 1984.

Bandopadhay, A., "A multiple channel model for the perception of optical flow." *Proceedings,* IEEE Workshop on Computer Vision: Representation and Control: Annapolis, MD, 78–82, 1984.

Bandopadhay, A., "A computational study of rigid motion perception." Ph.D. thesis, Dept. of Computer Science, University of Rochester: New York, September, 1986.

Barrow, H. G., & Popplestone, R. J., "Relational descriptions in picture processing." *Machine Intelligence, 6,* 1971. pp. 377–396.

Barrow, H. G., & J. M. Tenenbaum, "Recovering intrinsic scene characteristics from images." In *Computer Vision Systems,* A. R. Hansen & E. M. Riseman (Eds.), Academic Press: New York, 1978. pp. 3–26.

Brice, C. R., & Fennema, C. L., "Scene analysis using regions." *Artificial Intelligence, 1,* 205–226, 1970.

Brooks, M. J., & Horn, B. K. P. "Shape and source from shading." *Proceedings,* International Joint Conference on Artificial Intelligence-85: Los Angeles, CA, 932–936, August 1985.

Brown, C. M., Ballard, D. H., & Kimball, O. A., "Constraint interaction in shape-from-shading algorithms." 1982–93 Computer Science and Computer Engineering Research Review, Computer Science Department, University of Rochester: New York, 3–21, 1983.

Bruss, A., & Horn, B. K. P. "Passive nagivation." *Computer Vision, Graphics and Image Processing, 21,* 3–20, 1983.

Clowes, M. B. "On seeing things," *Artificial Intelligence 2,* 1, Spring, 1971, 79–116.

Davis, L. S., Wu, Z., & Sun, H., "Contour based motion estimation." *Computer Vision, Graphics and Image Processing, 23,* 313–326, 1983.

Fang, J. Q., & Huang, T. S., "Solving three-dimensional small-rotation motion equations: Uniqueness, algorithms, and numerical results." *Computer Vision, Graphics and Image Processing, 26,* 183–206, 1984.

Freuder, E. C., "A computer vision system for visual recognition using active knowledge." TR 345, MIT AI Lab, 1974.

Grimson, W. E. L. "Binocular shading and visual surface reconstruction." *Computer Vision, Graphics and Image Processing, 28,* 19–44, 1984.

Haralick, R. M., & Lee, J. S., "The facet approach to optical flow." *Proceedings,* DARPA Image Understanding Workshop: Arlington, VA, 84–93, June, 1983.

Hoffman, D. D., "Interpreting time-varying images: The planarity assumption." *Proceed-*

ings, IEEE Workshop on Computer Vision, Representation and Control, 92–94, August, 1982a.

Hoffman, D. D., "Inferring local surface orientation from motion fields." *Journal of Optical Society of America*, 72(7), 888–892, July 1982b.

Hoffman, D. D., & Flinchbaugh, B. E., "The interpretation of biological motion." *Biological Cybernetics, 42*, 195–204, 1982.

Horn, B. K. P., "Shape from shading: A method for obtaining the shape of a smooth opaque object from one view," (Tech. Rep. MAC-TR-79). Project MAC, MIT Press: Cambridge, MA, 1970.

Horn, B. K. P., "Obtaining shape from shading information." In *The Psychology of Computer Vision*, P. H. Winston (Ed.), McGraw-Hill: New York, 115–155, 1975.

Horn, B. K. P., "Understanding image intensities." *Artificial Intelligence, 8*(2), 201–231, 1977.

Horn, B. K. P., "Hill-shading and the reflectance map." *Proceedings*, DARPA Image Understanding Workshop: Palo Alto, CA, 79–120, 1979.

Horn, B. K. P., *Robot Vision*, McGraw-Hill: New York: 1986.

Horn, B. K. P., & Schunck, B. G., "Determining optical flow." *Artificial Intelligence, 17*, 185–204, 1981.

Horn, B. K. P., & Sjoberg, R. W., "Calculating the reflectance map." *Applied Optics, 18*, 1770–1779, 1979.

Huang, T. S., & Blonstein, M. "Robust algorithms for computing three-dimensional motion from image sequences," *Proceedings* IEEE-Computer Vision and Pattern Recognition Conference, pp. 301–316, 1985.

Huang, T. S., & Tsai, R. Y., "Image sequence analysis: Motion estimation." In *Image Sequence Analysis*, T. S. Huang (Ed.), Springer-Verlag: Berlin, 1981.

Huffman, D. A., "Impossible objects as nonsense sentences." In *Machine Intelligence, 6*, Meltzer, B. & Michie, D., (Eds.), Edinburgh University Press: Edinburgh, 295–323, 1971.

Ikeuchi, K., & Horn, B. K. P., "Numerical shape from shading and occluding boundaries," *Artificial Intelligence, 17*, 141–184, 1981.

Johansson, G., "Visual perception of biological motion and a model for its analysis," *Perception & Psychophysics, 14*(2), 201–211, 1973.

Kanade, T., "Camera motion from image differentials." *Proceedings*, Conference of the Optical Society of America: Lake Tahoe, NY, 1985.

Lawton, D., & Rieger, J. H., "The use of difference fields in processing sensor motion." *Proceedings*, Defense Advanced Research Projects Agency Image Understanding Workshop: Arlington, VA, June 1983.

Lesser, V. R., & Erman, L. D., "A retrospective view of the Hearsay-II architecture." *Proceedings*, International Joint Conference on Artificial Intelligence, 2, 790–800, 1977.

Longuet-Higgins, H. C., & Prazdny, K., "The interpretation of a moving retinal image." *Proceedings of the Royal Society of London, B 208*, 385–397, 1980.

Mackworth, A. K., "Interpreting pictures of polyhedral scenes." *Artificial Ingelligence, 4*(2), 121–137, 1973.

Marr, D., "Early processing of visual information." *Philosophical Transactions of the Royal Society of London* (Series B), *B 275*, 483–524, 1976.

Marr, D., "Representing visual information." In *Computer Vision Systems* A. R. Hanson & E. M. Riseman, (Eds.), Academic Press: New York, 1978. pp. 61–80.

arr, D., & Hildreth, E., "Theory of edge detection." *Proceedings of the Royal Society of London, B 207*, 187–217, 1980.

Marr, D., & Poggio, T., "A theory of human stereo vision." *Proceedings of the Royal Society of London, B 207*, 301–328, 1979.

Milenkovic, V. J. & Kanade, T. "Trinocular vision using photometric and edge orientation constraints," *Proceedings Defense Advanced Research Projects Agency, Image Understanding Workshop*, Miami, FL, 1985, 163–175.

Minsky, M., & Papert, S., "Artificial Intelligence Progress Report." AI Memo 252, MIT Press: Cambridge, MA, 1972.

Hagel, H.-H., "Displacement vectors derived from second order intensity variations in image sequences." *Computer Vision, Graphics, and Image Processing, 21*, 85–117, 1983a.

Nagel, H.-H., "Overview on image sequence analysis." In *Image Sequence Processing and Dynamic Scene Analysis*, T. S. Huang (Ed.), 1983b. pp. 2–39.

Pentland, A. P., "Finding the illuminant direction," *Optical Society of America, 72*(4), 448–455, April 1982.

Prazdny, K., "On the information in optical flow." *Computer Vision, Graphics, and Image Processing, 22*, 239–259, 1983.

Regan, D., & Beverley, K. I., "Visually guided locomotion: Psychophysical evidence for a neural mechanism sensitive to flow patterns." *Science, 205*, 311–313, 1979.

Richards, W., "Structure from stereo and motion," *Journal of the Optical Society of America*, A2:343–349, 1986.

Rosenfeld, A., Hummel, R., & Zucker, S. W., "Scene labeling by relaxation operations." *IEEE Transactions on Systems, Man and Cybernetics, 6*, 420–433, 1976.

Shirai, Y., "A context-sensitive line finder for recognition of polyhedra." *Artificial Intelligence, 4*, 95–119, 1973.

Stewart, G. W., *Introduction to Matrix Computations*, Academic Press: New York, 1973.

Strat, T. M., "A numerical method for shape from shading from a single image." M.S. thesis, Dept. of Electrical Engineering and Computer Science, MIT Press: Cambridge, MA, 1979.

Sugihara, K., & N. Sugie, "Recovery of rigid structure from orthographically projected optic flow, *Computer Vision, Graphics, and Image Processing, 27*, No. 3, 309–320, Sept. 1984.

Tenenbaum, J. M., & Barrow, H. G., "Experiments in interpretation-guided segmentation." *Artificial Intelligence, 8*(3), 241–274, 1977.

Tsai, R. Y., & Huang, T. S., "Uniqueness and estimation of three dimensional motion parameters of rigid objects with curved surfaces." *IEEE Trans. Pattern Analysis and Machine Intelligence, PAMI-6*, 13–27, January 1984.

Ullman, S., "The interpretation of structure from motion." *Proceedings Royal Society of London*, (Series B), *B 203*, 405–426, 1979a.

Ullman, S., *The Interpretation of Visual Motion*, MIT Press: Cambridge, MA., 1979b.

Waltz, D., "Understanding line drawings of scenes with shadows." In *The Psychology of Computer Vision*, P. H. Winston, (Ed.), McGraw-Hill: New York, 19–91, 1975.

Waxman, A., "Kinematics of image flows," *Proceedings*, Defense Advanced Research Projects Agency Image Understanding Workshop: Arlington, VA, June, 1983.

Waxman, A. M., & Sinha, S., "Dynamic stereo: Passive ranging of moving objects from relative image flows." *Proceedings*, Defense Advanced Research Projects Agency Image Understanding workshop, New Orleans, LA, 130–136, October, 1984.

Webb, J. A., "Shape and structure from motion of objects." Ph.D. thesis, University of Texas at Austin, 1981.

Webb, J. A., & Aggarwal, J. K., "Structure from motion of rigid and jointed objects," *Artificial Intelligence, 19*, 107–130, 1982.

Webb, J. A., & Aggarwal, J. K., "Shape and correspondence." *Computer Vision, Graphics, and Image Processing, 21*, 145–160, 1983.

Winston, P. H., "The MIT Robot." In *Machine Intelligence, 7*, B. Meltzer & D. Michie (Eds.), Edinburgh University Press: Edinburgh, 1972. pp. 431–464.

Woodham, R. M., "Relating properties of surface curvature to image intensity." *Proceedings*, 6th IJCAI, Tokyo, Japan, 971–977, 1979.

IMAGE FLOW THEORY: A FRAMEWORK FOR 3-D INFERENCE FROM TIME-VARYING IMAGERY

ALLEN M. WAXMAN
Boston University

KWANGYOEN WOHN
University of Pennsylvania

A major source of three-dimensional information about objects in the world is available to the observer in the form of time-varying imagery. Relative motion between textured objects and observer generates a time-varying optic array at the image, from which image motion of contours, edge fragments and feature points can be extracted. These dynamic features serve to sample the underlying "image flow" field. We present an overview of our work on image flow theory and its potential for the recovery of three-dimensional surface structure and space motions of rigid objects. Methods for flow recovery and segmentation stem directly from the analytic structure of image flow fields. New, closed-form solutions are given for the structure and motion of planar and curved surface patches from monocular image flow. The relationship between instabilities in the computation and visual illusions are also explored. Finally, the fusion of motion analysis and stereo vision is discussed in the context of "binocular image flows."

BACKGROUND AND OVERVIEW

Motion Psychophysics and Computer Vision

Ever since the pioneering experiments of Wallach and O'Connell (1953), Johannson (1975), and Braunstein (1976, 1983) made clear that an object's three-dimensional (3-D) structure could be revealed through two-dimensional (2-D) image motion, the significance of time-varying imagery in the perceptual process has become well established. The early theories of Gibson (1966, 1979) and Lee (1976, 1980) stressed the importance of "optical flow" (the time-varying optic array) as a source of navigational information, since the time-varying nature of the imagery was generally due to relative motion between the observer and objects in the scene. In fact, image motion reveals not only object structure, but this relative motion as well. Thus, its relevance to manipulation and locomotion, as well as object recognition should be obvious. A recent flurry of psychophysical experiments has illustrated that surface structure is perceived with very limited exposures (two frames) though several (three to five) frames lead to a more robust recovery process (Doner, Lappin, & Perfetto, 1984). And that, in fact, there are a wealth of distinct perceptual cues available in the time-varying domain (Todd, 1985). The phenomenon of dynamic illusions has also raised questions about the nature of the computations that underlie the recovery of "structure from motion" (Hildreth, 1983). Indeed, we shall describe how the realization and suppression of dynamic illusions has provided an important test of our own theory of "image flows."

The "computational approach to vision" championed by David Marr and his collaborators (Marr, 1982) placed motion analysis of time-varying imagery among the other sources of perceptual information (stereo, shading, texture, contour, shadow), which feed the "$2\frac{1}{2}$-D sketch," that viewer-centered depth map of the visual environment. It was in this computational climate that the important work of Ullman (1979) on the human visual system, no doubt inspired many computer visionaries among us to attempt to unravel the time-dependent projective geometry at the foundation of the "structure from motion" phenomenon.

Though our understanding of the mathematical issues associated with time-varying imagery has grown immensely in recent years, the overall problem is by no means solved. Thus, its potential role in machine vision systems has hardly been appreciated. Time-varying image analysis, united with control theory in a visual feed-back loop, paves the way to the interaction between robots and moving objects. This generalizes from parts manipulation and assembly to the visual coordination of multiple robot arms, from mobile platforms and autonomous vehicles to visual docking systems on the ocean surface and in space. Of course, other visual cues of three-dimensional shape are often available, and so motion analysis will ultimately be realized as a single, albeit important module in a complete machine vision system.

It is probably a mistake to think that "structure from motion" has now been liberated from the realm of psychophysics and neurophysiology and delivered solely into the domain of computer vision. Much analysis remains to be done and new formulations need to be explored; their motivations may well lie in the psychophysical arena. At this point in time there is not even general agreement on the basic "observables" that would serve as input to a "structure from motion" computation. The biological existence proof is humbling and should be both respected and exploited. No doubt that psychophysical inquiry can also illuminate the problems of coupling visual motion analysis to control theory for hand-eye coordination in a dynamic environment.

Problems and Approaches

There are various stages in motion analysis, and for each stage a variety of approaches have been adopted. Well, then which approach is utilized by the human visual system? Probably all, and then, probably none! That is to say, humans are, and machines must be, so robust that a variety of approaches are likely to be exploited in the proper instances, and that none of the approaches so far explored seem sufficiently robust to be worthy of the biological role. Perhaps we will have to be somewhat tolerant of our inept robots, if we are ever to teach them to see.

At the earliest stage there is simply motion detection and localization, which may serve to focus the visual attention of the perceptual system on some part of the scene, track the moving object across the field of view and activate a more elaborate motion analysis module. Approaches stem from detection of moving primitives, such as edges (Marr & Ullman, 1981) as well as intensity change in spatial frequency channels (Anderson, Burt, & van der Wal, 1985). Next, the extraction of quantitative measurements of image motion has led to a variety of methods and representations in terms of time-varying intensity (Adelson & Bergen, 1985; Fleet & Jepson, 1985; Horn & Schunck, 1981; Huang, 1983), feature point motions or token correspondences (Longuet-Higgins, 1981; Tsai & Huang, 1981a,b; Ullman, 1979), edge motions or normal flow (Buxton, Murray, & Williams, 1984; Hildreth, 1983; Waxman & Wohn, 1984), velocity fields (Gibson 1966, 1979; Horn & Schunck, 1981; Koenderink & van Doorn, 1975, 1976a; Longuet-Higgins & Prazdny, 1980; Schunck, 1986; Waxman & Ullman, 1983), and deformations (Hay, 1966; Koenderink & van Doorn, 1975, 1976a; Longuet-Higgins & Prazdny, 1980; Regan & Beverley, 1979b, Waxman, 1984; Waxman & Ullman, 1983; Wohn, 1984; Wohn and Waxman, 1986). Segmentation of the flow field has been addressed by Schunck (1984); Hildreth (1983); Waxman (1984); Adiv (1984); Wohn (1984); Wohn and Waxman (1986); and Murray and Buxton (1985). Finally, the recovery of three-dimensional information from these various representations has led to two rather different formulations in terms of either feature motions (Adiv, 1984; Hoffman & Bennet, 1985; Longuet-Higgins, 1981; Prazdny, 1980; Tsai & Huang, 1981a,b; Ullman 1979, 1983) or field variables, such as image velocity and its derivatives, that is, deformations (Kan-atani, 1985; Koenderink & van Doorn, 1975, 1976a; Longuet-Higgins & Prazdny, 1980; Waxman & Ullman, 1983). The uniqueness properties of these three-dimensional interpretations has been discussed in terms of point configurations (Longuet-Higgins, 1981; Tsai & Huang, 1981a), planar surfaces (Hay, 1966; Longuet-Higgins, 1984; Subbarao & Wax-man, 1985; Tsai & Huang, 1981b; Waxman & Ullman, 1983) and curved surface patches (Bandyopadhyay, 1985; Maybank, 1985; Waxman, Kamgar-Parsi & Subbarao, 1986; Waxman & Ullman, 1983).

The preceding analyses all concern monocular image motion. There has been recent interest in combining motion analysis with stereo vision, leading to a variety of binocular motion studies (Jenkin, 1984; Mitiche, 1984; Nagel, 1985; Richards, 1983; Waxman & Duncan, 1985; Waxman & Sinha, 1984). There is, in fact, psychophysical and neurophysiological evidence in support of a human binocular motion module (Regan & Beverley, 1979a). There remain, however, an enormous number of open questions in the area of stereo-motion fusion.

Image Flow Theory

In this chapter we describe the development of our "Image Flow" approach to the analysis of time-varying imagery. It is fundamentally a study of the time-varying projective geometry of physically identifiable features (e.g., texture edges) on surfaces moving through space. By measuring a set of *deformation parameters*, which characterize the relative image motions of these features as derived from a short image sequence, it is possible to recover the local surface structure (slopes and scaled curvatures) and three-dimensional rigid body motions (to scale) of the surface patch relative to the viewer. For nonrigid-body space motions, our flow analysis is still applicable, though the method for three-dimensional inference is not.

An outline of the theory is illustrated in Figure 3.1 (also see Waxman, 1984). A scene consists of several textured objects undergoing independent rigid body motions. The viewer, modeled as a single pinhole camera, records an image sequence under perspective projection. In order to detect the projected motion on the image plane of physical features on the object surfaces, edge detection is performed on each image. Edges must then be tracked over several frames (though points need not be put in correspondence), yielding a set of evolving image contours and edge fragments, which serve to sample the underlying image flow field. (Not all evolving contours are appropriate to include in the analysis, e.g., occluding boundaries and shadow edges. Fortunately our method allows for a consistency check among contours, and so one can discard inap-

STRUCTURE, MOTION & SEGMENTATION

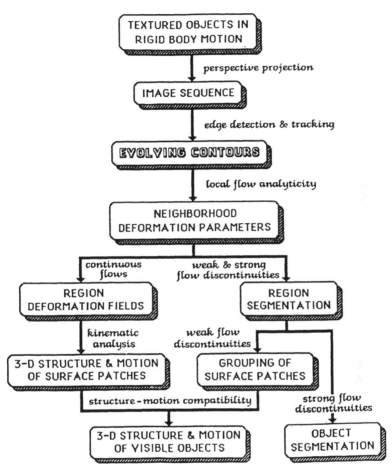

FIGURE 3.1. Steps in the computation which lead to the recovery of 3-D structure, motion, and segmentation from time-varying imagery. The methods of analyses leading from stage to stage are also shown.

propriate data.) In order to recover our representation of the local flow in an image neighborhood, we utilize a local model in the form of a second-order flow. This model is motivated by the projective geometry of the three-dimensional configuration and reflects the analytic structure of the local image flow field. The repreesntation we obtain is in the form of local deformation parameters. These parameters may then be used to

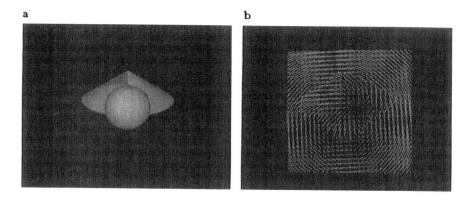

FIGURE 3.2. (a) A scene consisting of a sphere in front of a cone with background at infinity. (b) The image-flow field associated with a general rigid body motion of the camera.

reconstruct the flow fields in image neighborhoods, allowing for the detection of flow discontinuities, and hence, depth and orientation discontinuities. This leads to a segmentation of the flow field (and thereby, the scene). The deformation parameters are also used to recover the three-dimensional structure and rigid body motion of the surface patch that projected onto the corresponding image neighborhood. Of course, these computations should be implemented in parallel over a set of overlapping image neighborhoods. Finally, the separate three-dimensional solutions can be combined for surface patches sharing common three-dimensional rigid body motions and not separated by strong flow discontinuities. Thus, the three-dimensional structure and motion of visible objects, as well as their boundaries, can be recovered from the time-varying imagery.

An example configuration is shown in Figure 3.2 (created with a simulator developed by Sinha & Waxman, 1984). A sphere and cone are placed against a background at infinity in Figure 3.2a. If identifiable feature points were then painted on the entire scene, a moving observer would record a flow field as shown in Figure 3.2b. Actually, the observer would note the image space–time orbits of the feature points across the image sequence, from which instantaneous image velocities could then be derived. Note how the flow field varies smoothly where the surfaces are smooth, and how it exhibits discontinuities where the surface structures also jump. It should be clear that time-varying imagery is a rich source of three-dimensional information, for both humans and machines.

Organization of the Chapter

In this chapter, we describe in greater detail our ongoing investigation into image flows. First, we deal with the analytic structure of image flow fields, describing the local structure in terms of *deformations* and their global structure in terms of *boundaries of analyticity*. Our approach to flow recovery and segmentation follows. Then, the recovery of three-dimensional structure and motion is detailed; we give new closed-form solutions for both planar and curved surface patches. The next topic discussed is concerned with dynamic illusions and how they may manifest themselves as instabilities in our mathematical theory. We also outline our recent work on binocular image flows—an attempt to combine stereo vision and motion analysis into a new vision module. Finally, this chapter concludes with a description of future directions of investigation.

THE STRUCTURE OF IMAGE FLOWS

We shall first derive the relations between image velocity and three-dimensional structure and motion. This will expose the analytic structure of image flows. In a local neighborhood, we find it sufficient to model the flow in terms of second-order polynomials, the coefficients of which characterize *local deformations*. Moving from neighborhood to neighborhood in the image, the flow is realized as a slowly varying (in terms of image coordinates) vector field, forming an *analytic region*. Separate regions are divided by *boundaries of analyticity*, contours across which the second-order flow model does not hold. This description pertains to the instantaneous image flow field. However, the entire flow evolves over time in a coherent way, i.e., it is temporally analytic as well.

Image Velocity Relations

Our derivation follows that of Longuet-Higgins and Prazdny (1980) and Waxman and Ullman (1983). For each independent object in the scene we consider the equivalent problem of a stationary object and a moving, monocular observer represented by the spatial coordinate system (X, Y, Z) in Figure 3.3. The origin of this system is located at the vertex of perspective projection, and the Z-axis is directed along the center of the instantaneous field of view. The instantaneous rigid body motion of this coordinate system is specified by the translational and rotational velocities of its origin, V and Ω, respectively. The two-dimensional image sequence is created by the perspective projection of the object onto a

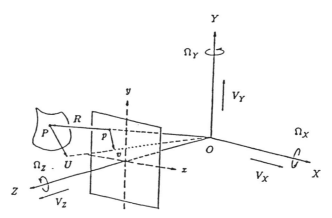

FIGURE 3.3. Spatial coordinate system (X, Y, Z) and image coordinates (x, y) in motion relative to a surface patch.

planar screen whose origin $(x, y) = (0, 0)$ is located in space at $(X, Y, Z) = (0, 0, 1)$; that is, the image is reinverted and scaled to a focal length of unity.

Due to the observer's motion, a point P in space (located by position vector $\mathbf{R}$) moves with relative velocity $\mathbf{U} = -(\mathbf{V} + \mathbf{\Omega} \times \mathbf{R})$. At each instant, point P projects onto the image at point p with coordinates $(x, y) = (X/Z, Y/Z)$. The corresponding image velocities are $(v_x, v_y) = (\dot{x}, \dot{y})$, obtained by differentiating the image coordinates with respect to time and utilizing the components of $\mathbf{U}$ for the time derivatives of the spatial coordinates. Thus, the image velocities are the projectives of spatial velocities of points in space. We find

$$v_x = \left[x\frac{V_Z}{Z} - \frac{V_X}{Z} \right] + [xy\Omega_X - (1 + x^2)\Omega_Y + y\Omega_Z] \tag{1a}$$

$$v_y = \left[y\frac{V_Z}{Z} - \frac{V_Y}{Z} \right] + [(1 + y^2)\Omega_X - xy\Omega_Y - x\Omega_Z]. \tag{1b}$$

These equations define an instantaneous image flow field, assigning a unique two-dimensional image velocity $\mathbf{v}$ to each direction (x, y) in the observer's field of view. For different objects with different space motions, the parameters describing the observer's relative space motion in Equation 1 are obviously different. Thus, changes in space motions will cause discontinuities in the image flow field. The shape of an object influences the image flow through the depth Z in Equations 1a+b. Conversely, we see that image flow reveals object shape only in the presence of a translation through space. Pure rotation of the observer yields no shape information. Moreover, discontinuities in depth or orientation give rise to discontinuities in the image flow or its first derivatives, respectively. Where depth varies smoothly, e.g., over a smooth surface, the flow is differentiable.

When describing whole visible surfaces in terms of surface patches, we shall find that it is sufficient to consider a local quadric approximation to a surface patch in the vicinity of the line of sight. (Surface patches not in the center of the field of view may be handled this way as well by utilizing a gaze transformation—this is discussed later in the chapter.) Consider first the planar surface patch. It can be described exactly in both spatial and image coordinate systems;

$$Z = Z_0 + pX + qY, \tag{2a}$$

$$Z^{-1} = Z_0^{-1}(1 - px - qy), \tag{2b}$$

where p and q are the slopes of the plane, that is, the plane's normal lies in the direction $(p, q, -1)$. The local quadric patch, given in spatial coordinates by

$$Z = Z_0 + pX + qY + \tfrac{1}{2}C_{XX}X^2 + \tfrac{1}{2}C_{YY}Y^2 + C_{XY}XY, \tag{3a}$$

may be *approximated* in image coordinates by

$$Z^{-1} = Z_0^{-1}(1 - px - qy - \tfrac{1}{2}k_{xx}x^2 - \tfrac{1}{2}k_{yy}y^2 - k_{xy}xy) + 0(x^3), \tag{3b}$$

with normalized curvatures defined by

$$(k_{xx}, k_{yy}, k_{xy}) \equiv Z_0(C_{XX}, C_{YY}, C_{XY}). \tag{3c}$$

We see from Equations 2 and 3 that local surface shape is characterized by a scale factor Z_0, the depth to the surface along the line of sight. From Equation 1 it is clear that this scale factor cannot be recovered from monocular flows as it always appears in ratio with the translational velocity. Thus, the translation will always be determined only up to a scale factor, V/Z_0; an obvious consequence of the projective geometry. A somewhat less obvious fact is that surface curvatures are *multiplied* by this scale factor when entering the flow equations, hence, curvature affects *grow* as distance to an object *increases;* (consider sailing over a flat Earth versus orbiting around a globe).

Second-Order Flows and Deformations

Equations 2b and 3b may be substituted directly into the velocity relations (Equation 1), and terms collected into ascending powers of x and y. In this manner, we recover the Taylor series of the image flow about the image origin. In the case of the planar patch (2b), we find the flow (1) to be given exactly by second-order polynomials in the image coordinates. For planes, the second-order flow model is globally valid since all higher-order Taylor coefficients vanish. For curved patches, Equation 3b is approximate and so a second-order flow model is only locally valid in this case. However, surface curvatures already influence the flow at second-order. This leads us to believe that *the second-order flow is the most fundamental image flow field*. It is exact for planes and locally valid for quadric patches. It also makes explicit the fact that curved patches should not be approximated by planar facets, unless the local radii of curvature are large compared to object distance.

Though the second-order flow model emerges from Equation 1, which was based on rigid body motions, it is not inappropriate to use the same flow model for nonrigid space motions; it merely expresses the local analytic structure of the flow. Of course the method for three-dimensional inference to be presented in the section will not suffice for nonrigid body motions. This is an important point because the method we will use for recovering the second-order flow model from evolving contours is then perfectly applicable to nonrigid as well as rigid body motions. Clearly, this generality would be important to the human visual system if flow recovery is a necessary precursor to three-dimensional inference.

Returning to the second-order polynomials that emerge from combining Equation 1 with Equations 2b or 3b, we note that the coefficients of the terms are related to the various partial derivatives of the image flow. Moreover, these coefficients are given in terms of the three-dimensional structure and motion parameters. Thus, the three-dimensional information is contained in the derivatives of the image flow through second order (Koenderink & van Doorn 1975, 1976a; Longuet-Higgins & Prazdny, 1980; Waxman & Ullman, 1983). We will consider these *kinematic relations* and their solutions in the following section.

We express the second-order flow approximation to the instantaneous, local image velocity field in the following way,

$$v(x, y) = \sum_{i=0}^{2} \sum_{j=0}^{2} v^{(i,j)} \frac{x^i}{i!} \frac{y^j}{j!} \qquad (4a)$$
$$(i + j \leq 2)$$

where

$$\mathbf{v}^{(i,j)} \equiv \frac{\partial^{i+j} \mathbf{v}}{\partial x^i \partial y^j} \bigg|_0 ; \qquad (4b)$$

partial derivatives (i.e., the Taylor coefficients) being evaluated at the image origin. Expression 4a represents the local flow in terms of 12 parameters, the six undetermined coefficients in each of the two poly-nomials. These coefficients will be determined from the data extracted from an image sequence. However, we wish to interpret these coeffi-cients in a geometric manner.

Expression 4a can be thought of as a (non-affine) mapping of the geometry of an image over time. This rearrangement of image features can be thought of as a sampling of the deformation going on in an image neighborhood. Consider Figure 3.4a in which an ellipse, parabola, and square grid evolve to the deformed state shown in Figure 3.4d. This geometric pattern was projected onto the image plane from a curved surface moving rigidly in space. Had only the ellipse and parabola been shown, their shape changes could have been summarized by the "normal flow" shown in Figure 3.4b; that is, only their displacements *perpendicular to the contours* could have been measured. (We will return to this "aper-ture problem" in the next section.) The point is that these contour mo-tions were merely sampling the complete underlying flow field, shown in

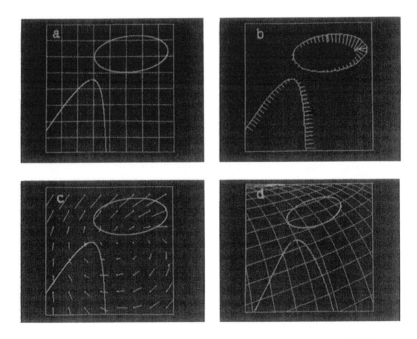

FIGURE 3.4. Contour deformation and image flow due to general rigid body motion of a quadric surface patch. (a) Contours embedded in a grid before the motion. (b) Normal flow along the contours. (c) Full flow in the neighborhood. (d) Deformed contours after a short interval; the grid ex-periences the same deformation.

Figure 3.4c, which manifests itself in the deformation of the entire grid and, hence, the whole neighborhood. (This is reminiscent of D'Arcy Thompson's [1917] transformational theory of morphogenesis.) It is well known in the continuum mechanics literature (e.g., Aris, 1962) that these neighborhood deformations can be interpreted via simple linear combinations of the Taylor coefficients of the velocity field, i.e., the coefficients of Expression 4a. These notions were applied to the image velocity field by Hay (1966), Koendrink and van Doorn (1975, 1976a), Longuet-Higgins and Prazdny (1980), Waxman and Ullman (1983), Wohn (1984), and Wohn and Waxman (1986).

The zeroth order terms in Equation 4a correspond to a uniform translation of the image pattern, no actual deformations of the pattern are induced. The first order terms correspond to an affine transformation and may be interpreted in the context of the Cauchy-Stokes Decomposition theorem (Aris, 1962). We form the image velocity-gradient tensor and decompose it into the sum of symmetric and antisymmetric parts. The elements of the symmetric rate-of strain tensor are given by

$$e_{xx} = v_x^{(1,0)}, \; e_{yy} = v_y^{(0,1)}, \tag{5a,b}$$

$$e_{xy} = e_{yx} = \tfrac{1}{2}\big[v_y^{(1,0)} + v_x^{(0,1)}\big]; \tag{5c}$$

the nonzero elements of the antisymmetric spin tensor are.

$$\omega_{yx} = -\omega_{xy} = \omega = \tfrac{1}{2}\big[v_y^{(1,0)} - v_x^{(0,1)}\big]. \tag{5d}$$

In this decomposition, e_{xx} corresponds to the rate-of-stretch of a differential-image line oriented along the x-axis, e_{yy} to the rate-of-stretch along the y-axis, e_{xy} to the rate-of-change of the angle between two line segments along the image axes, and ω to the rate-of-rotation (i.e., the spin) of the differential neighborhood of the image about the origin. Alternatively, one may consider the eigenvalues and eigenvectors of the rate-of-strain tensor (Koenderink & van Doorn, 1975, 1976a); whence, one finds that a circular neighborhood dilates according to the sum of the eigenvalues (equivalent to the trace $e_{xx} + e_{yy}$), undergoes a stretch and compression at constant area according to the difference of the eigenvalues (along mutually perpendicular axes aligned with the eigenvectors of the rate-of-strain) thereby deforming into an ellipse, and then rotates as a locally rigid area element according to the spin ω.

The second-order terms in Equation 4a correspond to the non-affine part of the image mapping; they are important in small but finite image neighborhoods. From Equation 4 we see that they correspond to the six independent second derivatives of the image-velocity field. Alternatively, we may adopt six independent first derivatives of the rate-of-strain and spin. Waxman and Ullman (1983) adopted the following six: $e_{xx,x} \equiv$

$\delta e_{xx}/\delta x$, $e_{xx,y}$, $e_{yy,x}$, $e_{yy,y}$, $\omega_{,x}$ and $\omega_{,y}$. These quantities represent the linear variation of the first-order deformation over a small but finite neighborhood. Wohn (1984) has argued that, on the basis of symmetry, one should replace the second-order terms $e_{xx,y}$ and $e_{yy,x}$ with the alternative terms $e_{xy,x}$ and $e_{xy,y}$. The symmetry becomes clear by noting that

$$\omega_{,x} = \tfrac{1}{2}\left[v_y^{(2,0)} - v_x^{(1,1)}\right], \tag{6a}$$

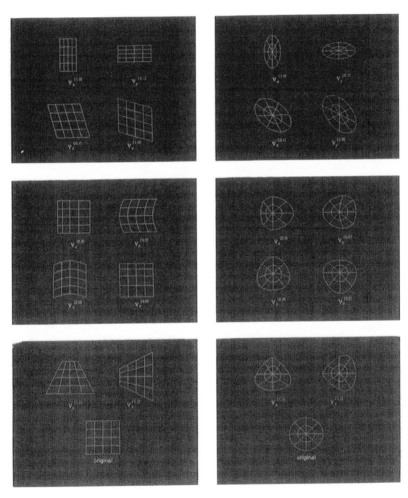

FIGURE 3.5. The class of deformations (through second-order) due to the Taylor coefficients. Left side illustrates deformations of a square neighborhood, right side for a circular neighborhood.

$$e_{xy,x} = \tfrac{1}{2}\big[v_y^{(2,0)} + v_x^{(1,1)}\big], \tag{6b}$$

$$\omega_{,y} = \tfrac{1}{2}\big[v_y^{(1,1)} - v_x^{(0,2)}\big], \tag{6c}$$

$$e_{xy,y} = \tfrac{1}{2}\big[v_y^{(1,1)} + v_x^{(0,2)}\big]. \tag{6d}$$

This symmetry among the second-order terms is not present in the ones adopted by Waxman and Ullman (1983).

Whether one adopts the original 12 Taylor coefficients, or the param-

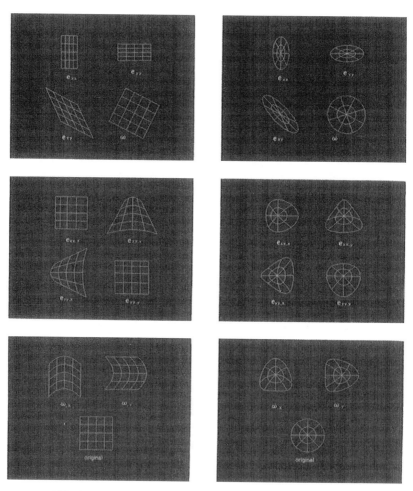

FIGURE 3.6. The class of deformations used in the original formulation of Waxman and Ullman (1983).

eters of Waxman and Ullman, or Wohn's symmetrized parameters, these *deformation parameters* may be thought of as forming a finite basis. Any local (i.e., second-order) flow field can then be decomposed into a set of 12 primitive deformations described by any one of these basis sets. (The kinematic relations in a later section will relate these basis elements to the three-dimensional shape and motion parameters.) We can visualize the deformation induced by the individual elements of each of these three bases by considering the second-order mapping induced by any

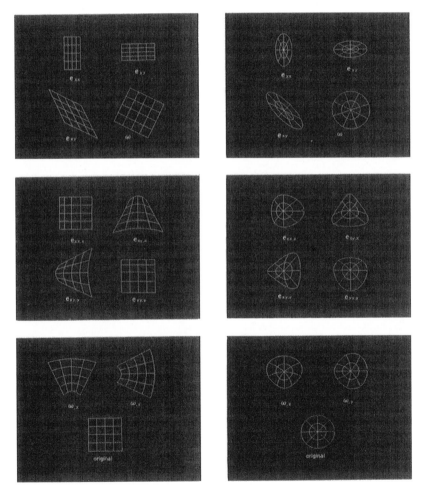

FIGURE 3.7. The class of deformations generated by Wohn's symmetrized parameters.

one element of a particular basis for which all other elements in that basis are zero. This is illustrated in Figures 3.5, 3.6, and 3.7 for both square and circular neighborhoods (the zeroth-order deformation, a translation, is not shown). The first- and second-order Taylor coefficients are shown in Figure 3.5, the deformation parameters of Waxman and Ullman in Figure 3.6, and the symmetrized deformations of Wohn in Figure 3.7.

From the point of view of visual perception, we may wonder if there is in fact a preferred basis of deformations. Are geometric deformations a more fundamental description than flow fields for the perceptual system? Sensitivity to the first-order deformations has been speculated upon by Koenderink and van Doorn (1975, 1976a) and Longuet-Higgins and Prazdny (1980). Evidence for their role in human visual perception has been put forth by Regan and Beverley (1979b, 1985). We then question whether the human visual system is sensitive to the second-order deformations, and if so, is there a preferred basis that may manifest itself in neural wetware?

Global Velocity Fields

The previous section described the image-flow field in a small neighborhood in terms of second-order polynomials; hence, second-order differentiability is insured. This will be valid in most neighborhoods of the velocity image. If we consider overlapping neighborhoods, inside each of which the flow is modeled as locally second-order, we will arrive at a global decomposition of a flow in the form shown in Figure 3.8. Individual neighborhoods are analytic in the sense of being twice differentiable. These neighborhoods are "continued" into analytic regions comprised of slowly varying (in the spatial sense) second-order flow fields. These analytic regions are then bounded by contours along which either the flow or its first derivatives are discontinuous (hence, its first or second derivatives are infinite, respectively). That is, the second-order flow approximation breaks down at these "boundaries of analyticity," which in turn, suggests a way of detecting them. As was noted following Equations 1, these discontinuities reflect important information about the three-dimensional structure of the scene, corresponding to jumps in space motion, depth, or surface orientation. Such discontinuities are apparent in the flow field of Figure 3.2b.

We summarize this section by stressing the importance of the analytic structure of image flow fields. Locally, a second-order flow model is necessary to describe the instantaneous image motion induced by a surface patch in space. This flow can be thought of as a set of deformations through second order, specified by twelve parameters. Globally, we think

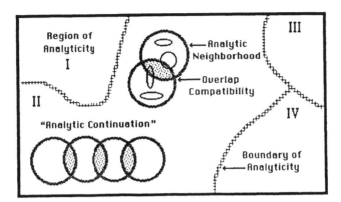

FIGURE 3.8. Partitioning of the velocity image into analytic flow regions separated by boundaries of analyticity. Analytic regions are comprised of overlapping neighborhoods in which the flow field is locally second-order.

of analytic flow regions and their boundaries of analyticity. As time progresses, both the local deformations and the boundaries of analyticity will generally evolve in a continuous fashion. That is, the temporal behavior of the flow will be analytic as well. Discontinuities in the temporal structure will be perceived as "events." The extension of the second-order flow model, Equation 4, to time-varying image flows are made explicit in the following section.

FLOW RECOVERY AND SEGMENTATION

Evolving Contours

Our approach to the recovery and segmentation of image flows begins with the detection and tracking of image features such as edge fragments and extended contours. In the first section of this chapter, we noted many studies that extract flow estimates directly from time-varying intensity. However, it is questionable under what circumstances such flow measurements actually reflect the mapping derived from the time-varying projective geometry (cf. Schunck, 1986). Insofar as edge features can be accurately localized and tracked from frame to frame, and *correspond to physically identifiable surface features* (e.g., texture boundaries or surface markings), geometrically useful flow measurements can be made. Of course, not all image contours correspond to physical surface events, (e.g., shadow, extremal and occluding boundaries). Fortunately, our method of recovering full flow fields has the potential to detect these

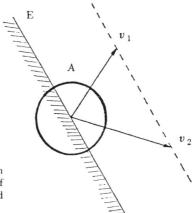

FIGURE 3.9. The "aperture problem in the small": Only the normal component of image motion of edge E can be determined by viewing E locally through aperture A.

inappropriate contours, as their motions are not consistent with the majority of surface markings in the context of a locally second-order flow.

Referring back to Figure 3.4, we recall that moving features such as contours serve to sample the underlying flow field in a neighborhood. That is, contour evolution is a manifestation of neighborhood deformation. We will establish under what conditions a contour or set of edges sufficiently samples a flow field in order that a local second-order flow model can be recovered. This, however, is a question in the "large" dealing with a local flow field and extended contours. We must realize that, in the "small," a moving edge fragment allows an estimate only of the component of flow perpendicular to the edge, our so-called "normal flow." Since correspondence between individual points along an edge cannot be established from frame to frame, the component of motion tangent to contours remains undetected. This is the well known "aperture problem" (Marr, 1982; Marr & Ullman, 1981) illustrated in Figure 3.9 (after Marr & Ullman, 1981, Figure 1). However, we call it the "aperture problem in the small" as it refers to a local indeterminacy. Later, we shall discuss a nonlocal indeterminacy due to insufficient structure of extended contours or edge distributions; it will be called the "aperture problem in the large." Such local aperture problems arise in the intensity-based approach as well (Horn & Schunck, 1981; Schunck, 1984).

Extracting Normal Flow

There are a variety of edge-detection techniques that can be used to extract contours and edge fragments from each frame in an image sequence (e.g., Canny, 1983; Marr & Hildreth, 1980). It can be argued that a temporal averaging of the intensity signal should be incorporated directly into the edge detection procedure (Buxton & Buxton, 1983). In any case, this procedure must be computationally inexpensive as it must be applied to each successive frame in a sequence.

Figure 3.10 illustrates a contour tracked from time t_0 to time $t_0 + \delta t$. An estimate of the normal flow at point P can be obtained from the measured displacement between contours along a line perpendicular to the contour at t_0. The ratio of measured normal displacement to time interval δt provides an estimate of normal flow to an accuracy of $0(\delta t)$. The error of $0(\delta t)$ can be related to the existence of the tangential component of image motion as well as to the finite difference approximation to the temporal derivative. By utilizing three frames at times $t_0, t_0 \pm \delta t$, one can modify this simple approach to use a time-centered difference in order to achieve an accuracy of $0(\delta t^2)$. It is simply an average of the normal velocities determined between $t_0 \to t_0 + \delta t$ and $t_0 \to t_0 - \delta t$. A further refinement can be achieved by utilizing five frames at times $t_0, t_0 \pm \delta t, t_0 \pm 2\delta t$. These five frames can be viewed as two sets of three frames measured on two timescales $(t_0, t_0 \pm \delta t)$ and $(t_0, t_0 \pm 2\delta t)$. Each set provides a time-centered difference estimate, but on different timescales. This allows us to assess the magnitude of the $0(\delta t^2)$ error and effectively extrapolate $\delta t \to 0$, providing a more accurate estimate of *normal velocity* from *normal displacement*. This philosophy is known as "Richardsonian extrapolation" in the numerical-analysis literature (Acton, 1970). Its performance with regard to normal flow estimation is currently under study.

The point of this discussion is that *multiple frames can, in principle, be used to obtain more accurate estimates of instantaneous normal flow along a contour.* We will have another opportunity to exploit multiple frames when we consider time-varying second-order flow models. These models will allow us to determine the *instantaneous three-dimensional structure and motion* more robustly.

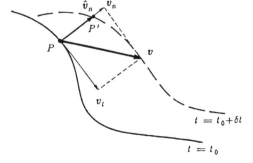

FIGURE 3.10. Normal flow can be estimated to $0(\delta t)$ using two frames and $0(\delta t^2)$ using three frames. Normal flow cannot be obtained exactly due to both tangential flow and discrete time sampling.

Velocity Functional Method

Our method for recovering the local image flow in a neighborhood utilizes the normal flow measured along contours and edge fragments. We simply require that our instantaneous normal flow measurements be consistent with a local second-order flow model of the form (Equation 4a); consistency can be imposed in the "least-squares" sense. This approach can be thought of as an analytic statement of coherence among sampled image velocities, we call it the "Velocity Functional Method" (Waxman & Wohn, 1984). It should be compared with the rater heuristic formulations of smooth velocity fields given by Horn and Schunck (1981) and Hildreth (1983). In the context of surfaces moving rigidly through space, the implicit assumption underlying the second-order flow model is that the sampled image velocities constituting an image neighborhood arise from the projection of a quadric surface patch. Surfaces with more geometric structure must be subdivided into simpler patches, and their corresponding image neighborhoods must possess sufficient texture to recover the second-order flow approximation in a robust manner. This, we feel, is the principle limitation of our approach!

Given measurements of normal flow along contours, $v_n(x, y)$, and the measured unit normal along contours $\mathbf{n}(x, y) = (n_x, n_y)$, we require that the data satisfy $v_n = \mathbf{n} \cdot \mathbf{v}$ in the least-squares sense. From Equation 4a,

$$v_n(x, y) = \sum_{\substack{i = 0 \\ (i+j \leq 2)}}^{2} \sum_{j = 0}^{2} \frac{x^i}{i!} \frac{y^j}{j!} [n_x(x, y) v_x^{(i,j)} + n_y(x, y) v_y^{(i,j)}] \tag{7}$$

provides one linear constraint (for each datum) among the 12 unknowns $v^{(i,j)}$. In principle, 12 normal flow measurements are the minimum required to determine the local second-order flow field. In practice, it is better to use many (perhaps hundreds of) measurements along a single or multiple contours in a neighborhood. Our approach can be described as a constrained minimization problem, the constraint being posed as a velocity functional, the second-order flow model.

Consistency of the data with Expression 7 provides us with a solution to the "aperture problem in the small." An example of flow recovery from synthetic data along a set of simple contours is shown in Figure 3.11. Given ideal data generated by a planar surface in motion, our methods gives the exact Taylor coefficients and hence, the exact flow field, since second-order flows are globally valid for planes. For a curved surface in motion, the recovered flow is subject to series truncation error even for ideal data; (recall curved surfaces generate flow fields in the form of infinite series). Generally, this error is a function of surface

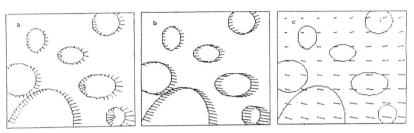

FIGURE 3.11. Multiple biquadratic contours on the image. (a) Normal flow along contours is the input. (b) Full flow along contours can be evaluated from the result. (c) Full flow in the neighborhood is recovered by the Velocity Functional Method.

curvature and angular extent of the neighborhood (Wohn & Waxman, 1985). However, it is usually dominated by noisy flow estimates.

In addition to the polynomial coefficients, our method provides a measure of "goodness of fit" between the data and the model in the form of the least-squares residual. Individual data points can then be assessed in light of this residual. In this manner, normal flow measurements, which are significant outliers from the determined model, can be removed from the sample and a new second-order flow model derived. Thus, the second-order flow model provides a means to sort the flow data, allowing removal of "incoherent data" such as that due to inappropriate contours (e.g., shadow and occluding boundaries).

We have tested the performance of our approach on synthetic data with multiplicative noise up to 30% for image neighborhoods ranging in extent from 5° to 40°. In all cases, the flow velocities are recovered to 5% or better and this is true of the first derivatives as well (Waxman & Wohn, 1984; Wohn & Waxman, 1985). However, the second derivatives are rather sensitive to noise, and they are required for the three-dimensional inference process. The sensitivity of the three-dimensional solution will be discussed in a later section.

Aperture Problem in the Large

The least-squares solution for the second-order flow based on constraint (Equation 7) leads to a set of 12 linear algebraic equations for the unknown derivatives $\mathbf{v}^{(i,j)}$. Solution of this system requires the corresponding coefficient matrix to have a rank of 12, otherwise the second-order model remains undetermined. We have shown that rank deficiency is associated with insufficient contour structure (Waxman & Wohn, 1984). That is, if the normal flow to contours and edge fragments does not sample sufficient variation in the underlying flow (due to the shape of contours), the flow cannot be recovered. We have called this indeterminacy the "aperture problem in the large" as it deals with extended contours or edge distributions, in contrast to the "aperture problem in the small," which occurs on a differential segment of contour.

An obvious example of this aperture problem occurs with a circular contour. Clearly, any spin of the circle about its center is undetected and cannot be recovered. In fact, any bi-quadratic contour (i.e., conic section) alone is insufficient to determine the second-order flow model. We have shown that the minimum structure required of a contour, in order that a rank of 12 be obtained, is that the contour's shape be described by a bi-quartic relation. An example of such a contour is illustrated in Figure 3.12.

In the case of known planar surfaces in motion, the flow field is exactly second-order, with only eight independent coefficients. That is, the exact flow satisfies the four conditions $v_x^{(0,2)} = v_y^{(2,0)} = 0$, $v_x^{(2,0)} = 2v_y^{(1,1)}$, $v_y^{(0,2)} = 2v_x^{(1,1)}$. In the solution for the flow we can impose these as additional constraints to be satisfied in the least-squares sense. Thus, even for known planar surfaces, we seek a rank of 12. Experiments with synthetic data lead to the following rank results for various contours:

contour type	rank (general)	rank (planar)
bi-quadratic	9	11
bi-cubic	11	12
bi-quartic	12	12
1 line segment	5	8
2 lines (nonparallel)	10	12
3 lines (nonparallel)	12	12

For linear segments we have not used the additional information associated with tracking their endpoints, only normal flow has been used.

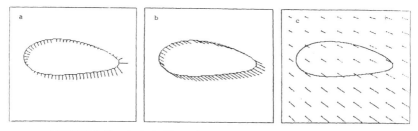

FIGURE 3.12. A single biquartic contour is the minimum structure required to recover a second-order flow model; it just overcomes the "aperture problem in the large."

Results for linear segments are particularly relevant to planar surfaces such as landing platforms at sea or in space, with polygonal boundaries. Such boundaries will generate admissable image contours as they correlate with physically identifiable surface features.

All of our experimental results on rank deficiency have been confirmed by an alternative analysis we call the "Contour Functional Method" (Waxman & Wohn, 1984; Wohn, 1984). The basic idea is that, given a contour of specified shape, a moment later it will be mapped, via a second-order flow, to a new contour of a predictable functional form. The coefficients of this functional are related to the Taylor coefficients $\mathbf{v}^{(i,j)}$. In order to obtain 12 independent coefficients for the evolved contour functional and so determine the second-order flow model, it is necessary to begin with a contour of at least bi-quartic structure.

Real images do not generally give rise to contours of simple shape, and moreover, the high-frequency components of contour structure are not very reliable. Our approach to flow recovery demonstrates that *the information necessary to reconstruct image flow fields is contained in the low-frequency components of contour shape.* It is only necessary to learn how to extract this information from real images.

Time-Varying Flow Fields

The second-order flow model of Expression 4a is meant to represent the instantaneous local image flow. As time passes, this flow will generally vary due to changes of surface geometry imparted by motion, as well as changes in the motion parameters themselves, though at each instant it will be second-order in image coordinates. This suggests that we allow the 12 Taylor coefficients $\mathbf{v}^{(i,j)}$ to vary linearly in time over a short image sequence. Hence, we generalize our flow model of Equation 4a to the form

$$\mathbf{v}(x, y, t) = \sum_{\substack{i=0 \\ (i+j \leq 2)}}^{2} \sum_{j=0}^{2} \sum_{k=0}^{1} \mathbf{v}^{(i,j,k)} \frac{x^i}{i!} \frac{y^j}{j!} \frac{t^k}{k!} \tag{8a}$$

where we now have 24 coefficients $\mathbf{v}^{(i,j,k)}$ to determime. We can utilize Expression 8a in the Velocity Functional Method, where the measured unit normal along contours is now time-varying as well, $\mathbf{n}(x, y, t)$. The time-varying normal flow measurements are constrained, in the least-squares sense, to satisfy

$$v_n(x, y, t) = \sum_{\substack{i=0 \\ (i+j \leq 2)}}^{2} \sum_{j=0}^{2} \sum_{k=0}^{1} \frac{x^i}{i!} \frac{y^j}{j!} \frac{t^k}{k!} [n_x(x, y, t) v_x^{(i,j,k)} + n_y(x, y, t) v_y^{(i,j,k)}]. \tag{8b}$$

Utilizing normal flow measurements over multiple frames will lead to a more robust determination of the second-order flow at any given instant, and hence, the instantaneous three-dimensional structure and motion. This is another way that temporal coherence can be exploited in the image domain.

Flow Segmentation

A number of investigators have addressed the problem of detecting and localizing discontinuities in image velocity. Hildreth (1983) has argued in favor of using the normal flow directly, though it is necessary to consider data falling into different orientations. Schunck (1984) utilized an iterative procedure consisting of velocity-field smoothing and "edge detection" in the separate components of velocity. Adiv (1984) has considered a grouping approach of a similar spirit to our own method. Motion vectors (derived from feature tracking) are grouped based on their consistency with a linear velocity field (whose parameters are determined by

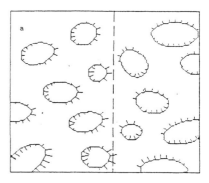

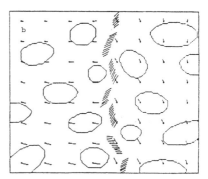

FIGURE 3.13. Two planar surfaces with a motion and depth discontinuity. (a) Input normal flows; dashed line indicates exact discontinuity (b) Recovered flow fields and strong discontinuity (hatch marks)

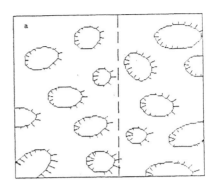

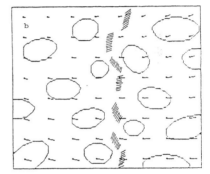

FIGURE 3.14. Segmentation of two planar surfaces with an orientation discontinuity moving as a rigid body (i.e., a dihedral angle).

a Hough voting procedure). These small groupings are further clustered based on compatibility with a flow field created by a planar surface patch (which is a special case of our general second-order flow). Murray and Buxton (1985) have considered the simultaneous segmentation and three-dimensional inference problem using methods from stochastic optimization.

Our approach to flow recovery gives rise to a natural means of segmenting image flow fields. Segmentation boundaries constitute the boundaries of analytic regions shown in Figure 3.8. They are contours across which the second-order flow model breaks down. Thus, if one attempts to impose the second-order flow model in neighborhoods and can detect its failure (say, through an unusually high residual), then the presence of segmentation boundaries can be detected.

As shown in Figure 3.8, analytic regions are decomposed into *overlapping neighborhoods*. Within each neighborhood we determine a second-order flow model and its corresponding residual per unit area (i.e., per data point). Within the overlap region, the flows determined by each neighborhood's second-order model should be compatible, that is, they

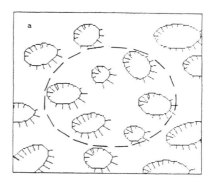

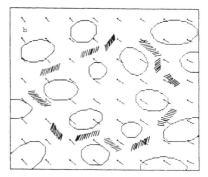

FIGURE 3.15. Segmentation of a bump on a plane moving as a rigid body.

should agree to the extent that the individual models agree with the data based on the residuals. Where they do not agree, a boundary is expected. In the image domain, boundaries cannot be localized to a degree finer than existing edge density permits.

Boundaries of analyticity delineate contours along which either image velocity exhibits a jump (a "strong" discontinuity) or the first derivatives of velocity jump (a "weak" discontinuity). Our approach is able to detect both kinds of discontinuities in the presence of 10% noise or more. When the noise becomes excessive (20% or so), it can mask the presence of a segmentation boundary because the residual measures can become large everywhere. Three examples of flow segmentation are illustrated in Figures 3.13, 3.14, and 3.15. Preliminary studies on real imagery (a scene of boxes with dots) have shown some promising results (Waxman & Duncan, 1985), but much work remains to be done to obtain a robust algorithm.

THREE-DIMENSIONAL INFERENCE

Kinematic Relations

The three-dimensional inference process attempts to recover the surface structure and space motion parameters of objects in the scene from the image velocity field. The relation between three-dimensional structure and motion, and image motion for *rigid bodies* is embodied in Equations 1a–b. Our approach addresses this problem in the context of small surface patches that project onto neighborhoods in the image domain, within which the second-order flow model is valid. (It is assumed at this point that flow recovery and segmentation has already been completed.) Thus, we first seek the *kinematic relations* between local surface structure, space motions, and the deformations parameters derived from the coefficients of the second-order flow model.

The kinetmatic relations for the deformations are obtained from linear combinations of the Taylor series coefficients, through second-order, of the image velocity relations (see Equation 1). These coefficients are easily obtained for a surface patch centered about the line of sight $(x, y) = (0, 0)$ by substituting Equation 3b into Equation 1 and collecting terms into ascending powers of x and y. For image neighborhoods that are not centered about the image origin, the local second-order flow can be easily transformed to the center of a new image plane coordinate system by a specified three-dimensional rotation about the vertex of perspective projection. This "gaze transformation" then maps a noncentered surface patch to an equivalent centered surface-patch problem (Waxman, 1984). (Alternatively, we could have chosen a hemispherical projection screen.) Such a transformation for a static image is a two-dimensional projective form, a *perspection* followed by a *section* (Winger, 1962). Its extension to image velocities and deformations is being utilized in the context of global three-dimensional solutions by Subbarao (1986). Thus, we need only consider the "centered-patch" problem.

We utilize the 12 deformation parameters of Waxman and Ullman evaluated at the origin, and adopt the following notation:

$$D_1 \equiv v_x^{(0,0)} \tag{9a}$$

$$D_2 \equiv v_y^{(0,0)} \tag{9b}$$

$$D_3 \equiv e_{xx} = v_x^{(1,0)} \tag{9c}$$

$$D_4 \equiv e_{yy} = v_y^{(0,1)} \tag{9d}$$

$$D_5 \equiv e_{xy} = \tfrac{1}{2}\left[v_y^{(1,0)} + v_x^{(0,1)}\right] \tag{9e}$$

$$D_6 \equiv \omega = \tfrac{1}{2}\!\left[v_y^{(1,0)} - v_x^{(0,1)}\right] \tag{9f}$$

$$D_7 \equiv e_{xx,x} = v_x^{(2,0)} \tag{9g}$$

$$D_8 \equiv e_{xx,y} = v_x^{(1,1)} \tag{9h}$$

$$D_9 \equiv e_{yy,x} = v_y^{(1,1)} \tag{9i}$$

$$D_{10} \equiv e_{yy,y} = v_y^{(0,2)} \tag{9j}$$

$$D_{11} \equiv \omega_{,x} = \tfrac{1}{2}\!\left[v_y^{(2,0)} - v_x^{(1,1)}\right] \tag{9k}$$

$$D_{12} \equiv \omega_{,y} = \tfrac{1}{2}\!\left[v_y^{(1,1)} - v_x^{(0,2)}\right]. \tag{9l}$$

The surface structure parameters enter from relations (Equation 3); they are the local slopes (p, q) and normalized curvatures (k_{xx}, k_{yy}, k_{xy}). The scale factor Z_0 is not recoverable and serves to define a normalized translational velocity $(V_x, V_y, V_z) \equiv Z_0^{-1}(V_X, V_Y, V_Z)$. The rotational velocity components $(\Omega_X, \Omega_Y, \Omega_Z)$ enter directly. We obtain the following 12 kinematic relations:

$$D_1 = -(V_x + \Omega_Y) \tag{10a}$$

$$D_2 = -(V_y - \Omega_X) \tag{10b}$$

$$D_3 = V_z + pV_x \tag{10c}$$

$$D_4 = V_z + qV_y \tag{10d}$$

$$D_5 = \tfrac{1}{2}(pV_y + qV_x) \tag{10e}$$

$$D_6 = -\Omega_Z + \tfrac{1}{2}(pV_y - qV_x) \tag{10f}$$

$$D_7 = -2(\Omega_Y + pV_z) + k_{xx}V_x \tag{10g}$$

$$D_8 = (\Omega_X - qV_z) + k_{xy}V_x \tag{10h}$$

$$D_9 = -(\Omega_Y + pV_z) + k_{xy}V_y \tag{10i}$$

$$D_{10} = 2(\Omega_X - qV_z) + k_{yy}V_y \tag{10j}$$

$$D_{11} = -\tfrac{1}{2}(\Omega_X - qV_z - k_{xx}V_y + k_{xy}V_x) \tag{10k}$$

$$D_{12} = -\tfrac{1}{2}(\Omega_Y + pV_z + k_{yy}V_x - k_{xy}V_y). \tag{10l}$$

With the formation parameters D_i obtained from the normal flow measurements using the Velocity Functional Method, relations (Equations 10a–l) form a closed set of 12 nonlinear algebraic equations among the 11 unknowns that comprise the local three-dimenstional inference. These equations are linear combinations of those derived by Longuet-Higgins and Prazdny (1980). The fact that these equations are nonlinear implies that multiple solutions may emerge; they correspond to ambiguous three-dimensional interpretations. We shall see that, in fact, there is the possibility of such ambiguities arising. However, they are three-dimensional interpretations of a local and instantaneous flow field, and hence, can be disambiguated by requiring global consistency or temporal continuity.

We next address the solution of Equations 10. The approach taken by both Longuet-Higgins and Prazdny (1980) to solve their related set of equations and Waxman and Ullman (1983) to solve Equation 10 involves a transformation of the image coordinates by a rotation about the center of the field of view. In Longuet-Higgins and Prazdny's case, this rotation was meant to orient one of the new image axes toward the focus of expansion $(x_{foe}, y_{foe}) = (V_X/V_Z, V_Y/V_Z)$; the rotation angle being the solution of a cubic equation. Unfortunately, their analysis was inapplicable for planar surfaces, seemed lacking in motivation for the case $V_Z \to 0$ (when the focus of expansion moves to infinity in an arbitrary direction), and was unable to reveal an important class of ambiguous cases. However, solutions were given in closed form. In Waxman and Ullman's case, the image rotation was meant to align the new image axes with the directions of maximum and zero slope on the surface; however, the rotation angle had to be found numerically as it was among the zeroes of a complicated function. Once the possible angles were obtained, the solution followed analytically. The method is valid for planar and curved surface patches and produces all possible ambiguous three-dimensional interpretations for a given set of deformation parameters (termed *observables* at that time by Waxman and Ullman).

In what follows, we shall present a solution procedure that unifies our interpretations of ambiguities in the planar and curved surface cases (cf. Waxman & Ullman, 1983); *all solutions emerge in closed form.* The approach follows from recent analytic work on the planar surface case by Longuet-Higgins (1984) and Subbarao and Waxman (1985). Its extension to the curved surface case is realized by solving for the tangent plane solution in a rotated coordinate system (Waxman, Kamgar-Parsi and Subbarao, 1986). Therefore, we shall solve the planar surface case first, and then the curved surface patch.

Planar Surface Patch

3-D solutions for planar surfaces in motion have been addressed by Hay (1966), Tsai and Huang (1981b), Waxman and Ullman (1983), Longuet-Higgins (1984), Buxton et al. (1984), and Subbarao and Waxman (1985). We present the method of Subbarao and Waxman, which utilizes the kinematic relations (see Equation 10). For planar surfaces, the normalized curvatures k_{xx}, k_{yy}, and k_{xy} vanish identically, simplifying Equations 10. The result is a set of 8 independent nonlinear equations (10a–

h) governing the surface slopes and space motions, and four equations (10i–l) that are linearly dependent on the first 8 (i.e., note $2D_9 = 4D_{12} = D_7$ and $\frac{1}{2}D_{10} = -2D_{11} = D_8$. This is a consequence of the fact that the globally valid second-order flow field generated by planar surfaces is specified by only 8 independent parameters and not 12. Therefore we need only consider Equations 10a–h in the absence of curvature terms. We have then,

$$D_1 = -(V_x + \Omega_Y) \tag{11a}$$

$$D_2 = -(V_y - \Omega_X) \tag{11b}$$

$$D_3 = V_z + pV_x \tag{11c}$$

$$D_4 = V_z + qV_y \tag{11d}$$

$$D_5 = \frac{1}{2}(pV_y + qV_x) \tag{11e}$$

$$D_6 = -\Omega_Z + \frac{1}{2}(pV_y - qV_x) \tag{11f}$$

$$D_7 = -2(\Omega_Y + pV_z) \tag{11g}$$

$$D_8 = \Omega_X - qV_z. \tag{11h}$$

Subbarao and Waxman (1985) prescribed a simple solution procedure for Equation 11; by elimination one obtains a cubic equation governing V_z, the remaining variables follow from back substitution. The procedure is derived assuming $V_z \neq 0$, however, it is valid in the limit $V_z \to 0$. We find that V_z satisfies the cubic equation

$$V_z^3 + C_1 V_z^2 + C_2 V_z + C_3 = 0, \tag{12a}$$

where

$$C_1 \equiv -(D_3 + D_4) \tag{12b}$$

$$C_2 \equiv -\frac{1}{4}[(D_1 - D_7/2)^2 + (D_2 - D_8)^2] - D_5^2 + D_3 D_4 \tag{12c}$$

$$C_3 \equiv \frac{1}{4}D_4(D_1 - D_7/2)^2 + \frac{1}{4}D_3(D_2 - D_8)^2 - \frac{1}{2}D_5(D_1 - D_7/2)(D_2 - D_8). \tag{12d}$$

All three roots of Equation 12a are real, but two are extraneous. Subbarao and Waxman demonstrated that the correct root of Equation 12a is the middle root (even when $V_z = 0$). Hence, V_z is obtained using any closed form solution for a cubic equation with real coefficients. (Similar results have been obtained from a different approach by Longuet-Higgins, 1984.) From V_z, we find two sets of solutions for the slopes given by

$$(p+, p-) = \left[(D_1 - D_7/2) \pm \sqrt{(D_1 - D_7/2)^2 - 4V_z(V_z - D_3)} \right] / 2V_z \tag{13a}$$

$$(q+, q-) = \left[(D_2 - D_8) \pm \sqrt{(D_2 - D_8)^2 - 4V_z(V_z - D_4)} \right] / 2V_z. \tag{13b}$$

Of the four possible combinations of $(p_\pm, q_\pm)$, only two are acceptable according to

$$(p_+, q_+) \text{ and } (p_-, q_-) \text{ for } S \geq 0 \tag{13c}$$

$$(p_+, q_-) \text{ and } (p_-, q_+) \text{ for } S < 0, \tag{13d}$$

where

$$S \equiv 4D_5 V_z + (D_1 - D_7/2)(D_2 - D_8). \tag{13e}$$

(For $V_z = 0$, we choose the unique values of p and q in Equations 13a,b, which yield finite results in the limit $V_z \rightarrow 0$. If the numerators of Equations 13a,b vanish as well, the slopes remain undetermined. This occurs when $\mathbf{V} \equiv 0$.) For each acceptable solution (p, q), we obtain the remaining unknowns as

$$V_x = pV_z - (D_1 - D_7/2) \tag{14a}$$

$$V_y = qV_z - (D_2 - D_8) \tag{14b}$$

$$\Omega_X = D_2 + V_y \tag{14c}$$

$$\Omega_Y = -D_1 - V_x \tag{14d}$$

$$\Omega_Z = -D_6 + \tfrac{1}{2}(pV_y - qV_x). \tag{14e}$$

We see that, in general, there are two three-dimensional interpretations of planar surfaces in motion for the same instantaneous second-order flow. This was first pointed out by Hay (1966) and independently rediscovered by a number of investigators. In fact, the solutions obey an interesting duality relation first specified by Waxman and Ullman (1983). For if one solution is denoted by $(\mathbf{V}, \boldsymbol{\Omega}, p, q)$ and the second by $(\hat{\mathbf{V}}, \hat{\boldsymbol{\Omega}}, \hat{p}, \hat{q})$, then the second can be written explicitly in terms of the first;

$$\hat{p} = -V_x/V_z, \quad \hat{q} = -V_y/V_z \tag{15a,b}$$

$$\hat{V}_x = -pV_z, \quad \hat{V}_y = -qV_z, \quad \hat{V}_z = V_z \tag{15c,d,e}$$

$$\hat{\Omega}_X = \Omega_X - (V_y + qV_z) \tag{15f}$$

$$\hat{\Omega}_Y = \Omega_Y + (V_x + pV_z) \tag{15g}$$

$$\hat{\Omega}_Z = \Omega_Z - (pV_y - qV_x). \tag{15h}$$

Notice how the slopes (p, q) and components of translation parallel to the image plane (V_x, V_y) play interchangeable roles in the dual solutions. These duality relations also make explicit the conditions under which a unique three-dimensional interpretation is found. A unique solution is obtained when $V_z = 0$, for in the limit $V_z \rightarrow 0$, we find $(\hat{p}, \hat{q}) \rightarrow \infty$. A planar surface with infinite slopes is oriented edge-on to the viewer and so is not visible. A unique solution is also found when the translational velocity is parallel to the surface normal (i.e., $V_x/V_z = -p$ and $V_y/V_z = -q$), in which case the duality relations (Equation 15) degenerate to identities. These limiting cases were illustrated graphically by Subbarao and Waxman (1985).

Generally, there is this two-fold ambiguity for planes and so we consider how to resolve it. It has been shown by Subbarao and Waxman (as well as Tsai & Huang, 1981b, and Longuet-Higgins, 1984) that global compatibility in the case of two or more planes moving rigidly, or simply continuity of the solutions over time, will single out the correct three-dimensional interpretation from the pair associated with each planar surface at each time instant. A third means of disambiguation has been pointed out by Longuet-Higgins (1984) (and B. Buxton in private conversation). Essentially, it requires that all points on the image plane that contributed flow data be consistent with a planar surface that lies in front of the viewer. Since the plane can be described in image coordinates by $Z = Z_0(1 - px - qy)^{-1}$ with $Z > 0$ for all visible features, a dual solution with slopes leading to $Z < 0$ for a visible feature (point or edge) at x, y is immediately ruled out. However, the viability of this disambiguation mechanism depends on the distribution of data over the image. It seems that, by far, the simplest means of selecting the correct three-dimensional interpretation is to require continuity of the solution over time.

Finally, we should note that, since planar surfaces in motion generate an image flow that is exactly second-order, our local analysis of the flow in small neighborhoods is actually globally valid. For ideal normal flow

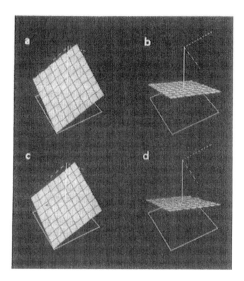

FIGURE 3.16. Dual planar configurations: line of sight along solid line, translational and rotational space motions indicated by dashed and dotted lines, respectively: (a) and (b) are exact solutions for ideal normal flow data, (c) and (d) are dual solutions for 10% noise.

data, our Velocity Functional Method recovers the exact flow field and exact deformation parameters. The dual three-dimensional interpretations recovered from Equations 11a–h are exact as well. Figure 3.16 illustrates dual three-dimensional interpretations for ideal and noisy (10%) data. We address the effects of noise in more detail later in this section.

Curved Surface Patch

Our new method of solving the kinematic relations (Equation 10) for curved surface patches is a direct extension of our solution for planar patches (Waxman, Kamgar-Parsi, & Subbarao, 1986). The approach also brings in elements of prior studies as well as obtaining all prior results with additional insight (cf. Longuet-Higgins & Prazdny, 1980; Waxman & Ullman, 1983). Note however, that the complete three-dimensional inference process for curved surfaces is not exact, even for ideal normal-flow data because the exact flow field is not second-order. The second-order flow model is a locally valid approximation, but it does introduce truncation errors to the deformation parameters; hence, the exact deformations are perturbed. Our closed form solution for the local three-dimensional interpretation will then be slightly perturbed as well, even for ideal flow data. If exact deformation parameters could be provided, our three-dimensional inference would be exact as well.

The key to solving Equations 10a–l is to realize that the curvatures (k_{xx}, k_{yy}, k_{xy}) can be decoupled from the structure and motion of the tangent plane in Equations 10a–h. We can then use the solution method for planar surfaces given previously to solve for the tangent plane. Finally, the curvatures are easily recovered from the remaining equations. We proceed as follows.

In Equations 10a–h, the curvatures enter only into 10g and 10h, and in both cases they are multiplied by the translational component V_x. If V_x were to vanish, the curvatures would decouple from 10a–h and so the structure and motion of the tangent plane could be recovered. This suggests that we seek a rotation of the image coordinates about the Z-axis by an angle α, that is, $(x, y) \xrightarrow{\alpha} (\bar{x}, \bar{y})$, such that in the new coordinate system $\bar{V}_x \equiv 0$. For any given $\mathbf{V}$, such a transformation always exists and is unique, except when $V_x = V_y = 0$, in which case $\bar{V}_x = 0$ for any rotation angle. Generally, the unique rotation is given by $\tan \alpha = -V_x/V_y$ (with $-\pi/2 < \alpha < \pi/2$), but of course this is not known ahead of time. The transform angle α must be determined from the deformation parameters themselves; it takes the place of $\bar{V}_x$ as an unknown that must be solved for. Thus, we consider Equations 10a–l in a rotated coordinate system, specified by an angle α which must be found, and for which $\bar{V}_x \equiv 0$. The rotation by α transforms the deformation parameters $D_i \xrightarrow{\alpha} \bar{D}_i$ as well as the three-dimensional parameters $\{\mathbf{V}, \boldsymbol{\Omega}, p, q, k_{xx}, k_{yy}, k_{xy}\} \xrightarrow{\alpha} \{\bar{\mathbf{V}}, \bar{\boldsymbol{\Omega}}, \bar{p}, \bar{q}, \bar{k}_{xx}, \bar{k}_{yy}, \bar{k}_{xy}\}$, and the transformation is invertable (cf. the Appendix at the end of this chapter for detailed expressions).

We will derive an expression for the transform angle α momentarily, but let us first note the rest of the solution procedure. For each possible transform angle (if there is more than one), we transform $D_i \xrightarrow{\alpha} \bar{D}_i$ and consider Equations 10a–h with $\bar{V}_x = 0$. These equations can be solved for $\bar{\mathbf{V}}, \bar{\boldsymbol{\Omega}}, \bar{p}, \bar{q}$ using the planar solution method. In fact, we generally obtain two (dual) solutions. There are constraints on the acceptability of these solutions. Both solutions have a common value for $\bar{V}_z$ (cf. Equation 15e), and from Equation 10c this is given directly by $\bar{V}_z = D_3$ (since $\bar{V}_x \equiv 0$). Thus, $\bar{D}_3$ must satisfy the cubic Equation 12a with coefficients ($\bar{C}_1, \bar{C}_2, \bar{C}_3$) if either dual solution is to be acceptable. (In fact, upon substituting $\bar{D}_3$ for $\bar{V}_z$ in Equation 12 and rearranging terms, one obtains exactly the expression for $Q_{pl}(\alpha)$ given by Waxman and Ullman (1983), the zeroes of which led them to the solution for planar surfaces!) If $\bar{D}_3$ does not satisfy Equation 12a, both solutions are rejected, (i.e., the value of α used was unacceptable). This helps us determine the correct value of α when more than one is possible. If $\bar{D}_3$ does satisfy Equation 12a, the value of α is acceptable, and we then have dual solutions for the tangent plane. However, we have defined the transformation according to $\bar{V}_x \equiv 0$, hence, we can accept only those solutions for which $\bar{V}_x$ determined by Equation 14a does indeed vanish. Of the two solutions for the tangent plane, usually only one satisfies $\bar{V}_x = 0$, the other is to be rejected. Sometimes it is possible for both solutions to satisfy $\bar{V}_x = 0$, this implies (Equation 15c) that the actual three-dimensional structure and motion satisfies $\bar{p} = \bar{V}_x = 0$. From Equation 10e we then see that $\bar{D}_5 = 0$ and realize that this is exactly the *structure-motion coincidence* of Waxman and Ullman (1983)! That is, some of our old notions about curved surface ambiguities actually emerge from the duality of the tangent-plane solutions. It is not surprising then, that explicit duality relations can be written for curved surface patches when $\bar{D}_5 = 0$. We give them in Equation 17.

We see that, for given α such that $\bar{V}_x \equiv 0$, Equations 10a–h provide us with eight nonlinear equations; seven are used to determine $\bar{V}_y, \bar{V}_z, \bar{\boldsymbol{\Omega}}, \bar{p}, \bar{q}$ governing the tangent plane, and one is used as a constraint on acceptable solutions. (Longuet-Higgins & Prazdny, 1980, have pointed out that the availability of such a constraint helps determine if a rigid body interpretation is at all appropriate. Unfortunately, for true planar surfaces there is no additional constraint.) The remaining four equations (10i–l) will be used to determine the three curvature parameters ($\bar{k}_{xx}, \bar{k}_{yy}, \bar{k}_{xy}$) and the transform angle α. For example, with $\bar{V}_x \equiv 0$ we find from (Equation 10i–k),

$$\bar{k}_{xx} = (2\bar{D}_{11} + \bar{\Omega}_X - \bar{q}\bar{V}_z)/\bar{V}_y \tag{16a}$$

$$\bar{k}_{yy} = (\bar{D}_{10} - 2\bar{\Omega}_X + 2\bar{q}\bar{V}_z)/\bar{V}_y \tag{16b}$$

$$\bar{k}_{xy} = (\bar{D}_9 + \bar{\Omega}_Y + \bar{p}\bar{V}_z)/\bar{V}_y. \tag{16c}$$

Clearly, if $\bar{V}_y = 0$ (as well as $\bar{V}_x = 0$) the curvatures cannot be determined from the local analysis. This is expected, for if $\bar{V}_x = \bar{V}_y = 0$ for some value of α, it will be true for all α because there is then no component of translation parallel to the image plane. From Equation 10 in the original image coordinate system we see that all curvature terms are multiplied by V_x or V_y, hence, if $V_x = V_y = 0$ curvatures remain undetermined, as pointed out by Waxman and Ullman (1983).

Using Expressions 16a–c for the curvatures, along with Expressions 15a–h for the duality of the tangent plane solutions and the transform relations from the appendix at the end of this chapter, we can derive the following duality relations (in the original coordinates) for curved surface patches, valid only when $\bar{D}_5 = 0$:

$$\hat{p} = -V_x/V_z, \quad \hat{q} = -V_y/V_z \tag{17a,b}$$

$$\hat{V}_z = -pV_z, \quad \hat{V}_y = -qV_z, \quad \hat{V}_z = V_z \tag{17c,d,e}$$

$$\Omega_X = \Omega_X - (V_y + qV_z) \tag{17f}$$

$$\Omega_Y = \Omega_Y + (V_x + pV_z) \tag{17g}$$

$$\Omega_Z = \Omega_Z - (pV_y - qV_x) \tag{17h}$$

$$\begin{bmatrix} \hat{T}_3 \\ \hat{T}_4 \\ \hat{T}_5 \end{bmatrix} = -\frac{1}{2V_z}\left(\frac{V_x}{p} + \frac{V_y}{q}\right)\begin{bmatrix} T_3 \\ T_4 \\ T_5 \end{bmatrix}. \tag{17i,j,k}$$

The duality of the tangent-plane solution is exactly that for planar surfaces, though the parenthetic Expression in 17h vanishes for $\bar{D}_5 = 0$ (since $\bar{p} = \bar{V}_x = 0$ corresponds to $p/q = V_x/V_y$). The duality relations for the curvatures is new. Again, the duality relations indicate when a unique solution exists (for the given transform angle α) even though $\bar{D}_5 = 0$. As was the case for planar surfaces, a unique solution exists when $V_z = 0$, for as $V_z \to 0$ the slopes and curvatures diverge. (That is, the dual solution elongates into a "needle" with zero radius of curvature at the tip, and so is invisible to the viewer.) Similarly, a unique solution is obtained when the translational velocity is parallel to the normal to the tangent plane ($V_x/V_z = -p$, $V_y/V_z = -q$), for then all of Equations 17 reduce to identities and the dual solutions degenerate. Another class of unique solutions arise for curved surface patches whose tangent planes are frontal, $p = q = 0$ (these were termed *specular points* by Koenderink and van Doorn, 1975). Indeed, such cases correspond to $\bar{D}_5 = 0$ since $\bar{p} =$

= 0 for all α and were found to be unique by Waxman and Ullman (1983), though it was not understood why. We now can see from Equations 17i, j, and k that, as $p \rightarrow 0$ and $q \rightarrow 0$, the curvatures of the dual solution diverge rendering it invisible (as an "elongated needle") to the viewer. These uniqueness results for curved surfaces are relevant for a given transform angle α. It remains to determine this angle, which we shall see leads to another source of ambiguity.

We can determine the possible transform angles α from the one remaining equation (10l) among the kinematic relations. Actually, we utilize a linear combination of Equations 10l and 10i to derive a constraint on the transform angle α which leads to $\bar{V}_x = 0$. Notice that with $\bar{V}_x = 0$, in the rotated coordinate system we have

$$2\bar{D}_{12}(\alpha) = \bar{D}_9(\alpha), \tag{18a}$$

where we have made explicit the dependence on α. Utilizing the transformation relations from the Appendix at the end of the chapter, for $\bar{D}_9$ and $\bar{D}_{12}$, we can reexpress Equation 18a in terms of the original (i.e., measured) deformation parameters and the transform angle. Collecting terms, we obtain the following simple equation for α:

$$(D_8 + 2D_{11})\tan^3 \alpha + (D_7 - 2D_9)\tan^2 \alpha + (D_{10} - 2D_8)\tan \alpha$$
$$+ (D_9 - 2D_{12}) = 0. \tag{18b}$$

With $-\frac{\pi}{2} < \alpha \leq \frac{\pi}{2}$, this equation has at most three real roots for α. For each real root then, we transform the deformation parameters using the expressions from the Appendix, utilize the solution procedure just described to obtain all solution sets $\{\bar{\mathbf{V}}, \bar{\mathbf{\Omega}}, \bar{p}, \bar{q}, \bar{k}_{xx}, \bar{k}_{yy}, \bar{k}_{xy}\}$, and finally, transform the three-dimensional solutions back to the original coordinate system. (This procedure requires only 25 msec of CPU time on a VAX 11/785.)

The fact that Equation 18b yields the required transform angle in closed form is substantial improvement over the method of Waxman and Ullman (1983), which required a numerical search for the transform angle. In fact, Equation 18b is exactly the cubic equation derived by Longuet-Higgins and Prazdny (1980, Equation A6) for their transform angle, which was chosen to orient one image axis toward the focus of expansion! In our case, it is chosen because it leads to a decoupling of the curvatures from the rest of the three-dimensional solution governing the tangent plant, allowing use of the planar solution method! Longuet-Higgins and Prazdny found this decoupling as well, but it was of no particular significance at the time. As was noted in our solution method for the planar surface patch (and by Longuet-Higgins and Prazdny as well), all coefficients in Equation 18b vanish in the case of planar surfaces; hence, the transform angle becomes irrelevant. Thus, when turning to solve Equation 18b for α one first computes the four coefficients and checks to see if they are vanishingly small. If so, turn directly to the planar solution method (i.e., either the surface is planar or there is no translation parallel to the image plane, in which case, surface curvature is not revealed). If all coefficients are nonzero, proceed with the curved surface solution as previously described. In either case, all solutions are obtained in closed form!

We now see that for curved surfaces patches, there are two sources of ambiguity. From Equation 18b we can find as many as three different transform angles, and for each angle there is the possibility of duality if $\bar{D}_5$ should vanish (cf. Equation 17). The question then arises, under what conditions can Equation 18b have more than one real root that leads to an acceptable solution? We can derive a very simple constraint that will isolate the problem somewhat. Condition 18a is a necessary but not sufficient condition to insure that $\bar{V}_x = 0$. It really implies that the product

$$\bar{V}_x \bar{k}_{yy} = 0, \tag{19a}$$

which arises from either

$$\bar{V}_x = 0 \tag{19b}$$

which leads to the desired root of Equation 18b $\tan \alpha = V_x/V_y$, or from

$$\bar{k}_{yy} = 0 \tag{19c}$$

which generates the two spurious roots of Equation 18b. An expression for k_{yy} can be derived from the expressions in the Appendix, giving rise to a quadratic equation for the two spurious roots which correspond to

$$\tan \alpha = k_{xy}/k_{xx} \pm \sqrt{(k_{xy}^2 - k_{xx}k_{yy})/k_{xx}^2}. \tag{19d}$$

(The curvatures in Equation 19d correspond to those of the correct solution, not the ambiguous solutions.) Now the parenthetic expression under the radicand of Equation 19d is proportional to the negative of the Gaussian curvature of the surface patch (McConnell, 1957). Therefore, the roots of Equation 19d will be complex conjugates for ovoid surface patches (positive Gaussian curvature), real and degenerate for cylindrical patches (zero Gauss curvature), and real for saddle patches (negative Gauss curvature).

We see then, that Equation 18b, for the transform angle, will have only one real root for ovoid surface patches, two real roots for cylindrical patches, and three real roots for saddle patches. The immediate implications of this are that ovoid surface patches (i.e., "bowls") are characterized by a unique transform angle; the only source of ambiguity being the possible duality of the structure–motion coincidence ($p/q = V_x/V_y$)

when $\bar{D}_5 = 0$. Hence, *ovoid surface patches almost always have a unique three-dimensional interpretation!* The possibility of multiple transform angles leading to acceptable solutions remains for nonovoid patches, where the spurious transformations align an image axis with an asymptotic line on the (correct) surface.

Unfortunately, the three roots of Equation 18b are not ordered in a manner in which the desired root is obvious. Indeed, there are cases in which multiple transform angles lead to several acceptable three-dimensional interpretations (e.g., specular points with a normalized mean curvature of -1 yield three solutions). As was noted in the solution procedure, acceptable solutions must satisfy the cubic (Equation 12a) with $\bar{V}_z = \bar{D}_3$. In fact, $\bar{D}_3$ must equal the middle root of the transformed cubic (Equation 12a). An analysis of this constraint using the spurious angles derived from Equation 19d is currently under way (Subbarao, 1986). However, as was the case with planar surfaces, there are additional means of disambiguating multiple-curved surface solutions by requiring global consistency with neighboring surface patches, temporal continuity, and positive depth for all data points. In fact, global consistency

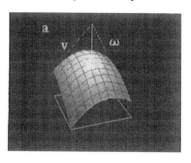
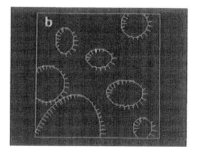
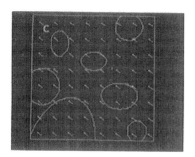
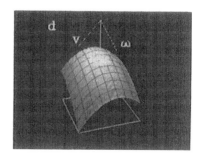

FIGURE 3.17. 3-D inference for a curved surface patch for ideal data. (a) Surface and motion used to generate the normal flow. (b) Normal flow along contours lying on the surface patch. (c) Full flow recovered in the neighborhood. (d) Surface structure and space motions reconstructed.

is very powerful here, since the presence of a single ovoid surface patch usually renders the global three-dimensional interpretation unique! Recent analyses by Bandyopadhyay (1985) and Maybank (1985) show that there can never be more than three global solutions, and for surfaces which are analytic, we have seen that such surfaces must locally be saddles.

Figure 3.17 illustrates the recovery of curved surface structure and space motion given ideal normal-flow data obtained along contours. The three-dimensional inference is not exact because the second-order flow approximation is only locally valid, hence, a series truncation error is introduced that perturbs the deformation parameters.

Sensitivity to Noise

We have tried to assess the sensitivity of our three-dimensional procedure to the effects of "noise" in the form of perturbations to the ideal normal flow. For a specified three-dimensional structure and motion, ideal normal flow was computed along the set of contours shown in

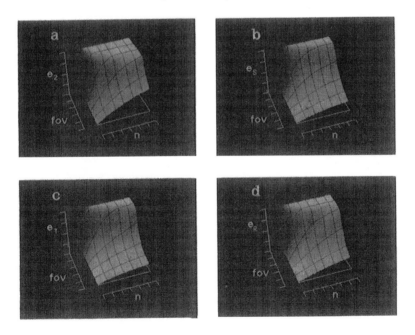

FIGURE 3.18. Noise sensitivity for planar surfaces in motion: $0 \leq e \leq 100\%$, $0 \leq n \leq 30\%$, $5° \leq fov \leq 40°$. (a) Accuracy of the second-order Taylor coefficients (b) The surface slopes (c) The translations (d) Rotations

Figure 3.11 for an image with specified field of view $5° \leq fov \leq 40°$. The
normal flow was then perturbed in magnitude and direction using a
random number generator scaled to a fixed percentage of noise, $0\% \leq n$
$\leq 25\%$. The Velocity Functional Method was used to obtain the 12
deformation parameters from which the three-dimensional inference
was derived. Many experiments were run in order to create the "error
surfaces" shown in Figures 3.18 and 3.19, for planar and curved surface
patches, respectively. We plot the percent error in the second derivatives
of flow, surface slopes and curvatures, and translational and rotational
motions, as functions of the noise and field of view. For planar surfaces
we find acceptable results for as much as 20% noise down to about 10°
fov. Curved surfaces are more sensitive to noise at small fields of view and
yield good results for 5% or less noise at around 10° *fov*. Further details
can be found in Wohn and Waxman (1985). Figure 3.20 illustrates the
three-dimensional inference following the flow segmentation shown in
Figure 3.15. At 20% noise the segmentation boundary is lost.

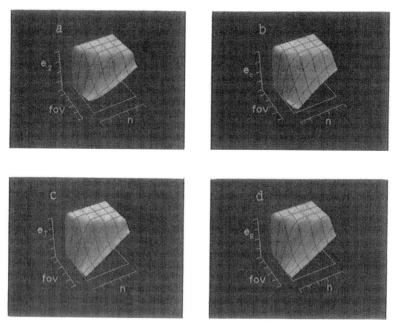

FIGURE 3.19. Noise sensitivity for curved surfaces in motion. (a) Accuracy of the second-order Taylor coefficients (b) The surface curvatures
(c) The translations (d) Rotations

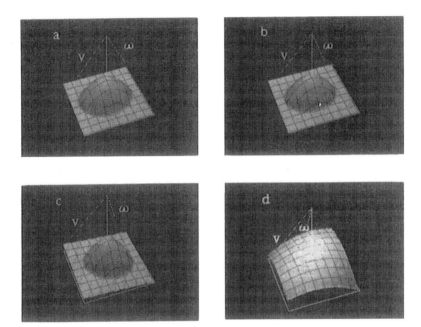

FIGURE 3.20. A bump on a plane in motion (cf. Figure 3.15). (a) The 3-D configuration used to generate the input normal flow (b) 3-D inference from ideal data (c) 3-D inference with 10% noise on the normal flow (d) 3-D inference with 20% noise where segmentation is lost.

Temporal Behavior in Three-Dimensions

Our approach throughout has been to concentrate on the instantaneous three-dimensional structure and motion of surface patches. We have noted where multiple frames may be exploited in the image domain to improve estimates of instantaneous normal flow or the instantaneous image velocity field. The instantaneous three-dimensional inference then follows. The only time temporal behavior in three-dimensions was utilized so far was in the context of resolving ambiguous solutions by temporal continuity. Some investigators have advocated the use of time-derivatives of flow fields for recovering three-dimensional solutions (Bandyopadhyay & Aloimonos, 1985; Subbarao, 1985; Wohn & Wu, 1986); however, it is always assumed that the space motion remains constant on the timescale of the evolving flow, which is questionable.

An alternative use of the temporal behavior of three-dimensional solutions is to exploit a *predict and verify strategy* in order to model "system noise." Given a surface patch approximated at any instant by the quadric

Equation 3a, it is straightforward to derive differential equations governing the evolution of the depth-scale factor and surface slopes due to the
instantaneous rigid body motions (cf. Subbarao & Waxman, 1985, the
Appendix for planar surfaces). We find

$$\frac{d\ln Z_0}{dt} = (\Omega_Y + V_x)p - (\Omega_X - V_y)q - V_z \tag{20a}$$

$$\frac{dp}{dt} = \Omega_Y + \Omega_Z q - \Omega_X pq + \Omega_Y p^2 + (\Omega_Y + V_x)k_{xx} - (\Omega_X - V_y)k_{xy} \tag{20b}$$

$$\frac{dq}{dt} = -\Omega_X - \Omega_Z p + \Omega_Y pq - \Omega_X q^2 + (\Omega_Y + V_x)k_{xy} - (\Omega_X - V_y)k_{yy}. \tag{20c}$$

Given an instantaneous three-dimensional interpretation, Equations 20b
and c can be used to predict the slopes of the same surface patch a
moment later. These predicted slopes can be compared to the newly
determined slopes for the same patch derived from the image flow at the
next instant. (This is particularly easy for planar surfaces as the slopes
are constant over the surface.) The verification of the predicted slopes
can be used to disambiguate multiple solutions when this arises. More
importantly, this comparison of predicted to determined slopes gives us
information about the noise in our system, quality of data, and inade-
quacies of our approach. It can then be exploited to improve the quality
of three-dimensional solutions at future instants; this is the basis of Kalman filtering (Kalman, 1960, Kalman & Bucy, 1961, Meinhold & Singpurwalla, 1983). These concepts may be most useful in a control context, for example, a robot arm placing an object onto a moving platform,
or a vehicle docking with a moving berth.

INSTABILITIES AND DYNAMIC ILLUSIONS

In the recent work of Hildreth (1983) on the recovery of image velocity
along a contour from normal flow measurements, a very interesting
point was raised concerning incorrect performance of a vision algorithm.
Could a computer-vision algorithm err in a manner similar to human
visual illusions, and does this lend support to the algorithm as a computational embodiment of a human visual task? We feel it is actually
appropriate to expand somewhat on the performance requirements if
one cares to pursue the machine–human vision analogy. In a discussion
with L. S. Davis on this point, we agreed that an impressive performance
test for an algorithm is that it produce (nearly) correct answers and be
robust when the human visual system perceives things correctly, and that
the algorithm err in an appropriate manner when the human perceives
an illusion! We decided to test our approach against the classical illusions

used by Hildreth—the rotating spiral and the rotating helix (i.e., the barberpole illusion). We were satisfied that our approaches to flow recovery and three-dimensional inference performed well given ideal data as well as data perturbed by several percent noise. And our study of the "aperture problem in the large" had revealed that a contour with just barely enough structure to fully determine the flow is very sensitive to noise, unlike sets of contours that tend to be quite robust. Moreover, we could also try to obtain the three-dimensional inference corresponding to a very perturbed flow field.

Unstable Contours

The case of the spiral contour on a frontal plane rotating about the line of sight is shown in Figure 3.21. Given the ideal normal flow, the Velocity Functional Method recovers the exact rotational flow; the three-dimen-

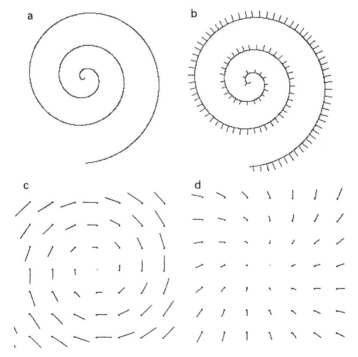

FIGURE 3.21. A spiral on a rotating frontal plane. (a) The spiral contour (b) The ideal normal flow along the contour (c) The exact rotational flow recovered using the Velocity Functional Method (d) The divergent flow recovered from the normal flow with 5% noise

sional inference yields the correct space motion without determining surface structure (tue to the absence of any translational space motion). However, given a normal flow perturbed even slightly (less than 1%), a divergent component of flow emerges in the full flow. Figure 3.21d illustrates the recovered flow for only 5% noise. The corresponding three-dimensional inference is also similar to the classical perception; it is a curved surface shaped like a bowl (somewhat off center), with the viewer approaching the bowl. The bowl sometimes curves toward the viewer and sometimes away.

Figure 3.22 illustrates the case of the helical contour rotating about its axis. The classical perception is not an axial rotation, but rather the contour seems to translate along the axis, (i.e., the barberpole illusion). Even for ideal data, our approach will not recover the correct flow in this case because the helix lies on a transparent cylindrical surface; the flow is not a simple second-order flow field (though it is probably well approximated by two interpenetrating second-order flows). A slightly perturbed normal flow (as derived from a sequence of orthographic projections) leads, via our Velocity Functional Method, to a strong translational component along the axis of the helix.

What both of these examples have in common is that the contour used is very sensitive to noise. The likely cause of this is that these contours can be well approximated by contours that have barely overcome the

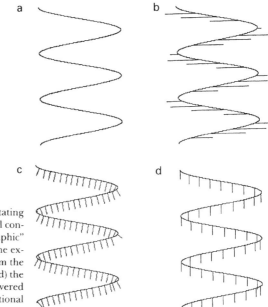

FIGURE 3.22. A helix rotating about its axis. (a) The helical contour (b) the exact "orthographic" flow along the contour (c) the exact normal flow derived from the orthographic flow as input (d) the translational flow recovered using the Velocity Functional Method.

aperture problem in the large. The spiral is much like portions of nearly concentric circles (which themselves exibit a classical illusion when rotated about the line of sight). Exactly concentric circles would be subject to this aperture problem. The helix in projection is nearly equivalent to two sets of exactly parallel lines, the sets being at some angle to each other. Two sets of exactly parallel lines would also suffer from the aperture problem in the large. It is striking, however, that the full flows recovered from perturbed normal flows seem qualitatively the same, regardless of the noise (as long as it is present). This is the telltale sign of an instability! Is it possible that dynamic illusions are a manifestation of an unstable process in the human visual system?

Conditions for Illusions

As our perception of a dynamic illusion is a three-dimensional one, it is not surprising that the conditions required to generate an illusion involve the three-dimensional configuration as well as the contour shape in projection. One condition that the various classical illusions share is that they correspond to three-dimensional configurations in which the structure is not well revealed by the image flow. For example, the purely rotational flow of the spiral is induced by a pure rotation in space; but shape information is revealed by spatial translations, not rotations. Similarly, the flow induced by the rotating helix is dominated by the spatial rotations, the translational part is small when the radius of the helix is small compared to the distance to the helix. This, of course, makes sense because if the true motion does not reveal shape then the three-dimensional percept will be driven entirely by the noise, via its influence on the recovered flow (or deformation parameters).

It is also necessary to have a source of noise which perturbs the normal flow. The method for estimating normal velocity, outlined earlier in this chapter is always subject to an error proportional to the ratio of tangential to normal velocity along the contour. Thus, an appreciable component of ideal flow oriented along a contour will serve as a source of noise. This is the case for the rotating spiral, nearly concentric circles, and helix.

The general conditions for a dynamic illusion then seem to be: (a) a noise source that perturbs normal flow estimates, (b) a contour that is particularly sensitive to noise, and (c) a space motion that does not clearly reveal the true three-dimensional structure in the image flow field.

Suppressed Illusions

We can carry the test of our theory one step further. If our algorithms do indeed reproduce visual illusions by means of instabilities, does the approach also suggest a way to suppress dynamic illusions? The answer would then be, "by stabilizing the apparent instability one suppresses the dynamic illusion." The instability of the flow recovery process can be removed by adding additional features to the scene that can be well tracked, such as dots moving with the rotational flow in the case of the spiral or nearly concentric circles. Even perturbed dot motions would lead to an improved determination of the full flow field, and so suppress the illusory three-dimensional percept somewhat.

A preliminary set of displays has been constructed using an Apple Macintosh with 512K of memory (which is really not bad for this kind of thing!). Image sequences corresponding to rotating spirals and nearly concentric circles give rise to vivid three-dimensional percepts of the illusory type. By adding a set of dots that moves with the image flow field, the illusion appears less pronounced. Our attempt at psychophysical experimentation is not very professional, but we may have learned something nonetheless.

BINOCULAR IMAGE FLOWS

The previous sections have dealt with the analysis of *monocular image flows* in order to obtain shape information about moving objects in the world. Another source of shape information that has commonly been studied is *shape from stereo* (Eastman & Waxman, 1985; Koenderink & van Doorn, 1976b; Marr & Poggio, 1979; Mayhew & Frisby, 1981; Pollard, Mayhew, & Frisby, 1985; Prazdny, 1985). However, when acting independently, each of these processes suffers from certain inherent difficulties; stereo is faced with a combinatorial correspondence problem plagued by the presence of occluding boundaries (Grimson, 1981; Poggio & Poggio, 1984), while motion analysis, as we have already seen, involves the solution of nonlinear equations and leaves the three-dimensional interpretation specified up to an arbitrary scale factor. There is evidence, however, for a separate channel of human visual processing in which stereo and motion analyses may come together much earlier than at the $2\frac{1}{2}$-D sketch. We describe here a theory of time-varying stereo in the context of "binocular image flows," where stereo and motion work closely in order to compensate for each other's shortcomings (Waxman & Duncan, 1985). Central to our approach is the notion of *relative flow* (or "binocular difference flow"), representing the difference between image velocities of a feature as seen in the left and right images separately. Neural organizations that perform this "computation" have already been proposed (Regan & Beverley, 1979a).

Stereo-Motion Fusion

The fusion of stereo and motion into a single module has been considered recently by others as well. Richards (1983) demonstrated recovery of structure from orthographic stereo and motion without knowledge of the fixation distance. He also pointed out the importance of measuring changes in quantities, such as disparity over time, relative to their current values. Jenkin (1984) considered a stereo-matching process driven by the three-dimensional interpretation of feature point velocities. Waxman and Sinha (1984) proposed a "dynamic stereo" technique based upon the relative flow derived from two cameras in known relative motion, valid in the limit of negligible disparity. The possibility of image motion facilitating the stereo-matching process was noted by Poggio and Poggio (1984); and as shown in the following steps, a correlation between binocular difference flow and disparity may support this possibility.

We suggest a decomposition of our stereo-motion module into five steps, which begins where low-level vision ends, that is, it follows the stage of edge and point feature extraction (and tracking over time) in the left and right images separately.

Step 1. Monocular image flow recovery and flow segmentation of the separate left and right image sequences utilizing the Velocity Functional Method and overlap compatibility. This procedure allows gross correspondence to be established between analytic-flow regions in the left and right images. It also reveals the depth and orientation discontinuities that often plague stereo-matching and surface-reconstruction algorithms.

Step 2. Establishing correspondence between (previously unmatched) left and right image features according to a correlation between binocular difference flow and stereo disparity. This process can be implemented in parallel over the binocular field of view in the context of "local support" within neighborhoods (Eastman & Wasman, 1985; Pollard et al., 1985; Prazdny, 1985). This correlation points to the importance of the ratio $\dot{\delta}/\delta$, rate of change of disparity $\dot{\delta}$ to disparity δ. The importance of this ratio was first noted by Richards (1983). A "rigidity assumption" for independently moving objects in the scene also enters here.

Step 3. Use of disparity functionals defined in overlapping neighborhoods to recover smooth surface structure between the discontinuities detected from the monocular flow analyses (Eastman & Waxman, 1985; Koenderink & van Doorn, 1976b).

Step 4. Recovery of rigid-body space motions corresponding to separate analytic-flow regions utilizing the determined surface structure and either monocular-image flow or cyclopean-image flow. Separate surface patches can then be grouped into rigid objects sharing the same space motions. This process entails solving only linear equations as a measure of its complexity.

Step 5. Use of the separate image flows to track features and discontinuities over time. This allows refinement of disparity estimates to "subpixel" accuracy by temporal interpolation. It also allows the *matching process to focus attention* onto areas where new image features will be unveiled and old ones will disappear, that is, at the discontinuities and periphery of the field of view.

This last step suggests that in the analysis of a time-varying stereo sequence, once an initial correspondence has been determined between left and right images, it is not necessary to establish correspondence anew for the entire image pair at subsequent times. Most of the image features merely flow to new locations, which can be predicted. Matching need only be performed on new features that enter the visible field from the periphery and from behind occluding boundaries.

Relative Flow–Disparity Relation

For simplicity, we restrict our analysis to the parallel stereo configuration illustrated in Figure 3.23. The left and right image planes lie in a common plane with the fixation point located at infinity (i.e., the cameras point straight ahead). The left and right coordinates, x_l, y_l and x_r, y_r, respectively, have their origins at the centers of their respective fields of view separated by a baseline of magnitude b along the common direction of the x-axes. Each image plane is positioned at a focal length of unity with respect to a pin-hole located at the vertex of projection for each separate camera. This stereo configuration is assumed to move rigidly with respect to other moving objects in the scene. No allowance has been made for vergence of the cameras (known or otherwise) in the current formulation (however, see Mitiche, 1984).

Consider the monocular flow analysis of Step 1, already performed separately on the left- and right-image sequences. The analytic-flow regions bounded by flow discontinuities are assumed to be brought into correspondence rather easily. This can be accomplished essentially by matching the flow discontinuities between left and right images. The correspondence is gross, but allows the binocular flow analysis to focus attention on individual regions. Each of these regions is assumed to correspond to a smooth surface of a rigid body. Thus, we may associate

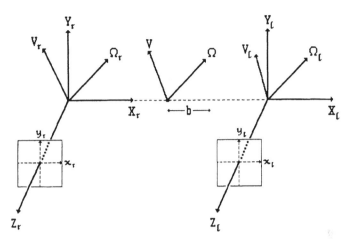

FIGURE 3.23. Spatial and image coordinate systems for the binocular configuration. Space motions are shown for the left, right, and cyclopean coordinate systems, which move as a rigid body.

with each region a set of relative rigid body-motion parameters. However, for the sake of analysis, if we ascribe the rigid body motion to the "monocular observer," as in Figure 3.3 and Equation 1, then the rigid body-motion parameters for a given region are different for the left and right cameras. This is due to the fact that the left and right cameras are in motion with respect to each other when relative motion between object and observer is ascribed to the observer. If according to the left coordinate system the rigid body-motion parameters of a region are $(\mathbf{V}_l, \mathbf{\Omega}_l)$, then in the right coordinate system that same region has motion parameters $(\mathbf{V}_r, \mathbf{\Omega}_r)$, where

$$\mathbf{\Omega}_r = \mathbf{\Omega}_l \tag{21a}$$

$$\mathbf{V}_r = \mathbf{V}_l - \mathbf{\Omega}_l \times b\hat{\mathbf{i}}, \tag{21b}$$

and $\hat{\imath}$ is a unit vector in the common x-direction.

Thus, the image-flow fields of the two cameras differ in magnitude as well as distribution (due to stereo disparity). And as both stereo disparity and monocular flow vary inversely with depth, we should not be surprised that binocular flow and disparity are related in a simple way. In fact, we shall see that binocular flow is synonymous with "rate-of-change of disparity."

Given the parallel stereo configuration, we have the simple case of corresponding features lying along horizontal epipolar lines. Thus, a feature located at position (x_l, y_l) in the left image at some instant of time is located at (x_r, y_r), in the right image, where $y_r = y_l$ and $\delta(x_l, y_l) \equiv x_r - x_l$ $= b/Z$, $\delta(x_l, y_l)$ being the angular disparity between right- and left-image positions. Now Equations 1 can be used to express the image velocity $\mathbf{v}_r(x_r, y_r)$ in the right image or $\mathbf{v}_l(x_l, y_l)$ in the left image. Waxman and Duncan (1985) defined the *relative flow* (or *binocular difference flow*) of corresponding features in the two images,

$$\Delta\mathbf{v}(x_l, y_l; \delta) \equiv \mathbf{v}_r(x_l + \delta[x_l, y_l], y_l) - \mathbf{v}_l(x_l, y_l). \tag{22}$$

Utilizing Equations 1 and 21, an expansion for Equation 22 can be obtained in terms of motion parameters and image coordinates of the cyclopean coordinate system located midway between the cameras (see Figure 3.23). The ratio of relative flow to disparity takes a particularly simple form,

$$\frac{\Delta v_x(x, y); \delta)}{\delta(x, y)} = \frac{V_Z}{b} \delta(x, y) + (y\Omega_X - x\Omega_Y) \tag{23a}$$

$$\frac{\Delta v_y(x, y; \delta)}{\delta(x, y)} = 0. \tag{23b}$$

These relations were verified against experimental data by Waxman and Duncan (1985).

If we consider the relative flow in a small enough neighborhood such that the underlying surface patch may be treated as locally planar, then we have a simple expression for the local disparity field,

$$\delta(x, y) \equiv \frac{b}{Z(x, y)} = \frac{b}{Z_0} (1 - px - qy), \tag{24}$$

where Z_0 is the depth to the plane measured along the center of the cyclopean field of view, and p and q are the components of the local slope. Substituting Equation 24 for the disparity on the right-hand side of Equation 23 yields the local relative flow to disparity relations,

$$\frac{\Delta v_x(x, y)}{\delta(x, y)} = \frac{V_Z}{Z_0} - \left(\frac{V_Z}{Z_0} p + \Omega_Y \right) x - \left(\frac{V_Z}{Z_0} q - \Omega_X \right) y \tag{25a}$$

$$\frac{\Delta v_y(x, y)}{\delta(x, y)} = 0. \tag{25b}$$

We see that locally, the relative flow to disparity ratio is a linear function of image coordinates with coefficients depending on the surface structure and relative motion between object and observer. We will describe how this correlation between relative flow and disparity can form the basis of a stereo matching procedure.

The correlation between relative flow $\Delta\mathbf{v}$ and disparity δ, presented in cyclopean coordinates in Equation 23 is simple to interpret. Recall that we are considering only a parallel stereo-imaging geometry, hence, the epipolar lines are horizontal (i.e., parallel to the x-axes). Now the relative flow $\Delta \mathbf{v}$ represents the rate of separation of a feature in one image from its match in the other image. It is the rate of change of vector disparity. As a feature and its match must always lie along some epipolar line, its vertical disparity must remain zero in this case. Thus, Relation 23b expresses the fact that a feature and its match must flow perpendicular to epipolars at the same rate in order to lie on a common epipolar. In general, the rate of change of vertical disparity must be such as to keep a feature and its match on an epipolar line.

For our parallel stereo configuration, we may then identify Δv_x with the rate of change of (horizontal) disparity and denote it by $\dot{\delta}$. Since disparity $\delta = b/Z$, we have

$$\dot{\delta} = -\frac{b}{Z^2}\dot{Z} = -\delta\frac{\dot{Z}}{Z}, \tag{26a}$$

and from $\mathbf{U} = -(\mathbf{V} + \mathbf{\Omega} \times \mathbf{R})$ we have $\dot{Z} = -V_Z - \Omega_X Y + \Omega_Y X$, hence,

$$\frac{\dot{Z}}{Z} = -\frac{V_Z}{Z} - (y\Omega_X - x\Omega_Y) = -\frac{V_Z}{b}\delta - (y\Omega_X - x\Omega_Y). \tag{26b}$$

Combining Equations 26a and b yields for $\dot{\delta}/\delta$,

$$\frac{\dot{\delta}(x, y)}{\delta(x, y)} = \frac{V_Z}{b}\delta(x, y) + (y\Omega_X - x\Omega_Y), \tag{26c}$$

which is identical with Relation 23a. Thus, this correlation between relative image flows and stereo disparity is, in fact, a relationship between disparity and its rate of change! Note that the ratio $\dot{\delta}/\delta$ is the inverse of the "time to collision," hence, collision time is a particularly simple function of (x, y, δ).

Facilitating Stereo Correspondence

In the case of a static stereo pair of images, many algorithms have been suggested for establishing correspondence between features (i.e., edges and points) in the left and right images. Knowledge of the stereo geometry constrains matches to lie along known epipolar lines (horizontal in the case of our parallel configuration). In addition to the "cooperative algorithm" of Marr and Poggio (1979), several algorithms based on the notion of *local support of disparity* have recently emerged (Eastman & Waxman, 1985; Pollard et al., 1985; Prazdny, 1985). Prazdny's algorithm attempts to embody the concept of "coherence" in the local disparity distribution, by assigning a weight to each potential match of a feature based on a measure of similarity between that disparity and potential disparities of other nearby features. Pollard et al. (1985) have developed a matching algorithm, which is driven by "local consistency with a prescribed disparity gradient limit" of unity (selected on the basis of psychophysical experiments). Again, potential matches of features are found, and the potential disparities of nearby points are tested for compliance with the disparity-gradient limit. The approach of Eastman and Waxman (1985) is based on the notion of "analytic disparity fields" in overlapping neighborhoods (motivated by our Velocity Functional Method). Potential matches between contours (i.e., extended edges) in the left and right images are established. Then, motivated by Equation 24, the implied disparities are fit to a linear functional form (in the least-squares sense) for potentially matched contours in a neighborhood, thereby yielding a locally planar interpretation along with the average residual (measuring goodness of fit). A match is then selected on the basis of minimizing this residual (and so maximizing local support) subject to the disparity gradient (derived from the functional) being less than a limit of unity. Our use of locally-analytic disparity fields is, in fact, a mathematical realization of "coherence". All of these "local support" algorithms may be implemented in a local and parallel manner.

For our case of time-varying stereo, we suggest the use of the binocular difference flow-disparity realtion (Equation 26c) to establish correspondence in neighborhoods. Of course, the static matching algorithms based on disparity alone may be used as well, but here we note the additional exploitation of flow to drive the matching procedure. We can implement the matching procedure in any of three ways, all of which embody the concept of "local support" for matching a neighborhood.

One implementation, motivated by Equation 25a, would seek matches in a neighborhood such that $\dot{\delta}/\delta$ is described locally by a functional form linear in image coordinates. Local support is maximized when the residual is minimized, and correspondence is thereby determined, (as was the case with disparity itself in Eastman & Waxman, 1985). A second implementation following Prazdny (1985) would be to compare potential values of $\dot{\delta}/\delta$ between pairs of neighboring features, relative to the angular separation of the features. (This is like a "directional derivative" of $\dot{\delta}/\delta$.) A weight is then assigned to the matches that participate, the weight decreasing with increasing derivative. Yet a third implementation could be based on the approach of Pollard et al. (1985). Correspondence being driven by local consistency with a gradient limit on $\dot{\delta}/\delta$. The existence of an isotropic gradient limit on disparity alone is well known for static stereograms (Burt & Julesz, 1980). But does such a gradient limit exist for dynamic stereograms? Could fusion be achieved with a dynamic stereogram for which the disparity gradient limit is exceeded?

We have yet to implement our matching strategy and so cannot comment on its possible strengths or weaknesses. But in keeping with Step 5, we expect that once correspondence is initially established, new features emerging from behind occluding boundaries and the periphery are easily matched. They are entrained into the local disparity field by a spreading of local support from previously matched features in the neighborhood.

Monocular–Binocular Flow Relations

In addition to the correlation that exists between binocular-difference flow and disparity, there are some interesting relations between this binocular and the monocular flow (e.g., as seen on the cyclopean image). The cyclopean-image velocity of a feature is the average of the corresponding feature velocities in the left and right images for this parallel stereo configuration. Equation 1 can be interpreted as the monocular flow in cyclopean-image coordinates, with space motion parameters and depth interpreted accordingly. Relations 23 and 24 are valid in cyclopean coordinates as well. Replacing $1/Z$ by δ/b in Equation 1 and combining with Equation 23, find

$$v_x - x\left(\frac{\Delta v_x}{\delta}\right) = -\Omega_Y + y\Omega_Z - \frac{V_X}{b}\delta \tag{27a}$$

$$v_y - y\left(\frac{\Delta v_x}{\delta}\right) = \Omega_X - x\Omega_Z - \frac{V_Y}{b}\delta \tag{27b}$$

$$-\left(\frac{\Delta v_x}{\delta}\right) = x\Omega_Y - y\Omega_X - \frac{V_Z}{b}\delta. \tag{27c}$$

Equations 27a–c have been written with "measurable" quantities on the left-hand side and unknown motion parameters as coefficients on the right-hand side. Note that Equations 27a–c require these combined monocular–binocular flow quantities to be linear functional forms in the variables (x, y, δ). Once correspondence is established between left and right images (as in Step 2), the measured disparities may be locally fit over small analytic neighborhoods to a linear form motivated by Equation 24, thereby determining local surface structure (as described in Step 3). Then Equations 27a–c may be used to fit linear forms to the measured flow quantities over analytic regions (in the least-squares sense), and thus determine the absolute rigid body motion parameters $\mathbf{V}$ and Ω for that region. This requires solving only linear equations. (Recall that structure and motion from monocular flow required solution of non-linear equations.) This corresponds to Step 4 of the stereo-motion fusion module described previously.

The obvious symmetries displayed by Equations 27a–c suggest that they may be written in vector notation. Corresponding to the three-dimensional space position vector $\mathbf{R} = (X, Y, Z)$ we introduce the three-dimensional image position vector $\mathbf{r} \equiv \mathbf{R}/Z = (x, y, 1)$. The three-dimensional image velocity is defined as $\mathbf{u} \equiv \dot{\mathbf{r}} = (v_x, v_y, 0)$. Then, recalling that $\Delta v_x \equiv \dot{\delta}$, we can rewrite Equations 27a–c as

$$\mathbf{u} - \frac{\dot{\delta}}{\delta} \mathbf{r} = - \left(\frac{V}{b} \delta + \boldsymbol{\Omega} \times \mathbf{r} \right). \tag{28}$$

It is not coincidental that Equation 28 bears a strong resemblance to the relation for three-dimensional space velocity of a point induced by an observer's rigid body motion (i.e., $\mathbf{U} \equiv \dot{\mathbf{R}} = -(\mathbf{V} + \boldsymbol{\Omega} \times \mathbf{R})$. In fact, Equation 28 is exactly this relationship for $\mathbf{U}/Z$! This same relation has recently been derived independently by Nagel (1985) for the purpose of recovering the parameters of space motion from time-varying intensity.

FUTURE DIRECTIONS

The analysis of time-varying imagery and recovery of three-dimensional interpretations has clearly come a long way in the last several years. Yet much remains to be done before motion analysis can truly be exploited by a machine vision system. In the context of our own approach, the low-level component has hardly been explored. Contour extraction, localization, and tracking need to be studied in the time-varying domain. The flow-segmentation algorithm needs to be automated with regard to neighborhood size and data density. Moreover, video-rate pipelined hardware or parallel processor arrays should be utilized if we are ever to achieve real-time capabilities. Similarly, parallel implementations of flow recovery and three-dimensional inference are necessary. A global pasting together of the recovered surface patches is then required. We have only scratched the surface of the stereo-motion fusion problem. Here, psychophysics may serve as a guide to future computational studies. Finally, the merging of motion analysis with conventional control theory may open new doors in robotic manipulation and navigation.

APPENDIX
THE TRANSFORMATION RELATIONS

In order to solve the kinematic relations for the three-dimensional structure and motion of curved surfaces, it is necessary to rotate the image axes about the line of sight by an angle α, that is, $(x, y) \xrightarrow{\alpha} (\bar{x}, \bar{y})$. The inverse transformation is given by

$$x = \bar{x} \cos \alpha - \bar{y} \sin \alpha$$

$$y = \bar{x} \sin \alpha + \bar{y} \cos \alpha, \tag{A1}$$

from which we find the partial derivatives transform as

$$\frac{\partial}{\partial \bar{x}} = \cos \alpha \frac{\partial}{\partial x} + \sin \alpha \frac{\partial}{\partial y} \tag{A2}$$

$$\frac{\partial}{\partial \bar{y}} = -\sin \alpha \frac{\partial}{\partial x} + \cos \alpha \frac{\partial}{\partial y} .$$

These relations determine the following transformation for the deformation parameters $D_i \overset{\alpha}{\to} \bar{D}_i$:

$$\bar{D}_1 = D_1 \cos \alpha + D_2 \sin \alpha \tag{A3}$$

$$\bar{D}_2 = D_2 \cos \alpha - D_1 \sin \alpha$$

$$\bar{D}_3 = D_3 \cos^2 \alpha + D_4 \sin^2 \alpha + 2D_5 \sin \alpha \cos \alpha$$

$$\bar{D}_4 = D_4 \cos^2 \alpha + D_3 \sin^2 \alpha - 2D_5 \sin \alpha \cos \alpha$$

$$\bar{D}_5 = D_5(\cos^2 \alpha - \sin^2 \alpha) + (D_4 - D_3) \sin \alpha \cos \alpha$$

$$\bar{D}_6 = D_6$$

$$\bar{D}_7 = D_7 \cos^3 \alpha + D_{10} \sin^3 \alpha + (3D_8 + 2D_{11}) \sin \alpha \cos^2 \alpha + (3D_9 - 2D_{12}) \sin^2 \alpha \cos \alpha$$

$$\bar{D}_8 = D_8 \cos^3 \alpha - D_9 \sin^3 \alpha + (D_{10} - 2D_8 - 2D_{11}) \sin^2 \alpha \cos \alpha - (D_7 - 2D_9 + 2D_{12}) \sin \alpha \cos^2 \alpha$$

$$\bar{D}_9 = D_9 \cos^3 \alpha + D_8 \sin^3 \alpha + (D_7 - 2D_9 + 2D_{12}) \sin^2 \alpha \cos \alpha + (D_{10} - 2D_8 - 2D_{11}) \sin \alpha \cos^2 \alpha$$

$$\bar{D}_{10} = D_{10} \cos^3 \alpha - D_7 \sin^3 \alpha - (3D_9 - 2D_{12}) \sin \alpha \cos^2 \alpha + (3D_8 + 2D_{11}) \sin^2 \alpha \cos \alpha$$

$$\bar{D}_{11} = D_{11} \cos \alpha + D_{12} \sin \alpha$$

$$\bar{D}_{12} = D_{12} \cos \alpha - D_{11} \sin \alpha.$$

The solution method yields the three-dimensional parameters in the rotated frame. To recover them in the original reference frame, we transform back $(\bar{\mathbf{V}}, \bar{\mathbf{\Omega}}) \overset{\alpha}{\to} (\mathbf{V}, \mathbf{\Omega})$ and $(\bar{p}, \bar{q}, \bar{k}_{xx}, \bar{k}_{yy}, \bar{k}_{xy}) \overset{\alpha}{\to} (p, q, k_{xx}, k_{yy}, k_{xy})$. Recall that our method is based upon $V_x \equiv 0$.

$$V_x = \bar{V}_x \cos \alpha - \bar{V}_y \sin \alpha \tag{A4}$$

$$V_y = \bar{V}_y \cos \alpha + \bar{V}_x \sin \alpha$$

$$V_z = \bar{V}_z$$

$$\Omega_X = \bar{\Omega}_X \cos \alpha - \bar{\Omega}_Y \sin \alpha$$
$$\Omega_Y = \bar{\Omega}_Y \cos \alpha + \bar{\Omega}_X \sin \alpha$$
$$\Omega_Z = \bar{\Omega}_Z$$

and

$$p = \bar{p} \cos \alpha - \bar{q} \sin \alpha \qquad\qquad (A5)$$
$$q = \bar{q} \cos \alpha + \bar{p} \sin \alpha$$
$$k_{xx} = \bar{k}_{xx} \cos^2 \alpha + \bar{k}_{yy} \sin^2 \alpha - 2\bar{k}_{xy} \sin \alpha \cos \alpha$$
$$k_{yy} = \bar{k}_{yy} \cos^2 \alpha + \bar{k}_{xx} \sin^2 \alpha + 2\bar{k}_{xy} \sin \alpha \cos \alpha$$
$$k_{xy} = \bar{k}_{xy} (\cos^2 \alpha - \sin^2 \alpha) - (\bar{k}_{yy} - \bar{k}_{xx}) \sin \alpha \cos \alpha.$$

ACKNOWLEDGMENTS

Much of this work was performed while the authors were with the Computer Vision Laboratory, Center for Automation Research, University of Maryland. Support of the National Science Foundation, the National Bureau of Standards, and the Defense Advanced Research Projects Agency during various phases of our research is gratefully acknowledged.

REFERENCES

Acton, F. S., 1970. *Numerical methods that work.* New York: Harper & Row.

Adelson, E. H., & Bergen, J. R., 1985. Spatiotemporal energy models for the perception of motion. *Journal of the Optical Society of America* A2, pp. 284–299.

Adiv, G., 1984 (October). Determining 3-D motion and structure from optical flow generated by several moving objects. *Proceedings of the DARPA Image Understanding Workshop,* pp. 113–129, New Orleans: SAIC.

Anderson, C. H., Burt, P. J., & van der Wal, G. S., 1985 (September). Change detection and tracking using pyramid transform techniques. *Proceedings of the SPIE Conference on Intelligent Robots and Computer Vision,* Boston.

Aris, R., 1962. *Vectors, tensors, and the basic equations of fluid mechanics.* Englewood Cliffs, NJ: Prentice-Hall.

Bandyopadhyay, A. 1985 (October). *Constraints on the computation of rigid motion parameters from retinal displacements.* University of Rochester, Dept. of Computer Science. Tech. Report 168.

Bandyopadhyay, A. and Aloimonos, J. 1985 (March). *Perception of rigid motion from spatiotemporal derivatives of optical flow.* University of Rochester, Dept. of Computer Science. Tech. Report 157.

Braunstein, M. L., 1976. *Depth perception through motion.* New York: Academic Press.

Braunstein, M. L., 1983 (April). Perception of rotation in depth: The psychophysical evidence. *Proceedings of the Workshop on Motion: Representation and Perception*, pp. 119–124, Toronto: ACM.

Burt, P., & Julesz, B., 1980. A disparity gradient limit for binocular fusion. *Science, 208*, 615–617.

Buxton, B. F., & Buxton, H. 1983. Monocular depth perception from optical flow by space-time signal processing. *Proceedings of the Royal Society of London, B218*, pp. 27–47.

Buxton, B. F., Buxton, H., Murray, D. W., & Williams, N. S., 1984. 3-D solutions to the aperture problem. *European Conference on Artificial Intelligence '84.*

Canny, J. F., 1983. Finding edges and lines in images. *M.S. thesis*, Department of Electrical Engineering and Computer Science. Cambridge, MA: MIT.

Doner, J., Lappin, J. S., & Perfetto, G., 1984. Detection of three-dimensional structure in moving optical patterns. *Journal of Experimental Psychology: Human Perception and Performance 10*, pp. 1–11.

Eastman, R., & Waxman, A. M., 1985 (October). *Using disparity functionals for stereo correspondence and surface reconstruction.* University of Maryland, Center for Automation Research: Tech. Report 145; also *Proceedings of DARPA Image Understanding Workshop*, December 1985, pp. 245–254, Miami: SAIC.

Fleet, D. J., & Jepson, A. D., 1985 (October). Velocity extraction without form perception. *Proceedings Workshop on Computer Vision: Representation and Control*, pp. 179–185, Bellaire: IEEE Press.

Gibson, J. J., 1966. *The senses considered as perceptual systems.* Boston: Houghton Mifflin.

Gibson, J. J., 1979. *The ecological approach to visual perception.* Boston: Houghton Mifflin.

Grimson, W. E. L., 1981. *From Images to Surfaces.* Cambridge, MA: MIT.

Hay, J. C., 1966. Optical motions and space perception: An extension of Gibson's analysis. *Psychological Review, 73*, pp. 550–565.

Hildreth, E. C., 1983 (April). The measurement of visual motion. *Ph.D. thesis*, Massachusetts Institute of Technology, Dept. of Electrical Engineering and Computer Science; also 1983 (April) Computing the velocity field along contours, *Proceedings of Workshop on Motion: Representation and Perception*, pp. 26–32, Toronto: ACM.

Hoffman, D. D., & Bennett, B. M., 1985. Inferring the relative three-dimensional positions of two moving points. *Journal of the Optical Society of America, A2*, pp. 350–353.

Horn, B. K. P., & Schunck, B. G., 1981. Determining optical flow. *Artificial Intelligence, 17*, pp. 185–203.

Huang, T. S., 1983. *Image sequence processing and dynamic scene analysis.* Berlin: Springer-Verlag.

Jenkin, M. R. M., 1984 (September). *The stereopsis of time-varying images.* University of Toronto, Dept. of Computer Science Tech. Report RBCV-TR-84-3.

Johansson, G., 1975. Visual motion perception. *Scientific American 232*, pp. 76–88.

Kalman, R. E., 1960. A new approach to linear filtering and prediction problems. *Journal of Basic Engineering, 82*, pp. 34–45.

Kalman, R. E., & Bucy, R. S., 1961. New results in linear filtering and prediction theory. *Journal of Basic Engineering, 83*, pp. 95–108.

Kanatani, K., 1985 (December). Structure from motion without correspondence: General principle. *Proceedings of the DARPA Image Understanding Workshop*, pp. 107–116, Miami: SAIC.

Koenderink, J. J., & van Doorn, A. J., 1975. Invariant properties of the motion parallax field due to the movement of rigid bodies relative to an observer. *Optica Acta, 22*, pp. 773–791.

Koenderink, J. J., & van Doorn, A. J., 1976a. Local structure of movement parallax of the plane. *Journal of the Optical Scoiety of America, 66*, pp. 717–723.

Koenderink, J. J., & van Doorn, A. J., 1976b. Geometry of binocular vision and a model for stereopsis. *Biological Cybernetcis, 21,* pp. 29–35.

Lee, D. N., 1976. A theory of visual control of braking based on information about time to collision. *Perception, 5,* pp. 437–459.

Lee, D. N., 1980. The optic flow field: The foundation of vision. *Philosophical Transactions of the Royal Society of London, B290,* pp. 169–179.

Longuet-Higgins, H. C., 1981. A computer algorithm for reconstructing a scene from two projections. *Nature, 293,* pp. 133–135.

Longuet-Higgins, H. C., 1984. The visual ambiguity of a moving plane. *Proceedings of the Royal Society of London B223,* pp. 165–175.

Longuet-Higgins, H. C., & Prazdny, K., 1980. The interpretation of a moving retinal image. *Proceedings of the Royal Society of London, B208,* pp. 385–397.

Marr, D., 1982. *Vision.* San Francisco, CA: Freeman.

Marr, D., & Hildreth, E. C., 1980. Theory of edge detection. *Proceedings of the Royal Society of London, B207,* pp. 187–217.

Marr, D., & Poggio, T., 1979. A computational theory of human stereo vision. *Proceedings of the Royal Society of London, B204,* pp. 301–328.

Marr, D., & Ullman, S., 1981. Directional selectivity and its use in early visual processing. *Proceedings of the Royal Society of London, B211,* pp. 151–180.

Maybank, S. J., 1985. The angular velocity associated with the optical flowfield arising from motion through a rigid environment. *Proceedings of the Royal Society of London, A401,* pp. 317–326.

Mayhew, J. E. W., & Frisby, J. P., 1981. Psychophysical and conputational studies towards a theory of human stereopsis. *Artificial Intelligence, 17,* pp. 349–385.

McConnell, A. J., 1957. *Applications of tensor analysis.* New York: Dover.

Meinhold, R. J., & Singpurwalla, N. D., 1983. Understanding the Kalman filter. *American Statistician, 37,* pp. 123–127.

Mitiche, A., 1984 (December). On combining stereopsis and kineopsis for space perception. *First Conference on Artificial Intelligence Applications,* pp. 156–160, Denver: IEEE Press.

Murray, D. W., & Buxton, B. F., 1985 (*preprint*). Scene segmentation: Finding the motions and dispositions of several moving planar surfaces from quasi-markov random optic flow fields: also *IEEE Pat. Anal. Mach. Intell.* 9, pp. 220–228, 1987.

Nagel, H.-H., 1983 (April). On the estimation of dense displacement vector fields from image sequences. *Proceedings Workshop on Motion: Representation and Perception,* pp. 59–65, Toronto: ACM.

Nagel, H.-H., 1985 (October). Dynamic stereo vision in a robot feedback loop based on the evaluation of multiple interconnected displacement vector fields. *Proceedings of the Third International Symposium on Robotics Research,* Gouvieux, Cambridge, MA: MIT.

Poggio, G. F., & Poggio, T., 1984. The analysis of stereopsis. *Annual Reviews of Neuroscience* 7, pp. 379–412.

Pollard, S. B., Mayhew, J. E. W., & Frisby, J. P., 1985. Disparity gradients and stereo correspondences. *Preprint,* Department Psychology, Sheffield University; *Perception* (in press).

Prazdny, K., 1980. Egomotion and relative depth map from optical flow. *Biological Cybernetics, 36,* pp. 87–102.

Prazdny, K., 1985. Detection of binocular disparities. *Biological Cybernetics, 52,* pp. 93–99.

Regan, D., & Beverley, K. I., 1979a. Binocular and monocular stimuli for motion in depth: Changing-disparity and changing-size feed the same motion-in-depth stage. *Vision Research, 19,* pp. 1331–1342.

Regan, D., & Beverley, K. I., 1979b. Visually guided locomotion: Psychophysical evidence for a neural mechanism sensitive to flow patterns. *Science, 205,* pp. 311–313.

Regan, D., & Beverley, K. I., 1985. Visual responses to vorticity and the neural analysis of optic flow. *Journal of the Optical Society of America, A2*, pp. 280–283.

Richards, W., 1983. Structure from stereo and motion. *M.I.T. Artificial Intelligence Laboratory Memo 731;* also *J. Opt. Soc. Amer. A2*, pp. 343–349 (1985).

Schunck, B. G., 1984 (April). Motion segmentation and estimation by constraint line clustering. *Proceedings Workshop on Computer Vision: Representation and Control*, pp. 58–62, Annapolis: IEEE Press.

Schunck, B. G., 1986 (May). Image flow continuity equations for motion and density. Submitted to *Workshop on Motion: Representation and Analysis*, Charleston: ACM.

Sinha, S. S., & Waxman, A. M., 1984 (July). *An image flow simulator*. University of Maryland, Center for Automation Research. Tech. Report 71.

Subbarao, M., 1985 (December). *Interpretation of image motion fields: A spatio-temporal approach*. University of Maryland, Center for Automation Research. Tech. Report 167.

Subbarao, M., 1986. *Interpretation of Visual Motion: A Computational Study*. Ph.D. thesis, University of Maryland, Department of Computer Science.

Subbarao, M., & Waxman, A. M., 1985 (October). On the uniqueness of image flow solutions for planar surfaces in motion. *Proceedings of Workshop on Computer Vision: Representation and Control*, pp. 129–140, Bellaire: IEEE Press.

Thompson, D. W., 1917. *On growth and form*. Cambridge University Press; see abridged (ed., J. T. Bonner) chap. 4, 1961.

Todd, J. T., 1985. Perception of structure from motion: Is projective correspondence of moving elements a necessary condition? *Journal of Experimental Psychology: Human Perception and Performance, 11*, pp. 689–710.

Tsai, R. Y., & Huang, T. S., 1981a. *Uniqueness and estimation of 3-D motion parameters of rigid objects with curved surfaces*. University of Illinois, Coordinated Science Lab. Report R-921.

Tsai, R. Y., & Huang, T. S. 1981b. *Estimating 3-D motion parameters of a rigid planar patch*. University of Illinois, Coordinated Science Lab. Report R-922.

Ullman, S., 1979. *The interpretation of visual motion*. Cambridge, MA: MIT Press.

Ullman, S., 1983. Maximizing rigidity: The incremental recovery of structure from rigid and rubbery motion. *M.I.T. Artificial Intelligence Laboratory Memo 721*. Cambridge, MA: MIT.

Wallach, H., & O'Connell, D. N., 1953. The kinetic depth effect. *Journal of Experimental Psychology, 45*, pp. 205–217.

Waxman, A. M., 1984 (April). An image flow paradigm. *Proceedings of Workshop on Computer Vision: Representation and Control*, pp. 49–57, Annapolis: IEEE Press.

Waxman, A. M., & Duncan, J. H., 1985 (October). *Binocular image flows: Steps toward stereomotion fusion*. University of Maryland, Center for Automation Research. Tech. Report 119; also *IEEE Pat. Anal. Mach. Intel. 8*, pp. 715–729, 1986.

Waxman, A. M., Kamgar-Parsi, B., & Subbarao, M. 1986 (February). *Closed form solutions to image flow equations for 3-D structure and motion*. University of Maryland, Center for Automation Research. Tech. Report 190.

Waxman, A. M., & Sinha, S. 1984 (October). *Dynamic Stereo: Passive ranging to moving objects from relative image flows*. Proceedings of DARPA Image Understanding Workshop, pp. 130–136, New Orleans: SAIC.

Waxman, A. M., & Ullman, S., 1983 (October). *Surface structure and 3-D motion from image flow: A kinematic analysis*. University of Maryland, Center for Automation Research. Tech. Report 24; also *Int. J. Robotics Research, 4*(3), pp. 72–94, 1985.

Waxman, A. M. & Wohn, K., 1984 (April). *Contour evolution, neighborhood deformation and global image flow: Planar surfaces in motion*. University of Maryland, Center for Automation Research. Tech. Report 58; also *Int. J. Robotics Research, 4*(3), pp. 95–108, 1985.

Winger, R. M., 1962. *Projective geometry*. New York: Dover.

Wohn, K., 1984 (September). *A contour-based approach to image flow.* Ph.D. thesis, University of Maryland, Department of Computer Science.

Wohn, K., & Waxman, A. M., 1985 (July). *Contour evolution, neighborhood deformation and local image flow: Curved surfaces in motion.* University of Maryland, Center for Automation Research. Tech. Report 134.

Wohn, K., & Waxman, A. M., 1986. *The analytic structure of image flows: Deformation and segmentation.* University of Maryland, Center for Automation Research. Tech. Report.

Wohn, K. and Wu, J. 1986, (January). Recovery of 3-D motion from first-order deformation. Harvard University, Robotics Laboratory Tech. Report.

AUTHOR INDEX

225

SUBJECT INDEX

A

Abstraction levels, 10–12
  communication between, 96
  processing in, 95
Albedo and shape, 159–160
Ambiguity,
  in flow, 196, 198, 201
  in images, 3–7
Analyticity, boundaries of, 171, 190
Aperture problem, 184–185
  in the large, 182, 185–187, 207, 209
  in the small, 182–183
Architecture for vision, 94–106
  requirements, 94–96
  specifications, 99–102
Array processing, 99–102
Associative processing, 97–102

B

Binocular optic flow, 210–218
Biquartic shape relation, 186
Blackboard, 69, 84, 101, 103
  error recovery, 88
  synchronization, 88
Boundaries of analyticity, 171, 190

C

CAAPP (Content Addressable Array Parallel Processor), 99–102

Cauchy-Stokes, 176
Clustering, 19–24
Color image understanding, 2
Combination of cues, see Fusion
Computing optic flow, 181–188
Cone, Processing, 14–16
Constraints,
  for reconstruction, 119–123
  flow, 182
  geometric, 56–66
  illuminant, 158
  image irradiance, 159
  shape-motion, 158
Content addressable processing, 99–102
Context in IU, 3–7
Contour,
  deformation, 181–182
  functional method for flow, 187
  information needed to find flow, 186
  instability, 207–209
Control of segmentation, 37, 73–76
Cooperative intrinsic images, 120–123
Correspondence,
  flow and disparity, 211–212, 215–217
  problem, 89, 135–136
  unnecessary, 137–141
Curvature,
  Gaussian, 201–203
  normalized, 192
Curved surface flow, 197–203

229

Printed and bound by CPI Group (UK) Ltd, Croydon, CR0 4YY

17/10/2024

01775688-0011